# Transitions

No
Limits

# University 101
UNIVERSITY OF SOUTH CAROLINA **Programs**

**Dottie Weigel, Dan Friedman**
Editors

**Erin Morris**
Design, Layout, Cover Art

We would like to acknowledge the special contributions of our dedicated and knowledgeable authors:
Chapter 1: Dan Friedman, Director, University 101 Programs
Chapter 2: Claire Robinson, Director, University Advising Center
Chapter 3: Dan Friedman, Director, University 101 Programs
Chapter 4: Dallin George Young, Assistant Director, National Resource Center for The First-Year Experience and Students in Transition
Chapter 5: Dottie Weigel, Assistant Director, University 101 Programs, and Kevin Clarke, former Assistant Director, University 101 Programs
Chapter 6: Stuart Hunter, Senior Fellow, University 101 Programs/ National Resource Center for The First-Year Experience and Students in Transition, Faculty Fellow, USC Connect
Chapter 7: Jennifer Latino, former Associate Director, University 101 Programs
Chapter 8: Dottie Weigel, Assistant Director, University 101 Programs and Kayla Lisenby, former Coordinator for Lesbian, Gay, Bisexual, & Transgender Programs, Multicultural Student Affairs
Chapter 9: Maegan Gudridge, Communications Director, Division of Student Affairs and Academic Support
Chapter 10: Amber Fallucca, Associate Director, USC Connect
Chapter 11: Vicki Hamby, Senior Associate Director, Career Center

We would also like to thank previous authors and contributors without whom we could not produce this publication: Frank Anderson, Debbie Beck, Mary Elizabeth Bridges, Kevin Clarke, Karen Brown, Michelle Burcin, Kimberly Dressler, Jimmie Gahagan, Gwen Geidel, Maureen Grewe, Mike Hix, Jessica Johnston, Jennifer Keup, Paul Millard, Jaime Shook Miller, Rodrick Moore, Eric Moschella, Marguerite O'Brien, Katherine Robinson, Timothy Simmons, Sandra Smith, Dawn Traynor, and Irma Van Scoy.

Copy Editors: Candace Chellew and Viki Fecas

Cover art based on photo by Julia Brown

How to cite this text:
Weigel, D., & Friedman, D. (Eds.) (2016). *Transitions*. Columbia, SC: University of South Carolina.

# CONTENTS

**CHAPTER 1** — 1
## An Introduction to University 101

**CHAPTER 2** — 13
## Academic Strategies

**CHAPTER 3** — 53
## Managing Time

**CHAPTER 4** — 73
## Academic Policies, Processes, and Resources

**CHAPTER 5** — 103
## Involvement and Engagement

**CHAPTER 6** — 129
## Positive Relationships

# ASSESSMENTS, FIGURES, AND TABLES

# An Introduction to University 101

*Dear First-Year Student,*

Congratulations on your acceptance to the University of South Carolina and your decision to enroll in our nationally recognized University 101 course. By signing up for UNIV 101, you have made a commitment to your own success and have paved the way for a smoother transition to college and a more rewarding first-year experience.

You probably have heard that University 101 has been consistently recognized by *US News and World Report* as "A Program to Look For," along with other schools, such as Princeton, Stanford, North Carolina, Michigan, and Yale. Back when *US News* ranked first-year seminars, South Carolina was selected as the #1 program in the country. You should be proud to attend a school that is continually recognized as the leader in the nation in helping students make a successful transition to college.

The University 101 course is designed to help you achieve academic success, discover all the resources Carolina has to offer, engage in the academic and cocurricular life of the University, and build important relationships with students and faculty. It will provide you with the tools and resources needed to succeed. I anticipate that this will be one of the most rewarding, meaningful, and engaging courses you will take as a college student.

As with most things in life, what you get out of this experience will be commensurate with what you put into it. This course, your instructor, and your peer and/or graduate leader, along with this edition of *Transitions*, are here to help you be as successful as you want to be. College comes with many new freedoms, which can be both exciting and daunting. But with these new freedoms come new responsibilities. Discovering how to manage and balance freedom and responsibility are important goals of this course.

If there is anything that I, or others in the University 101 office, can do to support you in this important transition, please do not hesitate to call on us 803-777-6029. I hope you have a wonderful first-year experience, and I wish you the very best.

Sincerely,

Dan Friedman
Director, University 101

# About University 101 at the University of South Carolina

Welcome to the University of South Carolina! We are excited that you are joining a great institution and have taken the first step to ensure success during your time here by enrolling in University 101. University 101 is essentially an extended orientation, and our goal is to give you the information, resources, and support you need at the time you need it. When you were here for Orientation, you may have been overwhelmed with information or concerned mostly with where you were going to live and what classes you would take. Now that you are a student on campus, you are probably more interested in learning about all the great opportunities this school has for you, how to manage your time effectively, or how to eat well on campus. This course was designed by staff, faculty, and students to meet these needs.

We know this course will help you be more successful. Students who take U101 earn higher first-year grade point averages (GPAs) than other students, come back for their sophomore year at greater rates, and are more likely to complete their degree at Carolina. In addition, University 101 students are more likely to report that they are satisfied with USC. More than 92% of UNIV 101 students responding to the 2014 National Survey of Student Engagement indicated that they would choose to attend USC again if they had it to do over (compared with 85.5% of participants who did not take UNIV 101).

Past students have raved about University 101. In fall 2015, the majority of first-year students said that they would recommend this course to other students. We expect that you will have a great experience as well. But as with anything in life, you will get out of it what you put into it. Here are a few tips from former U101 students on how to have a successful U101 experience:

1.  **Keep an open mind.** Some of the activities you do in U101 might seem odd or silly. But trust us; all these activities are intentional and have a purpose.

2. **Attend every class.** U101 is a seminar class, meaning that it is a group conversation. Your opinions, perspectives, and experiences are important.
3. **Take advantage of the small class experience by getting to know your classmates and your instructors.** This class is a great way to meet new friends and to have a resource and mentor in your instructor and peer leader.

# University of South Carolina – The National and International Leader in First-Year Seminars

New-student seminars have been part of the academic curriculum at American colleges and universities for more than 100 years. A first-year seminar was first offered in 1882 at Lees College in Kentucky, but the popularity of these courses has fluctuated since that time. After almost disappearing in the 1960s, the first-year seminar has enjoyed a gradual and steady rebirth across the nation since the mid-1970s, due largely in part to the model that was created here at the University of South Carolina in 1972. Following Carolina's lead, a majority of American colleges and universities have created similar courses. In fact, data from the 2012 National Survey on First-Year Seminars, sponsored by our very own National Resource Center for The First-Year Experience and Students in Transition, indicated that 87% of responding institutions offered some type of new-student seminar.

## *The Impetus for University 101*

University 101 at the University of South Carolina was born out of student activism. In the late 1960s and early 1970s, many college campuses experienced student protests against the Vietnam War and social injustices. Notable demonstrations occurred at The University of California at Berkeley and Kent State University in Ohio. Similarly, student unrest affected the University of South Carolina as students voiced their opinions to the faculty and administration in various ways.

In the spring of 1970, approximately 1,000 students turned out to protest the U.S. invasion of Cambodia in addition to other state and campus issues that had been brewing for months.

In the spring of 1970, the conflict came to a head when approximately 1,000 students turned out to protest the U.S. invasion of Cambodia in addition to other state and campus issues that had been brewing for months. The governor called out the National Guard, and although no shots were fired, the students responded by storming the office of President Thomas Jones and holding him a virtual prisoner for days (Morris & Cutright, 2005).

President Jones interpreted the students' protests as evidence that the University had "failed its students in some fundamental way, and it was incumbent on the institution to do a better job of assimilating students into university life, specifically USC's history, purposes, and traditions" (Morris & Cutright, 2005). Jones believed that the university could help students succeed during their time in college by enhancing their relationships with faculty and staff. In 1972, he introduced University 101 as a first-year seminar course that would focus on helping students be successful rather than on a specific discipline.

## University 101 Today

The University 101 course today has evolved from the course Jones introduced more than 40 years ago. However, the spirit of University 101 is the same: to promote student success through a small seminar, taught by caring faculty, and focused on transition needs. University 101 is designed to help students make a successful transition to the University of South Carolina, both academically and personally. It is a unique learning experience in that it is a course for first-year students, about first-year students.

University 101 is an elective for approximately 75% of the students enrolled; however, selected student populations such as Opportunity Scholars, Exercise Science majors, Teaching Fellows, and Capstone Scholars are required by their program to take the course. Annual student enrollment has risen to more than 80% of the first-year class.

University 101 is taught in small groups, comprised of 19 students, by faculty and staff members who have a special interest in first-year students. The small class size allows students to learn directly from each other as they share

Thomas F. Jones, Jr. was elected the 23rd president of USC in 1962 and served until 1974. He was one of the most influential and innovative presidents in USC history.

common experiences and establish personal relationships with a college instructor. University 101 is offered in the fall and spring semesters, although the vast majority of University of South Carolina-Columbia students enroll in the fall.

# University 101 Learning Outcomes

Each University 101 class may vary in terms of structure and content based on the needs of the students enrolled in the specific course section. Common learning outcomes, however, exist for all sections and are designed to guide student learning.

## I. Foster academic success

As a result of this course, students will:

- Adapt and apply appropriate academic strategies to their courses and learning experiences.
- Identify and apply strategies to effectively manage time and priorities.
- Identify relevant academic policies, processes, and resources related to their academic success and timely attainment of degree requirements.

## II. Discover and connect with the University of South Carolina

As a result of this course, students will:

- Identify and use appropriate campus resources and engage in opportunities that contribute to their learning within and beyond the classroom.
- Develop positive relationships with peers, staff, and faculty.
- Describe the history, purpose, and traditions of the University of South Carolina.

## III. Promote personal development, wellbeing, and social responsibility

As a result of this course, students will:

- Clarify their values and identity and articulate how these shape their perspectives and relationships

University 101 is taught in small groups of 19 students by faculty and staff members who have a special interest in first-year students.

with people who are similar to and different from themselves.

- Explore the tenets of the Carolinian Creed.
- Examine and develop strategies that promote wellbeing and explain how wellness impacts their academic and personal success.
- Initiate a process toward the attainment of personal and professional goals and articulate potential pathways to employability.

## Your University 101 Instructors

Each University 101 class is taught by a University faculty or staff member and may be co-taught by an outstanding upper-division undergraduate (peer leader) or second-year graduate student (graduate leader) who will serve as a mentor, resource, and facilitator for learning during the semester. There are more than 200 instructors from over 70 departments across campus teaching University 101, and what they all have in common is a desire to help first-year students be successful. University 101 instructors receive extensive training and have a strong desire to provide a high quality learning environment. You can consider your University 101 instructors as primary resources for both academic and cocurricular situations when you need help. If your instructors cannot assist you directly, they will know how to connect you with a campus expert who can.

## University 101 Peer Leader Program

The University 101 Peer Leader Program at the University of South Carolina has been an important component of the University 101 course since 1993. Outstanding rising junior and senior students are recruited to help incoming first-year students navigate their Carolina experience by serving as role models, mentors, and facilitators for learning. Peer Leaders model academic success and involvement in the Carolina community for new students, while helping them successfully begin their Carolina experience. A former UNIV 101 student reflected on her peer leader, "She gave

MY PEER LEADER GAVE GREAT INSIGHT BECAUSE SHE HAS BEEN THROUGH IT AND EXPERIENCED WHAT WE ARE GOING THROUGH NOW.

- Former University 101 student

great insight because she has been through it and experienced what we are going through now." Look to your University 101 Peer Leader for advice and guidance in the classroom and beyond!

## Get Involved!

If after this semester you are interested in continuing your involvement with the University 101 program and would like to assist with the teaching of a course in your junior and/or senior year, you are encouraged to apply to become a University 101 Peer Leader. University 101 Peer Leaders exemplify the principles of the Carolinian Creed, have a 3.0 or higher GPA, and are involved in a wide variety of campus groups and organizations.

# University 101 Awards

Each year, the University 101 Program recognizes and rewards outstanding students, faculty, and staff for their contributions to the first-year experience at Carolina. Students who have successfully completed University 101 in the past year may be nominated for a University 101 Scholarship. Faculty, staff, and students may also be nominated for the Outstanding Advocate for First-Year Students, and

University 101 Peer Leaders exemplify the principles of the Carolinian Creed, have a 3.0 or higher GPA, and are involved in a wide variety of campus groups and organizations.

University 101 students may recommend their University 101 instructor for the Teaching Award. All scholarship and Advocate Award recipients are recognized annually at the University of South Carolina Awards Day ceremony.

## University 101 Scholarships

University 101 scholarships recognize undergraduate students who have made major contributions to their University 101 class and who have incorporated the course ideals and values into their academic and cocurricular experiences. To apply for the scholarship, a student must first be nominated by his or her University 101 instructor. Instructors recommend students based primarily on the impact they have had on the overall success of the class. Nominated students are then invited to submit an essay demonstrating their unique contributions to their University 101 class and to the University community through their academic excellence, campus involvement, and community service. Each spring, the selection committee awards up to eight recipients a $500 scholarship to apply to their tuition the following academic year. Out-of-state recipients may also receive a tuition discount for the year as their award.

## Outstanding Advocate for First-Year Students Award

Many members of the University community take a very special interest in the welfare and success of first-year students. For the past 19 years, University 101 has given formal recognition to such individuals by honoring them as Outstanding Advocates for First-Year Students. A plaque honoring previous recipients of the award is displayed prominently in the Russell House.

If, during your first year at the University of South Carolina, someone makes an important and positive difference in your academic or personal life, you are encouraged to nominate this individual for the award. In the fall semester, a call for nominations will be posted on the University 101 website and featured on the university home page. Your nominee may be any member of the campus community whom you regard as an exceptional advocate for first-year students.

### *M. Stuart Hunter Award for Outstanding Teaching in University 101*

As one way of recognizing the great work of our instructors, University 101 Programs sponsors an award for outstanding teaching in University 101. This award was established to recognize one University 101 instructor annually who demonstrates exemplary teaching and achievement of course outcomes and has made a positive impact on student lives. All University 101 students, peer leaders, and graduate leaders at the USC Columbia campus are invited to nominate their University 101 instructor for this award following the completion of each fall semester. The award recipient is recognized at the annual Building Connections Conference in May and receives a $500 award and a plaque honoring this important achievement.

## Other Courses

University 101 Programs is an academic unit at the University of South Carolina that offers four courses that support students' transition into and through their college experience.

In addition to the University 101 course, University 101 Programs offers:

**University 201: Fundamentals of Inquiry**
University 201 is a three-credit hour course that uses inquiry-based approaches to promote integrative learning. Students practice integrating concrete experiences with theoretical foundations by reflecting and applying information. These courses focus on any of the four USC Connect Pathways. Previous UNIV 201 courses have included *Service to Youth, World of Work*, and *International Inquiry: Navigating Cultures*.

**University 290, Special Topics in Residential College**
This one-credit hour course for students in a living-learning community covers topics aligned with the mission and goals of the particular community. Recent courses have included the following communities: Capstone Scholars, Green Quad, Magellan Scholars, Healthy Carolina, Journalism, and Pre-Health Studies. Students enrolled have traveled to Seattle, Costa Rica, and Iceland!

M. Stuart Hunter, Senior Fellow with University 101 Programs and the National Resource Center for The First-Year Experience and Students in Transition, is a pioneer in the first-year experience movement.

**University 401, Senior Capstone Experience**

This seminar is designed to prepare juniors and seniors for the transition to their career or graduate school following graduation. Students enrolled in specific sections of University 401 usually share the same academic major and/or career goals. The course is designed to assist students in bringing closure to their college experience through systematic, intentional reflection on both the student's major and, in general, their liberal arts education. Recent courses have included: *Graduation with Leadership Distinction, Transitioning to Medical School, Pre-Law, Journalism, Synthesizing the Sciences, Preparing for a Career in Higher Education/Student Affairs,* and *Medical School Application Process.*

University 101 Programs is part of a larger department that also houses the National Resource Center for The First-Year Experience & Students in Transition. The National Resource Center serves as the trusted expert, internationally recognized leader, and clearinghouse for scholarship, policy, and best practice for all postsecondary student transitions. The primary purpose of the Center is to support and advance efforts to improve student learning and transitions into and through higher education.

University 101 and the National Resource Center work together as one functionally integrated academic unit to build and sustain a vibrant campus-based and diverse educational community committed to the success of first-year college students and all students in transition. University 101 achieves this through the University 101 seminar and its other academic courses. The National Resource Center carries this mission beyond the University campus by sponsoring a series of national and international conferences, online courses for educators, seminars, and workshops; publishing a peer-reviewed journal, an electronic newsletter, a monograph series, and other publications; and maintaining a resource website and several electronic mailing lists.

If you would like to learn more about the University 101 seminar, our other academic courses, or the work of the National Resource Center, you are invited to visit our office any time during regular office hours.

## UNIVERSITY 101 OFFICE

 803-777-6029

 sc.edu/univ101

 **1728 College Street**
Monday – Friday
8:30 a.m. – 5:00 p.m.

## REFLECTION QUESTIONS

1. Why did you decide to take University 101?
2. What are you hoping to get out of the experience?
3. Of the 10 learning outcomes listed on pages 6-7, which one are you most interested in exploring?
4. What role will you play to ensure a classroom dynamic that is healthy and meaningful?

## RESOURCES

**University 101 Programs** ............ (803) 777-6029
1728 College Street
http://www.sc.edu/univ101/

## REFERENCES

Morris, L.V., & Cutright, M. (2005). University of South Carolina: Creator and standard-bearer for the first-year experience. In B. O. Barefoot et al., *Achieving and sustaining institutional excellence for the first year of college* (pp. 349-376). San Francisco, CA: Jossey-Bass.

Page 4 photo - Student Protest: *University of South Carolina Libraries: Caroliniana Columns, 27,* p. 3. Copyright 2010 by the University of South Carolina. Reprinted with permission.

Page 5 photo - Thomas F. Jones, Jr.: http://library.sc.edu/socar/archives/finding_aids/jones.htm

# CHAPTER 2

# Academic Strategies

# UNIVERSITY OF SOUTH CAROLINA

## Dear First-Year Student,

Welcome to the University of South Carolina! Your decision to be a Gamecock is just the first of many important decisions you will make on your path to success. As the director of the Student Success Center, I am often asked, "What is the key to being a successful student?" My response consists of the things you might expect: attend every class meeting; get to know your instructors; carefully manage your time; and take care of your body with plenty of exercise, healthy food, and rest. However, I also explain that true academic success comes from understanding yourself as a learner.

Learning is a process. It takes time and has multiple steps. As learners, we are all different, progressing at different rates with different styles. The sooner we come to understand how we learn best, the more quickly we are able to adapt to the new college learning environment. Understanding your learning preferences can be helpful in saving you time and frustration when you study. Remember, when you are challenged by course material and are having trouble learning it, try something new. Different material can call for different study methods.

Unlike high school, courses at USC will require you to comprehend the big picture. Developing a conceptual understanding of complex material can be frustrating if in the past you were only required to memorize facts about a topic. Recognizing the different levels of knowledge you are being asked to demonstrate can help you study more efficiently and be properly prepared for the questions on your exams. Learn to look for clues in your text, lectures, and the feedback you receive on your graded work.

Developing personal strategies for note-taking, reading your texts, and taking exams will help you to process new information in ways that are meaningful to you. Pay attention to what works for you and be willing to explore new methods. Build an arsenal of skills, and you will always be prepared. There are many people on campus who want to help you do this. Your professors can provide insight on how to learn in their classes. The Student Success Center provides a variety of resources and services that can help you build that arsenal of study skills. Your University 101 instructor can guide you as you begin to explore college resources. Pay attention to your learning. It is an investment that pays off in time—time that you can spend taking advantage of all the exciting opportunities you will encounter as a Gamecock!

Best of luck,

Eric J. Moschella
Director, Student Success Center

**EVERY** year the University of South Carolina welcomes the biggest and brightest first-year class to our Columbia campus. The average student entering USC in fall 2015 earned an SAT score of 1210 (ACT = 27.3) and had an average high school GPA of a 4.0 (University of South Carolina Admissions, 2015). Without question, every student admitted to USC has the capability of being successful. However, even with these qualifications, college takes hard work...and a lot of it.

As a first-year student enrolled at the University of South Carolina you have a tremendous opportunity ahead of you. Nationally, you are a member of a select group of students enrolled at a four-year college. As shown in the chart below, only 66% of students who graduated high school went on to enroll in an institution of higher education. More striking, only 42% of all graduating high school seniors enroll in a four-year institution.

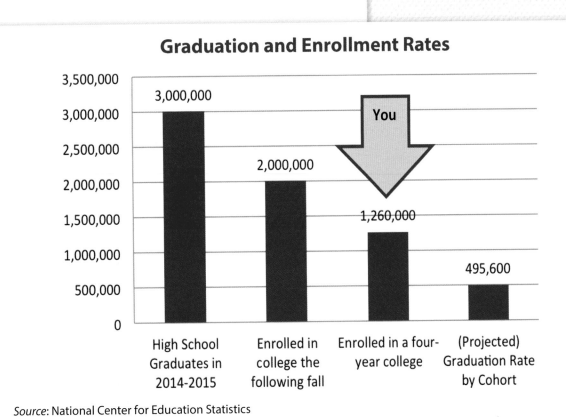

*Source*: National Center for Education Statistics

Your academic success, to this point, has enabled you to enroll at one of the best four-year public research institutions in the Southeast. However, consider this: Only 73% of Carolina students who started their bachelor's degree at USC in fall 2007 graduated within six years (University of South Carolina Admissions, 2015). With all of this in mind, one of the greatest challenges college students face is adjusting to a new academic environment. This chapter outlines some of these challenges and the essential academic strategies needed to succeed during your first year of college and beyond.

## I Never Studied in High School

High school and college are two different worlds. Many students proclaim they never studied in high school and still earned good grades. However, despite their former academic success, first-year students often experience *academic culture shock* or the reality that high school expectations of studying, writing, reading, and taking notes may no longer apply in college. For example, consider the differences in class expectations, attendance policies, participation, and assignment deadlines. High school classes have mandated attendance whereas college professors may never track attendance. Participation in class may be optional in high school but required in college. In college, you will likely receive a syllabus on the first day of class and then you are expected to track all deadlines for the remainder of the semester. Finally, perhaps the biggest academic culture shock of all is the amount of time and effort you will need to spend in order to be successful in college. In the 2014 Cooperative Institutional Research Program (CIRP) Freshman Survey, 53% of first-year students reported studying less than six hours a week in high school. In college, it is recommended that students study two hours for every one hour they are in class to be successful in their courses. Therefore, if you are enrolled in 15 hours, you should be studying at least 30 hours a week. High school graduates who do not enroll in college and instead enter the workforce likely spend an average of 40 hours per week at their job. Therefore, if you consider your college career as a full-time job, you should be spending at least 30-40 hours per week focusing on your

> IN COLLEGE, IT IS RECOMMENDED THAT STUDENTS STUDY TWO HOURS FOR EVERY ONE HOUR THEY ARE IN CLASS TO BE SUCCESSFUL IN THEIR COURSES.

academics. This requirement may be lighter in your first year, but it will quickly pick up in your sophomore year.

The " How is College Different than High School" table provides a snapshot of differences between high school and college. The components listed touch on some of the differences you are likely to encounter this semester.

In addition to these environmental differences, perhaps the main difference between high school and college is the concept of **self-regulated learning**. When reviewing the list on the following page, everything in the "college column" indicates it is the students' responsibility to navigate their own time, priorities, classes, schedule, and requirements. College students cannot exclusively rely on their teacher, parent, or advisor for answers (unlike in high school). The expectation that you will regulate your own learning is one of the biggest changes you will experience as a first-year student. Consider these examples. New college students may feel it is their professor's responsibility to teach them everything that will be on the test (not true). Or, they might expect their academic advisor will advise them on all registration, policies, and graduation requirements (also not true). In sum, self-regulated learning in college means it is the students' responsibility to navigate campus, ask questions, and be proactive in their education.

## Strategies versus Skills

In high school you probably heard the term "study skills." This likely includes things such as note-taking, reading comprehension, and time management. Indeed, all students should develop and adopt effective study habits to make the most of their college experience. However, consider for a moment the difference between a strategy and a skill.

> **Strategy**: a plan, method, or series of maneuvers for obtaining a specific goal or result.

> **Skill**: the ability to do something well.

Said another way, a *strategy* is something you practice or implement whereas a *skill* is something you develop or attain. Strategies are defined as a plan, method, or series of maneuvers for obtaining a specific goal or result. In high school and

# HOW IS COLLEGE DIFFERENT THAN HIGH SCHOOL?

| | HIGH SCHOOL | COLLEGE |
|---|---|---|
| **Cost** | High school is mandatory and usually free. | College is voluntary and expensive. |
| **Time** | Your time is structured by others. | You manage your own time. |
| **Permission** | You need permission to participate in extracurricular activities. | You decide whether to participate in co-curricular activities. |
| **Responsibility** | You can count on parents and teachers to remind you of your responsibilities and to guide you in setting priorities. | You must balance your responsibilities and set priorities. You will face moral and ethical decisions you have never faced before. |
| **Classes** | Each day you proceed from one class directly to another, spending 6 hours in class each day. This equals 30 hours per week in class. | You often have hours between classes; class times vary throughout the day and evening and you spend only 12 to 16 hours each week in class. |
| **Schedule** | Most of your classes are arranged for you. | You build your own schedule in consultation with your advisor. Schedules tend to look lighter than they really are. |
| **Graduation Requirements** | You are not responsible for knowing what it takes to graduate. | Graduation requirements are complex, and differ from year to year. You are expected to know those that apply to you. |
| **Guiding Principle** | You will usually be told what to do and corrected if your behavior is out of line. | You are expected to take responsibility for what you do and don't do, as well as for the consequences of your decisions. |

*Source*: Southern Methodist University:
"How is College Different than High School?"

college, you may develop good note-taking strategies in class (a method) so you will do well on a biology test (a result). Or, you develop effective test-taking strategies (a method) in order to do well in a class (a result). Perhaps you balance your course load (a method) in order to obtain a certain major or degree (a result). There are literally thousands of books on how to study in college outlining strategies such as the Cornell note-taking method, SQ3R reading technique, or outlining a paper. Strategies require planning, effort, and implementation. In other words, you are strategizing on how to be successful.

After you have practiced and implemented various strategies, you begin to develop a skill-set. These skills are what make you successful in college and your career. For example, after you have given several presentations you will develop strong public speaking skills. Once you have balanced 18 credit hours, a part-time job, and co-curricular activities, you will develop strong time management skills. You may use strategies in college such as a weekly time-log or a semester-at-a-glance. Those resources are there to help you develop the skills needed to successfully manage your time. A strong skill set will not only help you succeed in college, but also in your career. Skills often distinguish one candidate from another.

Finally, skills are actually fun to develop! Once you have acquired new skills, you develop greater confidence and can achieve more goals. College affords you some of the most concentrated time in your life to develop a solid skill-set. However, in order to obtain them you must be strategic. The following pages reveal some of the most effective strategies college students can use to do well in their academics.

## Study Strategies in College

This section discusses some of the tried-and-true academic strategies shown in the literature that equip students to do well in college. Keep in mind, not every strategy will work for every student. And, not every strategy will work with every class. (You do not study the same exact way for an anatomy class as you would for a philosophy class.) However, there

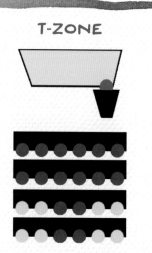

**T-ZONE**

The term action zone, or T zone, is used to refer to an area where the teacher is most likely to interact with his or her students. A study by M. Gail Jones at the University of North Carolina conducted observations between interactions with students in the action zone compared to students located outside of the action zone in 56 physical science and chemistry classes. The researcher observed that students located in the action zone, "dominated class interactions and received more direct questions, teacher-afforded conversation, and sustaining feedback" (Jones, 1989).

are decades of research on how to study in college and how people learn. The following are a list of academic strategies and suggestions on how you can implement them.

## Attend Class

This may seem so simple, but attending class is imperative to success in college. In order to fully understand the material your professor wants you to learn, you need to hear it from the source. While your instructor may not notice your absence in a large lecture, when you skip a class you miss critical information not covered in the text. Research studies have found a strong negative correlation between absences and final grades (Gump, 2005), meaning if you skip class your grades are likely to be significantly lower than if you attend class. In fact, Crede et al. (2010) found that attendance is a stronger predictor of high marks in college than any other predictor, including study habits, study skills, and high school grade-point average.

If grades are not enough of a motivator, consider the financial cost of skipping class. Regardless if your reasons are excused or unexcused, every time you skip class you are throwing money out the window. The "How Much is Skipping Class Costing You graphic?" illustrates this concept.

- Estimate that current in-state USC tuition is $11,000 (University of South Carolina Office of Financial Aid, 2015).
- The average student enrolls in 15 credit hours per semester, which equals 10 courses per year.
- Each course costs approximately $1,100.
- Tues/Thurs courses typically meet 29 times per semester.
- $1,100 divided by 29 = $38.00 per class.

This means, if you are paying in-state tuition, you are *wasting* **$38.00 every time you skip class**. If you are paying out-of-state tuition (approximately $29,000 per year) this cost per class translates to **$100 per course**. Keep in mind these figures are tuition only. Add in housing, meals, books, and forgone employment, and the cost goes up significantly. Clearly, college is a big investment.

# How much is skipping class **costing** you?

Estimate that the current USC Tuition is
**$11,000** (in-state) FY 15-16
**$29,900** (out-of-state) FY 15-16

The average student enrolls in **15 credit hours** per semester, which equals 10 courses per year.

Thus, each course costs approximately
**$1,100** (in state)
**$2,990** (out-of-state)

Courses typically meet **29** times per semester.

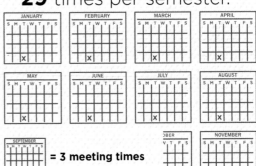

= 3 meeting times

Cost of each course divided by 29 =
**$38** per class (in state)
**$103** per class (out-of-state)

**Student Success** Center
University of South Carolina

In addition to attending class, you should sit where you can see the instructor and where the instructor can see you. You will find that sitting near the instructor will benefit you significantly. You can see and hear all material and notice where he or she places emphasis within the subject matter. An added perk is that your professor may begin to recognize your face, creating the opportunity for you to develop a strong student/faculty relationship that can pay dividends in the future. Faculty also benefit from your seating placement in that they can gain an understanding of whether you are learning the material by your facial expressions and visual cues.

Research indicates that *where* students sit in class is a predictor of course grades. Consider a lecture-style course where all seats are facing forward toward the professor as opposed to a seminar course like U101, where students are typically facing each other and sitting in a circle. In a lecture course, students who regularly sit in the front or down the middle aisle may earn higher grades than those who sit in the back. Why? These seats allow students an opportunity to stay engaged with the material, make eye contact with the professor, and avoid distractions.

## Limit Distractions

One of the hardest skills for college students to master is concentration. America's lifestyle has been described as a culture of distraction. Social media, cell phones, and instant information constantly compete for our attention. In fact, the learning literature suggests that the average adult cannot pay attention in a passive learning environment for more than 15 minutes. As Medina (2008) pointed out, "The story is consistent: Whether you are an eager preschooler or a bored-out-of-your-mind undergrad, better attention always equals better learning. It improves retention of reading material, accuracy, and clarity in writing, math, science – every academic category that has ever been tested" (p. 74).

What can you do to ensure you are getting the most out of your study time?

> SUCCESS IN LIFE IS A MATTER NOT SO MUCH OF TALENT OR OPPORTUNITY AS OF CONCENTRATION AND PERSEVERANCE.
>
> - Wendte

### When

- Study your hardest or "boring" subjects first. You will feel less overwhelmed once you have tackled the most challenging aspect of your study session.
- Find the time of day that you can focus the best, whether that is before the sun is up, after it goes down, or between your classes. By experimenting with different times throughout the day for studying, you can find the best time for you.

### Where

- Find a spot on campus where you can focus, whether that is in your residence hall, the library, or at a local coffee shop.
- Train your body and mind that a certain location correlates to work being done. You can master this skill by frequently studying in the same location.
- DO NOT study in your bed. Just like you can train your mind that the library means homework, your body and mind are trained that your bed means sleep. You can't get much work done if you are dozing off.

### How

- Turn off your cell phone.
- Write down your goals for your study session. (e.g., "Read 50 pages and outline the chapter.")
- Keep a "worry pad." Write down any stray ideas that pop into your head while you are reading or writing.
- Get up and get moving during study breaks; this simple action gets your blood flowing which can help you retain more information and keep you alert.
- Keep a positive attitude about your study goals and reward yourself once you have completed them.

## Read, Recite, Review

In college you will be asked to read more than you may have ever read before. Keeping up with the reading for all your courses can be one of the most challenging and daunting tasks. And, if you find yourself falling behind in the syllabus, trying to catch up may be very anxiety provoking. Be sure to read the required readings before class. This allows you to

## COUNSELING AND PSYCHIATRY

Anxiety can inhibit your ability to concentrate. Therefore, if you find yourself getting overwhelmed or severely stressed, you should seek help from USC Counseling and Psychiatry.

 sa.sc.edu/shs/cp/

understand the big picture for the lecture content and helps you ask knowledgeable questions of your professor. Sometimes an instructor will choose to only highlight major parts of the text in a lecture but will test your knowledge on the lecture and readings. Ask your professors what they expect you to gain from the readings; whether big picture, definitions, key issues, or supplemental understanding. A reading strategy that can help you read faster and retain more is the SQ3R Method. The letters refer to the five steps, which Hirsch (2001) described as:

- *Survey* the chapter you are getting ready to read. This means literally flip through all the pages quickly so you can see the outline the author presents, section headings, and so on.
- *Question* yourself by asking "What do I already know about this subject?" The best way to really learn something is by associating it with prior knowledge and experiences. Try to make analogies between the new content and things you already know. Throughout your reading, continue to develop questions about the material. This will help you stay engaged, concentrate, and prepare for tests.
- *Read* the chapter as thoroughly as you can and be sure to keep the questions you have in the back of your mind.
- *Recite* any important information (the more ways you work with the material, the better). This can be as simple as stopping your reading, making sure you remember the key points of the section you read, and then continuing on.
- *Review* - be sure to go back over the questions you listed and make sure you can answer them. If you can't, it's important to go back and review that section again to continue to build your understanding.

Practice the SQ3R method often. Once you have made the SQ3R a habit, you will realize you automatically use it without having to review the model!

# Take Notes

Taking notes in class and during your reading is one of the best ways to stay engaged in the lecture, capture important information, and ultimately do well in the class. Some professors post their lecture notes on Blackboard. If they do, print them or have them accessible electronically during class. Bringing outlines of chapters or pre-written notes is one of the best ways to keep focused, organized, and stay on track during a lecture. Below are a few more tips when it comes to taking notes.

- **Abbreviate**. It is not realistic or advisable to write down every word your professor says. Use abbreviations that work for you. Invent one or two letter symbols for common words and phrases. For example, put a star next to notes that the teacher mentions are important or that will be on the test.
- **Label and date** all of your notes with the course title, number, and lecture topic. Stay organized.
- **Rewrite or type** your notes to better understand and remember the content.
- **Identify important concepts**. Highlighting draws attention to important concepts; however be careful of "over" highlighting as this reduces the degree to which you remember the information. Researchers recommend highlighting no more than one sentence per paragraph (Wollen, Cone, Britcher, & Mindemann, 1985).
- **Review, review, review!** Review your notes from previous lectures or the assigned reading before class. Take 10 minutes after class to glance over your notes and clarify any unclear points (e.g., abbreviations or shorthand symbols).

Many students take notes in class on their laptop. But is this a good strategy? In addition to the temptation to "multitask" by taking a quick peek at a text message or social media site during the lecture, an emerging body of research suggests that taking notes on your laptop is not as effective for learning and retaining information as handwriting on paper. In a study published in the academic journal, *Psychological Science*, Mueller and Oppenheimer (2014) studied

## NOTE-TAKING SHORTCUTS

| WORD OR TERM | ABBREVIATION OR SYMBOL |
|---|---|
| About | ~ |
| Amount | Amt. |
| And | & |
| Chapter | Ch. |
| Company | Co. |
| Continued | Cont'd. |
| Decrease | Decr. |
| Definition | Def. |
| Economic | Econ. |
| Example | Ex. or X or e.g. |
| General | Gen. |
| Government | Gov. |
| Hour/hourly | Hr., hrly. |
| Illustrate | Illus. or e.g. |
| Important | Imp. |
| Increase | Inc. |
| Information | Info. |
| Introduction | Intro. |
| Months | Mo(s.) |
| Number or Pound | # |
| Organization | Org. |
| Page(s) | Pg., p., pp. |
| Psychology | Psyc. |
| Principal | Princ. |
| Significant | Sig. |
| Social or sociology | Soc. |
| Summary/ summarize | Sum. |
| Versus | Vs. |
| Volume | Vol. |
| Year | Yr. |
| Equal/Not Equal | = and ≠ |
| Less than/more than | < and > |
| Positive/negative | + and − |
| With/without | w/ and w/o |

the note-taking methods of college students at Princeton and UCLA. They looked at students who took notes by hand and those who typed notes on a laptop and found that while the two groups performed similarly on questions that involved recalling facts, students who took notes by hand outperformed the laptop group on conceptual questions requiring them to apply what they've learned.

Why is that? Perhaps simply transcribing what was said leads to shallow processing rather than allowing students to make sense of the material by reframing and summarizing in their own words. It also leads to a deluge of words. Handwritten notes generally contain fewer words, especially since laptop note takers tend to try to type every word in the lecture. The handwritten notes, which should contain only the most important information, makes studying for exams much more efficient. Regardless of the note-taking method employed, it is important to summarize the content in your own words and seek to make connections to the material by applying it to what you already know.

A win-win strategy would be to take notes by hand during the lecture and then later that evening or the next day, go back and type your notes. This will allow you to have an electronic copy which makes it easier to study from and also allows you the opportunity to experience the material again, leading to greater understanding and mastery. You could also type notes from your readings and combine with the lecture notes (Mueller & Oppenheimer, 2014). Regardless of the methods you try, your first semester in college is the best opportunity to try them all and see which one fits with how you learn.

## Using High Impact Learning Strategies

In order to best utilize your study time, it is helpful to understand the learning strategies that are proven to be most effective. Unfortunately, many students are committed to using strategies that do not work very well. The literature is quite clear that highlighting and re-reading material is of limited use in understanding and retaining information. So,

what does work? In a meta-analysis of the research on learning techniques, researchers (Dunlosky et al. 2013) determined that the two most effective strategies to promote learning are (1) practice testing and (2) distributing learning over time (as opposed to cramming).

## Practice Tests

Practice testing includes strategies such as flashcards, completing practice problems available in online modules or textbooks, or making your own quizzes. Practice testing is effective because it promotes retrieval and recall of information, which has long been known to be an effective strategy (all the way back to Aristotle!). It is the practice of retrieval that makes information stick rather than mere re-exposure. Thus, simply re-reading your book or lecture notes is not as effective as making practice tests or using flash cards. In their book *Make it Stick: The Sciences of Successful Learning*, Brown, Roediger, & McDaniel (2014) noted that "it makes sense to reread a text once if there's been a meaningful lapse of time since the first reading, but doing multiple readings in close succession is a time-consuming study strategy that yields negligible benefits at the expense of much more effective strategies that take less time" (p. 15).

## Learning over Time

A second effective strategy is to spread the learning out over time. Many students believe that cramming can work for them. While it may be better than not studying at all, "distributing learning over time (either within a single study session or across sessions) typically benefits long-term retention more than does massing learning opportunities back-to-back or in relatively close succession" (Dunlosky et al, 2013, p. 35). As the memory curve depicted in the sidebar illustrates, people forget information quickly if it is not reviewed on a regular and recurring basis. You can do this by reviewing your notes on a regular basis, taking notes on your readings and merging those with your lecture notes, and applying the practice and recall strategies such as using flashcards to restudy the material, and developing practice quizzes.

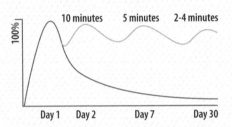

## MEMORY CURVE

The figure above represents the amount of information you forget in a 30-day period, depending on the amount of time you spend reviewing the information from your notes.

On Day 1, you begin with little to no knowledge of the subject, but after the lecture you know 100% of the information instructors have shared with you (or relatively close to 100% considering a few questions are expected). However, if you do not review your notes and other materials for just a few minutes within the first 24 hours following the lecture, you will forget 50%-80% of the information by Day 2. Rather, if you spent just 10 minutes on Day 2 reviewing your notes, you would retain closer to 90% of the information you learned the day before.

*Source: The University of Waterloo, Counseling Services*

## Stay Motivated

Knowing why you are in college and what you're striving to become down the road can provide you with a wellspring of motivation for anything from finding the determination to complete one study session or finishing an entire paper. College can be one of the most memorable, fun, and impactful times of your life. However, college also presents many distractions. Parties, dating, friends, Netflix, social media, and hundreds of other non-academic activities will compete for your time. In order to be successful in college, you need to balance these competing priorities. Motivation is what gets you moving. And, it helps you prioritize what's important. To gauge your current level of motivation, ask yourself these three questions:

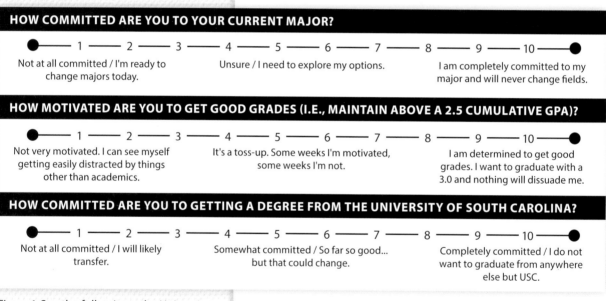

**HOW COMMITTED ARE YOU TO YOUR CURRENT MAJOR?**

1 — 2 — 3 — 4 — 5 — 6 — 7 — 8 — 9 — 10

Not at all committed / I'm ready to change majors today.

Unsure / I need to explore my options.

I am completely committed to my major and will never change fields.

**HOW MOTIVATED ARE YOU TO GET GOOD GRADES (I.E., MAINTAIN ABOVE A 2.5 CUMULATIVE GPA)?**

1 — 2 — 3 — 4 — 5 — 6 — 7 — 8 — 9 — 10

Not very motivated. I can see myself getting easily distracted by things other than academics.

It's a toss-up. Some weeks I'm motivated, some weeks I'm not.

I am determined to get good grades. I want to graduate with a 3.0 and nothing will dissuade me.

**HOW COMMITTED ARE YOU TO GETTING A DEGREE FROM THE UNIVERSITY OF SOUTH CAROLINA?**

1 — 2 — 3 — 4 — 5 — 6 — 7 — 8 — 9 — 10

Not at all committed / I will likely transfer.

Somewhat committed / So far so good... but that could change.

Completely committed / I do not want to graduate from anywhere else but USC.

*Figure 1:* See the full quiz on the University Advising Center's website, sc.edu/advising. Your First-Year Advisor will ask you these three questions and more.

Your answers to these questions will hint at your current level of motivation and commitment to your major, grades, and USC in general. You are encouraged to share your answers with your U101 instructor and/or another trusted faculty or staff member at USC. In addition, make sure you seek out the appropriate resources if you are on the fence about graduating from USC, changing your major, and getting good grades. Ultimately, these decisions are up to you, but there are dozens of offices on campus and people you can meet with to discuss your options.

# Use Tutoring, Supplemental Instruction, and Study Groups

Successful students will make use of the wealth of resources available to them. Almost every student at USC will take advantage of at least one academic resource during their time in college. The three most common are tutoring, Supplemental Instruction, and informal study groups.

| TUTORING |
| --- |
| • Peer tutors provide 1:1 support |
| • Tutors have taken the class before, have earned an A, and are trained to work with you |
| • Tutors hold hours that students can schedule time to meet with them |

| SUPPLEMENTAL INSTRUCTION |
| --- |
| • SI Leaders attend the class with students and work with the instructor |
| • Group sessions where students help answer questions and SI leader facilitates |
| • SI sessions are held regularly, usually in the same classroom space |

| STUDY GROUPS |
| --- |
| • Created by students in a class |
| • Learning happens in both the discussion of topics and sharing of ideas |
| • Meet on an as-needed basis, but recommended to be a regular occurrence |

So which should you pick? As with all study strategies, use what works best for you. If you are in a class and you're finding the material difficult, Tutoring or SI would be a good starting point for you. A tutor can help you learn specifics, and SI can assist in understanding the larger concepts and reinforcing what you learned in class. If you are studying for a test and find that you're not retaining the information on your own, you might consider forming a study group which can help you in the give-and-take of a discussion, give you a chance to learn more of the material, and hear a different perspective.

Keep in mind that each choice has its own drawbacks as well. Tutoring can be readily available, or all tutors may be booked out several weeks and not able to help you before your next test. If you don't enjoy large group settings for studying, SI may not be the best environment for you to thrive in. And, as you might expect, sometimes study groups can go off the rails onto a subject that has nothing to do with your class! Finding a balance between all three methods is the solution.

# College Students are measured on Four "Products"

College student performance is measured in four main ways: exams, papers, presentations, and group work. When you get your syllabus on the first day of class, you will see a breakdown of how these products are assigned, quantified, and measured. The following is a brief overview of these four college products and some items for consideration as you embark on college-level coursework.

# Product #1: Exams

The most frequently used method of assessment in education is examinations (e.g., tests and quizzes). There are two main types of exams you will encounter: objective exams and subjective exams. Objective exams have a clear, right/wrong answer and you need to identify it. **True-false, multiple choice, matching, and fill-in-the-blank** are examples of exams where you must know the information verbatim in order to do well on the test. Strategies to help prepare for objective tests include flashcards and self-quizzing. Subjective exams require students to interpret, explain, and/or synthesize material. The most common exam types are **essay or short answer**. When preparing for subjective exams, students must be able to build on their knowledge of the subject and demonstrate application. See the advice on the following page for various strategies for tackling different exam types.

# ADVICE FROM PEER LEADERS

University 101 Peer Leaders were asked to identify their top study strategies that contribute to their academic success. Following is a summary of their responses in order of their frequency:

## 1 FLASHCARDS

"Quizlet is great."

"I go through flashcards and separate them into piles of ones I know and don't know. I do this until get them all right."

## 2 DO PRACTICE PROBLEMS

## 3 REVIEW AND REWRITE NOTES

"Rewrite notes to better understand material."

"Draw pictures to go with my notes."

"Organize notes into categories or tables."

"Draw an unlabeled diagram. Try to label it an hour later."

"State concepts out loud to myself."

"Define key words."

"Type abbreviated notes of all the lectures, print them out, and write on them/highlight."

"Highlight notes / color code by topic."

"Read notes out loud to someone."

"Condense notes into small study guides."

"Type and print some sort of fill in the blank outline."

"Look at learning outcomes and see how much I know."

## 4 FORM A STUDY GROUP

"Discuss with a group the opinions of readings/ solutions to homework questions."

"Discuss main concepts."

## 5 CREATE AND REVIEW OUTLINES FOR MY CHAPTERS/READINGS

"Summarize the material."

"Make up mnemonic devices to remember words, sequences, and phrases."

## 6 TAKE NOTES WHILE READING

"For literature classes, draw a plot/character map based off notes."

"Annotate readings."

"Write textbook reading in own words."

## 7 SET ASIDE A BLOCK OF TIME SOLELY FOR STUDYING EVERY DAY - AND STICK TO IT!

"Have a bunch of snacks on hand to keep you going."

"Turn off phone."

"Study a little each night rather than a lot right before test."

## 8 MEET WITH PROFESSOR

"Professors love to get to know their students."

"The professors at USC are the best of the best."

## 9 RELATE MATERIAL TO REAL LIFE

# GENERAL TEST-TAKING STRATEGIES

**Multiple-Choice Test Format:**

- Formulate your own answer before reading the options
- Eliminate unlikely answers first
- Select numbered answers from the middle range, not the extremes
- Select answers that are longer and more descriptive
- Watch out for similar answers
- Watch out for "Not True"

**True-False Test Format:**

- When you don't know the answer, mark it as true
- Look for any factor that will make a statement false
- Look for extreme modifiers that tend to make the question false
    - Extreme modifiers: "Always", "All", "Never", "Only"
- Qualifying words tend to make the question true
    - Qualifying words: "Seldom", "Often", "Many"
- Negative words or prefixes complicate the statement
- Questions that state a reason tend to be false
- There is no substitution for the truth

**Matching Test Format:**

- Examine both lists to determine the types of items and their relationships
- Use one list as a starting point and go through the second list to find a match
- Move through the entire list before selecting a match because a more correct answer may follow
- Cross off items on the second list when you're certain you have a match
- Don't guess until all absolute matches have been made because you'll likely eliminate an answer that could be used for a later choice

**Sentence Completion/Fill-in-the-blank Test Format:**

- Concentrate on the number of blanks in the sentence and the length of the space
- Provide a descriptive answer when you can't think of the exact word or words

**Short Answer/Essay Question Test Format:**

- Organize your thoughts before you begin to write
- Paraphrase the orginial question to form your introductory statement
- Use the principles of English composition
- Write clearly as the instructor needs to be able to read it
- Use lists or bullets whenever possible
- Identify the verbs or words in the question that give you direction

**Student Success** Center
University of South Carolina

@UofSCSSC  **University of South Carolina Student Success Center**

803.777.1000
sc.edu/success

# Product #2: Papers

The second most frequently used measure of college students are papers (e.g., essays, journals, reflection papers, research papers). Many new students often think of writing as a one-shot process, where they sit down, type up their thoughts, and then turn in that first draft. College level writing is much more substantial and should take a greater amount of time and effort than writing papers in high school. Professors will tell you over and over to make sure you spread your work on a paper across several weeks (if possible). One of the main reasons is to allow time to incubate. This means once you get a portion of the paper written – or the entire rough draft – leave it alone: save and close the file, put the paper down, step away from the computer! Given your brain time away from what you have written and come back to it a few days later. This incubation time allows for you to have a fresh and usually more objective view of your work. Not only will it strengthen your thoughts and ideas, but it will result in better writing as well. Making sure you have time to use this method is key in your time management strategies. When writing papers, consider the following steps:

## STEP 1: PRE-WRITING

Also known as the thinking stage of writing. Here, you should focus on generating ideas for writing without worrying about the organization, wording, or expression.

## STEP 2: DRAFTING

Once you have done some initial research and thinking about their topics, you are ready to begin drafting. Focus on getting the main ideas down on paper and supporting them without worrying too much about style, punctuation, or grammar.

## STEP 3: REVISING

In some ways, this step is a continuation of the drafting stage. You will need to reread your first draft with a critical eye, taking into consideration any feedback you may have received from your peers or instructor. Make sure you have a clearly stated thesis, that the main ideas are related to the thesis, and that you have adequate support for your argument. At this stage, you may also begin reworking sentence structure, incorporating transitions, and experimenting with different words or expressions to make the essay flow better and make the meaning more clear.

## STEP 4: EDITING

You may have begun editing during the revision stage, but once the major content issues are resolved, turn your attention fully to the word and sentence level to fine tune your essay. Focus on word choice, make sure that you have adequate transitions within and between paragraphs, and rephrase sentences so that there is a good variety of sentence types and lengths in the essay. Identify and correct major grammatical problems, such as fused or incomplete sentences.

## STEP 5: POLISHING THE FINAL PRODUCT

At the final stage, carefully proofread the essay and correct errors in punctuation, spelling, capitalization, or grammar. Also check to see that you have observed all formal requirements of the assignment (e.g., margins, font size, tables, and charts).

## *Use Your Resources*

The Writing Center is a valuable resource available to all members of the USC community. Many people think the Writing Center provides assistance for "poor" writers. But all writers, from beginners to professionals, benefit from having other people review their work. At the Writing Center, no matter your level of writing expertise, you will find experienced assistants to help you with all phases of your writing process:

- **Getting started**: choosing a topic, developing a thesis, writing an introduction.
- **Editing a draft**: checking organization, the clarity of your argument, sentence structure, punctuation, usage.
- **Revising a paper your instructor has returned**: deciphering symbols and comments, finding more effective ways of developing the topic.

Writing Center consultants will help you improve not only writing for any class but also personal writing, such as letters for scholarships, personal statements for professional school applications, and cover letters and résumés for job applications.

Writing Center consultants work with you, not for you. Because dropping off your paper to have someone "fix" it is not an option, you must schedule an appointment. To make sure you can schedule an appointment when you need it, call at least two or three days ahead, and after mid-term, at least a week or two ahead. There are 25 and 50 minute appointments available, and there is no limit on the number of times per week a student can schedule an appointment.

## Evaluating Information Sources

Many college papers will require the use of appropriate sources. With the rapid growth in technology and the variety of sources of information available (e.g., through libraries, community resources, media, Internet), it is increasingly important to be information literate so that you can sift through this overabundance of sources to find useful information and know that it is accurate and reliable, and to avoid bias, misinformation, or false facts. Every day, thousands of sites are added to the Internet by individuals, companies, researchers, organizations, and the government, and there are no standards in place to ensure the accuracy and authority of the content. Anyone anywhere can develop a website and put anything on the Internet. Books and articles are important information sources, but not all books and articles are valid or reliable. The criteria below can be used as a checklist to help you determine if an information source is suitable for your research needs or personal use.

**WRITING ASSISTANCE**

**The Writing Center**

 803-777-2078

 artsandsciences.sc.edu/write

 Find the Writing Center in the Byrnes Building, Room 703

**Student Success Center (Peer Writing)**

 803-777-1000

 sc.edu/success

**Writer's Hotline**

 803-777-2078

## Authority

Be skeptical and use good judgment. Authors who are proud of their work will provide contact information and tell you who they are and why they are experts on a particular topic. Ask yourself the following questions:

- Is biographical or background information on the author(s) provided?
- Is an institutional or organizational affiliation provided? If so, what can I find out about that institution or organization?
- What are the basic values or goals of the organization or institution?
- What are the possible biases of the author or organization?
- Has the author written anything else?
    - Use the biographical information located in the publication itself to help determine the author's affiliation and credentials.
    - You can also use biography databases and resources available from the University Libraries.
- Is there a way of verifying the legitimacy of the content creator? Did the author(s) provide full contact information (e.g., phone number or postal address)? Using only an e-mail address is not enough, since they are easily obtained and difficult to verify.
- If the source is an Internet site, what is the domain?
    - .gov indicates a government site
    - .edu indicates an educational site
    - .org indicates a nonprofit, advocacy, or public interest site
    - .com indicates a commercial site such as news, business, or marketing

## Accuracy and Reliability

As a general rule of thumb, never quote from an unknown source, and do not use information that you cannot verify. Use the points below to help you determine the accuracy and reliability of your information.

- Are the sources for any factual information clearly listed so they can be verified in another source?

- Is there documentation provided in the form of a bibliography or citations in the text, and is it enough to verify the information?
- Is the information free of errors (e.g., grammatical, spelling, typographical)? If the information source is an Internet source, does the source have a sponsor?
  o What is the purpose of the content (e.g., to instruct, entertain, inform, persuade, sell)?
- Is the author's name familiar (e.g., mentioned by your instructor or cited in other sources)? Respected authors are cited frequently by other scholars. For this reason, always note those names that appear in many different sources.

## Relevancy

It may often seem easier to adopt a grab-and-go method of research, for example using the first five articles you find; however, you may find yourself overwhelmed with information since your results may have very different information or may not relate directly to your specific research question. Your results may be too broad or too narrow to adequately answer your questions. Therefore, while reviewing a wide breadth of articles, think about what you specifically need by asking:

- Is there adequate information?
- Is the content written in understandable language?
- Does it add to what I have retrieved elsewhere?
- Is my topic covered or does the information source just happen to contain some of the same keywords or phrases?

## Currency

Depending on your topic, when an information source was published may or may not have an impact on the validity of the information. For example, the data from current research studies may contradict conclusions from an older study (even one held to be a classic in the field) because of newly discovered information or methods that are now accepted as the new industry or field standard.

To determine the currency of an information source, ask yourself the following questions:

- Can I tell when the information was published?
- For websites, do I see a date that lets me know that someone is monitoring the site? Are the sources listed current, do the links work, or are there other clues that indicate the information is current?
- Is this a first edition of this publication? Multiple editions indicate a source has been revised and updated to reflect changes in knowledge, include omissions, and harmonize with its intended reader's needs. Also, many printings or editions may indicate that the work has become a standard source in the area and is reliable.

## Objectivity

Many information sources are produced by people or organizations with a particular agenda, for a specific group, or with a political or religious message. Therefore you need to be aware of bias when selecting information to use. Ask yourself these questions when considering a resource:

- Does the content present scholarly information or personal opinion?
- Is the content fact or opinion?
- Is the coverage balanced—presenting multiple sides of an issue?
- From whose viewpoint or perspective is the content presented? Bias is not necessarily negative, especially if you are seeking a strong viewpoint. What is important is whether the author hides a bias.
- Is advertising, sponsorship, or funding evident? For example, if the information source is a scholarly article reporting the results of a study, is there a statement about how the study was funded?
- Are ads clearly delineated and separated from the informational content?
- If the information source is a website, does the organization or business posting the information have a financial interest in the information posted? For instance, a car company may state safety test

results in a format that is advantageous for sales. However, you need to compare the results with those posted by the government or consumer agency that performed the tests.

- Who is the publisher, and what other types of work have they distributed? If the source is published by a university press, it is likely to be scholarly. Although the fact that the publisher is reputable does not necessarily guarantee quality, it does show that the publisher may have high regard for the source being published.

The faculty and staff employed by the University Libraries are here to help and can assist you in a variety of ways, including (a) locating information needed for papers and projects, (b) demonstrating how to select and use article databases, (c) obtaining books and articles not available from the University Libraries, and (d) providing procedures for checking out a key to an individual or group study room. University Libraries has access to a vast amount of resources and librarians are willing to assist you.

## Academic Attribution and Plagiarism

Once you have found reliable and relevant information for your paper or presentation, you will need to ensure that you provide the proper attribution. In other words, you will need to appropriately cite your sources. Providing appropriate citations is a cornerstone of academic work. Citing sources (a) helps establish context for material, (b) allows the reader to identify and locate additional information, and (c) gives the reader an idea as to the legitimacy of your claims. It also acknowledges authors that have made previous contributions to your topic. Research and scholarly inquiry involve ongoing conversations with the academic community, whereby ideas and knowledge are advanced and developed. Citing the relevant previous research on your topic gives credit to those that came before you and demonstrates how your contribution adds to the body of knowledge. For all these reasons, academic honesty is essential in ensuring the integrity of information and protecting scholarly inquiry.

 USC LIBRARIES

The University is home to six libraries:

**Thomas Cooper Library, Reference Department**
803-777-4866

**South Caroliniana Library**
803-777-3132

**Business Library**
803-777-6032

**Music Library**
803-777-5139

**Hollings Special Collections Library**
803-777-3847

**Moving Image Research Collections**
803-777-6841

## What Is Plagiarism?

The failure to properly cite your sources is considered plagiarism. The Office of Academic Integrity at the University of South Carolina defines plagiarism as the act of taking another's ideas, writings, or work and presenting it as your own in whole or in part. Plagiarism includes the following:

- Copying and pasting words, sentences, ideas, conclusions, and/or examples from any source (e.g., book, article, website, or even another student) and submitting it as your own work, without properly acknowledging the source
- "Sloppy" or improper paraphrasing- only changing a few words here and there in an otherwise directly copied passage so that the passage still retains the same thought as intended by the original author
- Patch-writing words, sentences, and/or examples from a source without proper acknowledgment
- Submission of another person's completed assignment, term paper, and/or exam as your own
- Knowingly aiding another student in any of the actions listed above

## Why Do Students Plagiarize?

There are many reasons why students plagiarize. Some students run out of time while working on a project; some are uninspired by the assignment; some are driven by intense competition; while still others simply may not understand the material. The predominant reason, though, is that many students do not *fully* understand *what* they must cite nor *when to do so*. It is important for you to know the general guidelines for when to cite, as well as strategies for avoiding this form of academic dishonesty.

## When and What to Cite

A common concern among new scholars is determining when and what to cite. You should cite in text when:

**You provide statistics, data, or other factual information taken from a source.** This is important so your reader knows how to find this information. The source can be a clue as to the validity of the data. Readers may also want to be able to

## A NOTE ABOUT SELF-PLAGIARISM

Acts of "self-plagiarism" such as when a student recycles or resubmits materials they have previously used for another class or assignment, actually falls under the "Lying" policy of the University of South Carolina's Honor Code. While you might have been the original author, unless you clear it with your professor first, avoid reusing old assignments!

Professors typically expect original work that fulfills the criteria for that assignment... not one you did years ago! If your professor does give you permission to use your previous work, make sure you properly cite yourself! If you are not sure how to do this, just ask your professor.

see the context of the study that provided the data to ensure that the statistics are being used appropriately.

> Between 1971 and 2000, the average price at public four-year institutions rose by 121 percent (Baum, 2001).

**You use a direct quotation from someone else.** Anytime you use someone else's words, you must put them in quotation marks (or a block quote for long passages) and cite the original source along with the page number so the reader can easily find the original text.

> Morphew (2002) found that "since 1990, more than 120 public and private four-year colleges have changed their names and became universities" (p. 207).

**You summarize or paraphrase someone else's words, ideas, or concepts.** When paraphrasing, you do not need to use quotation marks, but you must cite the author(s).

> Massy (1999) argued that prestige is viewed as a surrogate for higher education's contribution to society.

**Citing information or text you found quoted or cited by another work that you have not read.** In this case, you need to give attribution to both sources.

> These trends created what Pat Callan of the National Center for Public Policy in Higher Education referred to as the "perfect storm" (as cited in Ehrenberg, 2006).

You do *not* need to cite in text when:

**The information is commonly known (either by the general population, or within the particular discipline).**

While there is no absolute list of criteria to make this determination, generally, common knowledge includes information that is:

- Familiar (e.g., South Carolina is a coastal state)
- Easily available in various sources, such as encyclopedias (e.g., Abraham Lincoln was the 16th president of the United States)
- Not arguable or in question (e.g., smoking is hazardous to your health)

## SAFEASSIGN

You may submit assignments and papers on your course Blackboard site using SafeAssign, a plagiarism prevention tool. SafeAssign will review your assignment and identify any areas of possible plagiarism.

## TIPS FOR MANAGING YOUR CITATIONS

**Use proper citations when citing material.**
Review the Reference Department online citation guides at http://guides.library.sc.edu/citationguides. There are also many software programs available that make citing your sources quick, easy, and accurate. Tools like Endnote or Zotero (a free plug in for some web browsers) allow you to create a database of the sources you use for your papers and will automatically format your in-text citations and works cited or bibliography. Microsoft Word also has a built-in citations manager that will automatically format your in-text citations and reference page.

**Keep track of citations when writing your rough draft.**
When writing, highlight your citations in a different font color. This gives you a visual cue to help you keep track of where your citations are, what sources you are using, and how much of the current work is actually your own. This also helps when making your reference page!

guides.library.sc.edu/
citationguides

Remember that what *you* may think is common knowledge may *not* be as common as you think!

**It is your own original thought or opinion.**

When in doubt, cite! You will not be accused of plagiarism for too much citing. Keep in mind, however, that you want to find your own voice in your writing rather than over-relying on other people's words.

## How to Avoid Plagiarism

Hunt and Birks (2008) offer some practical solutions for making sure you do not inadvertently plagiarize. Here are their suggestions:

1. Have varied and quality sources to work from.
2. Take good notes from your sources.
   - Write down keywords, not whole phrases.
   - Include the page number and source if you write down a whole phrase so you can cite it later if you use it verbatim. Be sure to put the phrase in quotation marks to remind yourself that the wording is identical to the original source.
   - Write notes from each different source on separate sheets of paper, with the citation for the source at the top. It is much easier to remember where you got the information if you do it this way.
   - Write from your notes, not the sources you have used.
   - It is less tempting and not as easy to plagiarize if you are writing from your notes. However, your notes must be well-written and organized.
3. Write in your own words.
   - Many students are concerned about grammar or vocabulary, and they lift whole sentences from other people's writing because they are afraid of making mistakes.
   - Write simple sentences; short is okay.
   - Concentrate on getting your meaning across in the simplest way.

4. Give yourself plenty of time to complete the paper. Do not try to research and write all at the same time.

# Product #3: Presentations

Ever find yourself getting nervous about doing a presentation in class? You're not alone. You can have the best visual aid ever created and understand the material well, but your desire to present is just not there. It takes time, and more importantly, experience, to get better and hopefully get over those butterflies. The reality is that you're going to have to present in a class at some point, and to that end, here are six distinct steps you can take to get ready:

## Step One: Clarify your objective.

- What is the purpose of your presentation?
- What do you want your audience to know, believe, or do when you are finished?

## Step Two: Analyze your audience.

- Who are my audience members?
- What do they already know about my topic?
- What do they want or need to know?
- What are their attitudes toward me, my ideas, and my topic?

## Step Three: Collect and organize your information.

- Make a list of all possible points you may want to include and choose the 3-5 most important main points that you are going to cover in your presentation.
- Slides with paragraphs of information are distracting to the audience and hard to follow.
- Find appropriate and reliable source material to support your main points.
- Arrange your main points in a way that guides your listeners and best meets the objective of your presentation.

### Step Four: Choose your visual aids.

- Using visual aids are useful in helping you organize the material and helping the audience better understand and recall what they are hearing.
- Visual aids can include PowerPoint slides, handouts, posters, or video clips.
- Be sure to include your sources on each slide.
- Limit the amount of information you include on each slide and consider using graphics and images in place of text.

### Step Five: Prepare your notes.

- Do not write out your speech; the temptation to read directly from your notes will be hard to resist.
- Do not try to memorize your entire speech. Make sure to have notes to refer to if your memory fails.
- Do have a brief speaking outline from which you can speak extemporaneously.

### Step Six: Practice your delivery.

- Rehearse your presentation aloud several times.
- Do not read directly from the slides.
- Rehearse your presentation in front of an audience – your roommate, a classmate, your parents, or yourself in a mirror – to help you get a feel for what it will be like to have an audience before the actual presentation.

Source: Gardner, J. N., Jewler, A. J., & Barefoot, B. O. *Your College Experience: Strategies for Success, 8th edition.* Copyright(c) 2009 Bedford/St. Martin's. Used with permission of Bedford/St. Martins.

Above all, when it comes to presentations, preparation is key. Know your materials, understand what your presentation requirements are, and practice!

# Product #4: Group Work

Another way college student performance is measured and practiced is through group work. While this is often a source of frustration for students, there is certainly a method to the madness. In addition to preparing you for the realities of the working world, "students taught in a manner that incorporates small-group learning achieve higher grades, learn at a deeper level, retain information longer, are less likely to drop out of school, acquire greater communication and teamwork skills, and gain a better understanding of the environment in which they will be working as professionals" (Brent et. al, 2004, p. 9). However, for many students group work can be daunting and frustrating. Keeping everyone on track, finding a time to meet that works with everyone's schedule, and making sure everyone participates equally can be extremely challenging. However, this challenge is *exactly* why professors make these types of assignments. No matter what you do after college, you will work with different people for the rest of your career and life. It is important that you develop strong communication skills, develop effective ways to establish expectations, and work with people towards a common goal. Group work helps you accomplish all these things.

Dozens of skills can be gained for students who participate in group work. Project management, delegation, task accomplishment, goal achievement, and effective communication are all essential components of working in a group setting and are ultimately some of the best transferable skills. However, working in a group often presents challenges. The "Coping with Hitchhikers and Couch Potatoes on Teams" article, on pages 47-49, presents advice on how to handle certain types of group members that do not pull their own weight.

# Adopting a Growth Mindset on Academic Success – You Can Do This!

As a college student, you will have some challenges ahead of you in your first year and beyond. But, don't think of these as insurmountable: consider them learning opportunities and a chance to improve your skills and learn new strategies using a growth mindset. Having a growth mindset means you are not fixed in your beliefs about yourself and you understand you are capable of developing and improving upon your existing skill sets. People with a growth mindset believe that their intelligence and success are largely within their control, as opposed to people with a fixed mindset who believe that their abilities were set at birth. When faced with failure or an obstacle, individuals with a fixed mindset tend to attribute the failure to their own inabilities, while growth-minded individuals choose to interpret the failure as the result of insufficient effort or ineffective strategies, and then dig deeper and try different approaches (Brown et al., 2014). Research is quite clear that a student's ability to be successful in college (and in life) are not dictated by innate abilities and intelligence, but rather through discipline, grit, resilience, and having a growth mindset (Brown et al., 2014, Dweck, 2006).

All students accepted to the University of South Carolina have the opportunity to develop the skills needed to succeed. Make a habit of identifying and implementing new study strategies, utilizing the many campus resources available, and making the most out of every learning experience you encounter.

# COPING WITH HITCHHIKERS AND COUCH POTATOES ON TEAMS

You will usually find your university teammates as interested in learning as you are. Occasionally, however, you may encounter a person who creates difficulties. This handout is meant to give you practical advice for this type of situation. To begin with, let's imagine you have been assigned to a combined homework and lab group this semester with three others: Mary, Henry, and Jack. Mary is okay-she's not good at solving problems, but she tries hard, and she willingly does things like get extra help from the professor. Henry is irritating. He's a nice guy, but he just doesn't put in the effort to do a good job. He'll sheepishly hand over partially worked homework problems and confess to spending the weekend watching TV. Jack, on the other hand, has been nothing but a problem. Here are a few of the things Jack has done:

- When you tried to set up meetings at the beginning of the semester, Jack just couldn't meet, because he was too busy.

- Jack infrequently turns in his part of the homework. When he does, it's almost always wrong - he obviously spent just enough time to scribble something down that looks like work.

- Jack has never answered phone messages. When you confront him, he denies getting any messages. You e-mail him, but he's "too busy to answer."

- Jack misses every meeting. He always promises he'll be there, but never shows up.

- His writing skills are okay, but he can't seem to do anything right for lab reports. He loses the drafts, doesn't reread his work, leaves out tables, or does something sloppy like write equations by hand. You've stopped assigning him work because you don't want to miss your professor's strict deadlines.

- Jack constantly complains about his fifty-hour work weeks, heavy school load, bad textbooks, and terrible teachers. At first you felt sorry for him-but recently you've begun to wonder if Jack is using you.

- Jack speaks loudly and self-confidently when you try to discuss his problems- he thinks the problems are everyone else's fault. He is so self-assured that you can't help wondering sometimes if he's right.

Your group finally was so upset they went to discuss the situation with Professor Distracted. He in turn talked, along with the group, to Jack, who in sincere and convincing fashion said he hadn't really understood what everyone wanted him to do. Dr. Distracted said the problem must be the group was not communicating effectively. He noticed you, Mary, and Henry looked angry and agitated, while Jack simply looked bewildered, a little hurt, and not at all guilty. It was easy for Dr. Distracted to conclude this was a dysfunctional group, and everyone was at fault-probably Jack least of all.

The bottom line: *You and your teammates are left holding the bag. Jack is getting the same good grades as everyone else without doing any work. And yes, he managed to make you all look bad while he was at it.*

## WHAT THIS GROUP DID WRONG: ABSORBING

This was an 'absorber' group. From the very beginning they absorbed the problem when Jack did something wrong, and took pride in getting the job done whatever the cost. *Hitchhikers count on you to act in a self-sacrificing manner.* However, the nicer you are (or the nicer you think you are being), the more the hitchhiker will be able to hitchhike their way through the university, and through life. By absorbing the hitchhiker's problems, you are inadvertently training the hitchhiker to become the kind of person who thinks it is all right to take credit for the work of others.

continued on next page

# COPING WITH HITCHHIKERS AND COUCH POTATOES ON TEAMS

## WHAT THIS GROUP SHOULD HAVE DONE: MIRRORING

It's important to reflect back the dysfunctional behavior of the hitchhiker, so the hitchhiker pays the price - not you. Never accept accusations, blame, or criticism from a hitchhiker. Maintain your own sense of reality despite what the hitchhiker says (easier said than done). *Show you have a bottom line: there are limits to the behavior you will accept.* Clearly communicate these limits and act consistently on them. For example, here is what the group could have done:

- When Jack couldn't find time to meet in his busy schedule, even when alternatives were suggested, you needed to decide whether Jack was a hitchhiker. Was Jack brusque, self-important, and in a hurry to get away? Those are suspicious signs. Someone needed to tell Jack up front to either find time to meet, or talk to the professor.

- If Jack turns nothing in, his name does not go on the finished work. (Note: if you know your teammate is generally a contributor, it is appropriate to help if something unexpected arises.) Many professors allow a team to fire a student, so the would-be freeloader has to work alone the rest of the semester. Discuss this option with your instructor if the student has not contributed over the course of an assignment or two.

- If Jack turns in poorly prepared homework or lab reports, you must tell him he has not contributed meaningfully, so his name will not go on the submitted work. No matter what Jack says, stick to your guns! If Jack gets abusive, show the professor his work. Do this the first time the junk is submitted, before Jack has taken much advantage – not after a month, when you are really getting frustrated.

- Set your limits early and high, because hitchhikers have an uncanny ability to detect just how much they can get away with.

- If Jack doesn't respond to e-mails, answer phone messages, or show up for meetings, don't waste more time trying to contact him. (It can be helpful, particularly in industry, to use e-mail for contacting purposes, because then a written record is available about the contact attempt. Copying the e-mail to Jack's supervisor or other important people can often produce surprisingly effective results.)

- Keep in mind the only one who can handle Jack's problems is Jack. You can't change him - you can only change your own attitude so he no longer takes advantage of you. Only Jack can change Jack and he will have no incentive to change if you do all his work for him.

People like Jack can be skilled manipulators. By the time you find out his problems are never-ending, and he himself is their cause, the semester has ended and he is off to repeat his manipulations on a new, unsuspecting group. Stop allowing these dysfunctional patterns early in the game - before the hitchhiker takes advantage of you and the rest of your team!

## HENRY, THE COUCH POTATO

But we haven't discussed Henry yet. Although Henry stood up with the rest of the group to try to battle against Jack's irrational behavior, he hasn't really been pulling his weight. (If you think of yourself as tired and bored and really more interested in watching TV than working on your homework everyone has had times like these - you begin to get a picture of the couch potato.)

You will find the best way to deal with a couch potato like Henry is the way you deal with a hitchhiker: set firm, explicit expectations - then stick to your guns. Although couch potatoes are not as manipulative as hitchhikers, they will definitely test your limits. If your limits are weak, you then share the blame if you have Henry's work to do as well as your own.

## BUT I'VE NEVER LIKED TELLING PEOPLE WHAT TO DO!

If you are a nice person who has always avoided confrontation, working with a couch potato or a hitchhiker can help you grow as a person and learn the important character trait of firmness. Just be patient with yourself as you learn. The first few times you try to be firm, you may find yourself thinking, "but now he/she won't like me—it's not worth the pain!" But many people just like you have had exactly the same troubled reaction the first few (or even many) times they tried to be firm. Just keep trying - and stick to your guns! Someday it will seem more natural and you won't feel so guilty about having reasonable expectations for others. In the meantime, you will find you have more time to spend with your family, friends, or school work, because you aren't doing someone else's job along with your own

## COMMON CHARACTERISTICS THAT ALLOW A HITCHHIKER TO TAKE ADVANTAGE

- Unwillingness to allow a slacker to fail and subsequently learn from their own mistakes.

- Devotion to the ideal of 'the good of the team' without common-sense realization of how this can allow others to take advantage of you. Sometimes you show (and are secretly proud of) irrational loyalty to others.

- You like to make others happy even at your own expense. You always feel you have to do better-your best is never enough. Your willingness to interpret the slightest contribution by a slacker as 'progress.' You are willing to make personal sacrifices so as to not abandon a hitchhiker-without realizing you are devaluing yourself in this process. Long-suffering martyrdom - nobody but you could stand this. The ability to cooperate but not delegate.

- Excessive conscientiousness.

- The tendency to feel responsible for others at the expense of being responsible for yourself.

## A RELATED CIRCUMSTANCE: YOU'RE DOING ALL THE WORK

As soon as you become aware everyone is leaving the work to you - or doing such poor work that you are left doing it all, you need to take action. Many professors allow you the leeway to request a move to another team. (You cannot move to another group on your own.) Your professor will probably ask some questions before taking the appropriate action.

## LATER ON: OUT ON THE JOB AND IN YOUR PERSONAL LIFE

You will meet couch potatoes and hitchhikers throughout the course of your professional career. Couch potatoes are relatively benign, can often be firmly guided to do reasonably good work, and can even become your friends. However, hitchhikers are completely different people-ones who can work their way into your confidence and then destroy it. (Hitchhikers may infrequently try to befriend you and cooperate once you've gained their respect because they can't manipulate you. Just because they've changed their behavior towards you, however, doesn't mean they won't continue to do the same thing to others.) Occasionally, a colleague, subordinate, supervisor, friend, or acquaintance could be a hitchhiker. If this is the case, and your personal or professional life is being affected, it will help if you keep in mind the techniques suggested above.

---

Source: Randall (1997, 2004). Reprinted with Permission.

# STUDENT SUCCESS CENTER

The Student Success Center (SSC) is a comprehensive one-stop-shop for academic support services on campus. All of the center's programs and initiatives are free to undergraduate students at the University of South Carolina. The administrative office is located in the Thomas Cooper Library (Mezzanine Level), and three satellite offices are located in these residence halls: Bates House, Columbia Hall, and Sims at Women's Quad.

## COURSE SPECIFIC ACADEMIC SUPPORT

**Supplemental Instruction (SI):** Weekly collaborative study sessions for students enrolled in traditionally challenging first and second year courses. SI sessions integrate what to study with how to study in a structured peer-led environment.

**Peer Tutoring:** One-on-one tutoring that provides quality, course-specific academic support to students. Every semester Peer Tutoring supports over 80 courses.

**Drop-in Peer Tutoring:** Peer tutoring that is conveniently located in several residence halls and academic buildings and does not require an appointment.

**Online Learning:** Provides students with online peer tutoring and one-on-one support.

## OUTREACH AND EARLY INTERVENTION

**Financial Literacy:** Provides free one-on-one financial consultations to help students adjust to handling all the responsibilities that come with managing money in college.

**Transfer and Veteran Services:** Connects undergraduate transfer students and student veterans to support resources that promote successful transitions at Carolina.

**Out-to-Lunch:** Gives students an opportunity to invite professors to lunch on campus, encouraging interaction outside of the classroom.

---

 803-777-1000

 sc.edu/success

 Thomas Cooper Library, Mezzanine Level
Office Hours: 8:30am - 5:00pm
Service Hours: 9:00am - 10:00pm

## REFLECTION QUESTIONS

1. The chapter opens with the following statistic: 73% of Carolina students who started their bachelor's degree in fall 2007 graduated within six years (University of South Carolina Admissions, 2015). What do you think prevents students finishing their degree at USC?

2. The chart on p. 18 discusses several ways that high school is different than college. Please provide at least three examples of ways you have seen this play out in your own experience.

3. The chapter describes several strategies that promote academic success in college (e.g., Limiting Distractions, Read, Recite, Review, Taking Notes). Which strategies did you find most helpful and why?

4. Think about the courses that you are currently enrolled in or ones you plan to take. In what ways can Tutoring, Supplemental Instruction, or Study Groups contribute to your academic success?

5. What academic strategies (described in the chapter) could you implement to improve your performance with exams, papers, presentations, and group work?

6. What strategies can you implement into your academic work to avoid plagiarism?

7. The chapter includes ways to cope with "hitchhikers and couch potatoes" on teams. What goals or strategies can you implement to avoid frustration within group work?

## RESOURCES

**University Advising Center** . . . . . . . . . . (803) 777-1222
Close-Hipp Building, Suite 102
http://www.sc.edu/advising/

**Math Tutoring Center**
LeConte College, Room 105
http://www.math.sc.edu/mathlab.html

**Student Disability Services** . . . . . . . . . . (803) 777-6142
Telecommunications Device for the Deaf
(TDD) . . . . . . . . . . . . . . . . . . . . . . . . . . (803) 777-6744
LeConte College, Room 112A
http://www.sa.sc.edu/sds/

**Student Success Center** . . . . . . . . . . . . . . (803) 777-0684
Thomas Cooper Library-- Mezzanine Level
http://www.sa.sc.edu/ssc/

**Writing Center** . . . . . . . . . . . . . . . . . . . . . . . (803) 777-2078
702 Byrnes Building
http://www.cas.sc.edu/write/

**Writers' Hotline** . . . . . . . . . . . . . . . . . . . . . . (803) 777-2078

# REFERENCES

Brent, R., Elhajj, I., Felder, R. M., Oakley, B. (2004). Turning student groups into effective teams. *Journal of Student Centered Learning, 2*. Retrieved from http://bie.org/object/document/turning_student_groups_into_effective_teams

Brown, P. C., Roediger, H. L., McDaniel, M. A. (2014). *Make it stick: The science of successful learning*. Cambridge, MA: The Belknap Press of Harvard University Press.

Cooperative Institutional Research Program (CIRP). (2015). The American freshman: National norms fall 2014. Retrieved from: http://www.heri.ucla.edu/monographs/TheAmericanFreshman2014.pdf

Crede, M., Roch, S., & Kieszczynka, U. (2010). Class attendance in college: A meta-analytic review of the relationship of class attendance with grades and student characteristics. *Review of Educational Research, 80*(2), 272-295.

Dunlosky, J., et al. (2013). Improving students' learning with effective learning techniques: Promising directions from cognitive and educational psychology. *Psychological Science, 14*, 5-58.

Dweck, C. (2008). *Mindset: The new psychology of success*. New York, NY: Ballentine Books.

Gardner, J. N., Jewler, A. J., & Barefoot, B. O. (2009). *Your college experience: Strategies for success* (8th ed.). Boston, MA: Bedford/St. Martin's.

Gump, S. (2005). The cost of cutting class: Attendance as a predictor of success. *College Teaching, 53*, 21-26.

Hunt, F., & Birks, J. (2008). More hands-on information literacy activities. New York, NY: Neal-Schuman Publishers.

Jones, M. G. (1989). T-zone, target students and science classroom interactions. Paper presented at the Annual Meeting of the National Association for Research in Science Teaching, San Francisco, CA.

Medina, J. (2008). *Brain rules: 12 principles for surviving and thriving at work, home, and school*. Seattle, WA: Pear Press.

Mueller, P., & Oppenheimer, D. (2014). The pen is mightier than the keyboard: Advantages of longhand over laptop Notetaking. *Psychological Science, 25*, 1159-1168.

Odhiambo, E. (2010). How teacher positioning in the classroom affects the on-task behavior of students. *E-Journal of Student Research, 2*, 1-9.

Randall, V. (1997, 2004). Coping with Hitchhikers and Couch Potatoes on Teams. Retrieved from http://academic.udayton.edu/legaled/online/exams/group04.htm

Southern Methodist University. (2015). How is college different from high school? Retrieved from http://www.smu.edu/Provost/ALEC/NeatStuffforNewStudents/HowIsCollegeDifferentfromHighSchool

University of South Carolina Office of Financial Aid. (2015). Cost, tuition, and financial aid. Retrieved from: http://www.sc.edu/apply/cost_tuition_financial_aid/

University of South Carolina Office of Institutional Research and Assessment. (2015). Annual retention and graduation report, 1995-2013 cohorts, Columbia campus. Retrieved from: http://www.ipr.sc.edu/retention/retent.public.pdf

University of South Carolina Admissions. (2015). Office of undergraduate admissions. Retrieved from: http://sc.edu/admissions/apply/first_year_students/default.html

University of South Carolina Advising Center. (2015). Undergraduate advising at USC-Columbia. Retrieved from: http://www.sc.edu/advising/

University of South Carolina Student Success Center. (2015). Retrieved from: http://www.sc.edu/success/

Wollen K. A., Cone, R. S., Britcher, J. C., Mindemann, K. M. (1985). The effect of instructional sets upon the apportionment of study time to individual lines of text. *Human Learning, 4*, 89-103.

# CHAPTER 3

# Managing Time

Dear First-Year Student,

Welcome to the University of South Carolina! As a faculty member in the English department, I spent years directing the university's English 101 and 102 classes, which thousands of first-year students complete each year. I notice that most successful students on our campus aren't always the most naturally gifted scholars or those with the best high-school preparation—but rather those who make productive use of their time.

Time management skills do not come naturally to most college students, though. With all the opportunities and obligations you need to juggle during your first semester on campus, it is normal to feel over-committed. Although no single strategy works for everyone, here are a few recommendations to consider as you plan for a successful first year:

- Create a system. Time management experts agree: keeping a calendar, whether it's a traditional agenda book or an app on your phone, helps you to chart out your obligations. Enter major deadlines and obligations first, so that you can plan around them.
- Put academic obligations first. You'll be pleased to find out that going to class and doing your work when assigned actually saves you time and stress! Plan to spend two hours outside of class for every hour you spend in class, and block this time into your calendar. Then show up—not only for class, but also for your appointed study time.
- Make time for other activities. No one can (or should) study all the time; time spent with friends or exploring non-academic interests is an important part of your college experience. You'll learn to strike a balance—and that starts with the word "no." This is your first semester. Give yourself some breathing room and don't try to do everything that interests you (save some things for later!).
- Take care of your health. Research on learning and the brain shows that exercise, getting enough sleep and eating right not only keeps you feeling well, it also helps you learn. So, when you're scheduling your time, you'll want to plan for sleep, exercise and healthy eating.
- Expect the unexpected. No plan is perfect, and emergencies happen. You might have two exams and a paper due on the same day, and then come down with the flu. Do the best you can, and if you need advice or support, don't hesitate to ask for help. Campus resources such as the Academic Centers for Excellence coaches in the Student Success Center specialize in helping students enhance their study and time management skills.

When you look at how you spend your time this academic year, remember to go after what you want most, not what seems most pressing this minute. That means you'll have to pass up some things from time to time—but don't worry. By keeping the truly important things a priority, you'll be better able to enjoy your friends and your university when you are free from the stress of undone work and over-whelming deadlines.

Best wishes for a great first year on campus.
Sincerely,

Christy Friend

Christy Friend
Professor of English; Director, Center for Teaching Excellence

**ONE** of the greatest challenges first-year college students face is managing their time effectively. In high school, you may have followed the same schedule every day or were reminded by teachers and parents about deadlines and responsibilities. Your parents and teachers may have also helped to keep you on task and motivated. In college, you are responsible for setting your own schedule and determining how you will spend your time, which is both exciting and sometimes overwhelming. This new freedom also means that "the opportunity for more distractions exists" (Mullendore & Hatch, 2000, p. 9). These distractions often make it difficult for first-year students to juggle all their responsibilities which can include 12-18 hours of class, work, co-curricular activities, and sometimes multiple hours of downtime throughout the week. As students transition from high school to college, they must learn how to deal with unstructured time and competing demands. This is often challenging, as approximately 91% of first-year students at Carolina last year indicated that they frequently or occasionally felt overwhelmed by all they had to do. Developing solid time management strategies will be vital to your success in college and beyond.

## Time Management

Time management refers to your ability to balance responsibilities, manage priorities, and work toward your goals, while maintaining a lifestyle that is healthy and satisfying. Time management is a crucial skill to develop when you are in college. The ability to effectively manage time has been found to be positively correlated with grades (Gortner Lahmers, & Zulauf, 2000) and overall health. Misra and McKean (2000) found that students who practiced time-management behaviors, including starting tasks before due dates, breaking down large tasks, and completing tasks on a regular schedule, experienced lower academic stress as a result.

Covey (1989) noted in his book *The 7 Habits of Highly Effective People* that the term *time management* is really a misnomer. The challenge is not to manage your time, but to learn to manage yourself. Thus, time management is really less about technique and more about motivation,

discipline, and self-regulation. Self-regulation refers to the extent to which people are motivated and able to stick to their goal and persist into action towards the goal even when they are confronted with competing motivations (Kuhl & Fuhrmann, 1998). Covey also suggested that the key is not simply spending time, but in investing in it. Given that time is a finite resource, how will you effectively invest in yourself and your time? In other words, how will you use your limited amount of time and energy to accomplish your goals and manage your responsibilities? Thus, to effectively begin managing your time, you must first identify what you want to accomplish.

## Aligning Your Goals and Values

How you spend your time is often determined by your goals and values. Everyone spends 168 hours each week devoting their time and energy to various tasks; how are you spending your time? As a new student at Carolina, you will have to decide how to balance your time in order to be successful. Setting goals is a great first step in determining where you need to spend your time. Have you ever set goals for yourself only to find months later that you did not accomplish those goals? The key to effective goal setting is aligning your goals with your values. Unless you know why you want something, you are not likely to invest time discovering that particular goal. For example, you may be motivated to do well in organic chemistry because you know it will help you achieve your goal of getting in to medical school. Also, you might be motivated to maintain a 3.0 GPA because that is what you need in order to keep your scholarships. Reflecting on what you value will help you recognize what is important in your life and act as a means of evaluating what decisions to make.

## Goal Setting

Setting goals often provides a long-term goal with short-term motivation. It's good to set both minor and major goals.

Examples of minor goals are:
- Completing a homework assignment

THE KEY TO EFFECTIVE GOAL SETTING IS ALIGNING YOUR GOALS WITH YOUR VALUES.

- Reading a chapter of your textbook before lunch
- E-mailing your professor about the topics on your midterm

Setting and fulfilling minor goals gives you a sense of accomplishment and the motivation to create and tackle major goals.

Examples of major goals are:
- Earning a 3.6 GPA at the end of your first year
- Being admitted to pharmacy school
- Securing a summer internship with a reputable organization or business

Major goals, often, are distant and future-focused. They are meant to motivate and inspire you to reach a target. For some students, setting major goals might come naturally, and for others, the process might seem scary and daunting. Even though goals will vary widely from student to student, all major goals come from same the place—the things you want and need. Choosing your goal might just seem like choosing an occupation, but in reality, it is about knowing yourself and what you value most in life (Owens & Pauk, 2008).

## S M A R T Goals

When creating goals, it is important to move beyond the lofty dreams and wishes you may have had since you were a child. As a college student, you need to set goals that are specific (S), measurable (M), attainable (A), realistic (R), and timely (T). When creating goals, think of the destination and the process that will help you get there and use these criteria.

*Specific* – Goals that are too general are less likely to be accomplished. A specific goal answers these six questions: (a) Who is involved? (b) What do I want to accomplish? (c) Where is the location? (d) When will it happen? (e) Which requirements and restraints are needed? and (f) Why should I pursue this goal?

*Measurable* – For a goal to be measurable, you need to establish criteria for assessing your progress. By measuring your goal, you are more likely to stay on track, reach your target dates, and know the feeling

of success after you have completed the steps along the way.

*Attainable* - Once you have identified your goals, it is time for you to plan your steps, develop a positive attitude, and identify the abilities and skills you need. By doing this, you will be able to accomplish almost any goal!

*Realistic* - A realistic goal is one that you are able to work toward. You are the only one who can decide whether or not your goal meets this standard.

*Timely* - Giving your goal a time frame provides you a clear target to work toward. Without a time frame, there is no urgency or commitment to take action.

## How do you spend your time?

Once you have identified what you want to accomplish, the next step in managing time is to align your priorities with your allocation of time and energy. Do you have a good sense of where your time goes? Just like it's a best practice to budget and track your spending, it's also equally important to do the same with your time. Both money and time are finite resources, so consider treating them comparably. Personal data analytics are all the rage these days. Many people use tools like a Fitbit or iPhone to track their steps or calories. Self-tracking and assessment is important to better understand what we do and then make a plan to be more healthy or effective. Consider using the activity on page 61 to track how you spend your time. Choose a typical week in the semester and track your time for one week. Include all relevant categories, including sleep, study, leisure, and work. After tracking your time, make a graph to see a visual display of your time. That will make it easier to analyze the results. See the figure below for the typical breakdown of activities for a first-year student at Carolina. What is your ratio of free time to study time? To what extent is the use of your time aligned with your priorities and goals? Often, many students find that the challenge with time management in the first year of college is not that there is not enough

ONE PARADOXICAL KEY IS TO STAY BUSY. ACKERMAN AND GROSS (2003) FOUND THAT STUDENTS WITH LESS FREE TIME HAVE A SIGNIFICANTLY HIGHER GPA THAN THOSE WITH MORE FREE TIME.

# Academic Goal Setting Sheet

| CLASS/ASSIGNMENT | S.M.A.R.T. GOAL | STRATEGIES | DEADLINE |
|---|---|---|---|
| | | | |
| | | | |
| | | | |
| | | | |
| | | | |
| | | | |
| | | | |

time, but rather finding the motivation and discipline to use time wisely. It's easy to discover ways in which you may "waste" time. Many University 101 students report that their biggest time waster in college is Netflix. But how do you motivate yourself and hold yourself accountable to turn off Netflix and start studying for your classes? While there is no magic formula or answer, this could be a great discussion question to ask other students in your University 101 class or residence hall to find out what strategies may work for you. One paradoxical key is to stay busy. Ackerman and Gross (2003) found that students with less free time have a significantly higher GPA than those with more free time. Being busy compelled students to improve their time-management and study skills.

According to Chickering and Gamson (1987), students who are most successful devote an appropriate amount of time to academic tasks. The only way to learn new information or develop new skills is to practice and spend time doing it.

# TYPICAL FIRST-YEAR STUDENT WEEKLY TIME CHART

SLEEP
60 HOURS

EXERCISE
3 HOURS

WORK
5 HOURS

LEISURE
23 HOURS

PERSONAL CARE
9 HOURS

CO-CURRICULAR
10 HOURS

STUDY
20 HOURS

OTHER
11 HOURS

CLASS
15 HOURS

EATING
12 HOURS

*Note*: Data were gathered from a University 101 class.

# Weekly Schedule

| TIME | MON | TUES | WEDS | THURS | FRI | SAT | SUN |
|---|---|---|---|---|---|---|---|
| 6:00 am | | | | | | | |
| 7:00 am | | | | | | | |
| 8:00 am | | | | | | | |
| 9:00 am | | | | | | | |
| 10:00 am | | | | | | | |
| 11:00 am | | | | | | | |
| noon | | | | | | | |
| 1:00 pm | | | | | | | |
| 2:00 pm | | | | | | | |
| 3:00 pm | | | | | | | |
| 4:00 pm | | | | | | | |
| 5:00 pm | | | | | | | |
| 6:00 pm | | | | | | | |
| 7:00 pm | | | | | | | |
| 8:00 pm | | | | | | | |
| 9:00 pm | | | | | | | |
| 10:00 pm | | | | | | | |
| 11:00 pm | | | | | | | |
| midnight | | | | | | | |
| 1:00 am | | | | | | | |
| 2:00 am | | | | | | | |
| 3:00 am | | | | | | | |
| 4:00 am | | | | | | | |
| 5:00 am | | | | | | | |

Gladwell (2008) reported that what separates one performer or athlete from another is not natural talent but time devoted to practicing the task! For true expertise, 10,000 hours of practice is required to develop a level of mastery. While you may not spend 10,000 hours on your undergraduate studies, the more time you devote, the greater the expertise you will develop.

# Procrastination

Despite the clarity of goals and desire to focus on productive activities, the reality is that everyone procrastinates about something at some point. However, not everyone is a procrastinator. The term procrastination comes from Latin procrastinare, meaning to put off or postpone to another day (Ferrari, Johnson, & McCown, 1995). Generally, people put off the tasks that are harder and less enjoyable. Boice (1996) defined procrastination as "opting for short-term relief through acts that are easy and immediately rewarding, while generally avoiding even the thought (and its anxiety) of doing more difficult, delayable, important things" (p. 6). Thus, many people occupy time by staying busy with easy and short tasks, which can lead to feelings of accomplishment because short-term items are getting checked off the to-do list. However, this can also mean that more important tasks are getting less attention.

Whether procrastination becomes a problem or not depends on how it impacts your life (Ferrari, 2010). It might be acceptable to procrastinate cleaning your room, but delaying on major academic projects, such as your papers or preparing for exams, could significantly impact your grades.

Research indicates that while about 20% of the U.S. population are considered chronic procrastinators, about 75% of college students procrastinate on academic tasks such as studying, reading, and keeping appointments, and 50% reported doing it regularly and consider it a problem (Ferrari, 2010; Burka & Yuen, 2008). Piers Steel (2011), a leading scholar on procrastination, suggested that college students may be more prone to procrastination because academic tasks are viewed as unpleasant, the due date is generally far

## PROCRASTINATOR'S CLOCK

If you are you always running late to class or other meetings, try downloading a "procrastinator's clock." This computer program will display a digital clock that runs up to 15 minutes fast. The trick is the clock speeds up and slows down, assuring that you can't game the system.

away, and there are a lot of exciting enticements on a college campus that provide alternatives to studying.

Procrastinators tend to be more impulsive, and are easily bored and distracted (Ferrari, 2010). They often believe that they do their best work under the pressure of last minute deadlines, which provides a rush of adrenaline to complete the task. The assumption is that procrastination stems from a need to increase excitement and reduce boredom. Thus, procrastinators begin to make excuses about deferring to the last minute and believe that they will perform better under those circumstances. However, research shows that procrastinators do not do well under time limitations. They tend to make more mistakes and complete less of a task than non-procrastinators when there is a time limit (Ferrari, 2010).

So what can procrastinators do to break this habit? Get started! In their best-selling book *Switch: How to Change Things When Change is Hard*, professors Chip and Dan Heath (2010) told a story about the 5-minute room rescue. As with most people, you have probably put off a tedious task such as cleaning your room. The idea of the 5-minute room rescue is that you set the timer for five minutes and try to get as much cleaning accomplished as possible. How much cleaning can you get done in five minutes? Probably not a lot. However, starting an unpleasant task can be worse than seeing it through, and once you get going you may not have to stop when the timer rings. Try this with the academic tasks that you are inclined to put off. Set a timer for five minutes and tell yourself to work on that project until the buzzer rings. You may find that the initial step of getting started will give you the momentum you need to keep going.

It might also be helpful to set an action trigger for assignments and tasks. Alerts can be programmed into cell phones to grab your attention and remind you to start the task. If you are you always running late to class or other meetings, try downloading a free version of the "procrastinator's clock." This computer program will display a digital clock that runs up to 15 minutes fast. The trick is the clock speeds up randomly, assuring that you can't game the system. If you struggle with getting distracted by your phone or computer, try installing software such as Keep Me Out or Freedom

that will automatically limit your social media time or will not allow you to surf the web while you are writing. Other applications and web browser add-ons can be found by searching "block online distractions" on Google.

Ultimately college faculty members have much higher expectations for performance than high school teachers, so waiting until the last minute to write a paper or study for an exam will not lead to the best results. Many procrastinators in college underestimate the amount of time it will take to successfully complete a project. Some students will figure this out the hard way and make adjustments, but the price can be a lower first-semester GPA. The bottom line is to recognize when you are procrastinating and find a way to motivate yourself to get started.

## Multitasking

Many people in today's fast-paced and plugged-in world believe they can effectively multitask by focusing their attention on multiple stimuli at one time. For example, many students believe they can listen to a lecture or read their textbook while checking Instagram or texting their friends. However, the research (e.g., Cantor, 2011) is fairly clear that the belief in our ability to multitask is misguided. Simply stated: You cannot effectively multitask. Individuals can shift their focus from one priority to the next, but it is very difficult to do two things well at once. Paul Dux (n.d.), a neuroscientist at the University of Queensland, stated that "Despite the immense processing power of the human brain, it is severely capacity limited: Humans can barely attend to more than one stimulus at a time and have extreme difficulty undertaking multiple tasks concurrently" (para. 1).

This reality is problematic when trying to learn new information. In a study by Junco and Cotton (2011), 93% of students admitted to using Instant Messenger or another chatting device while doing academic work. Of these students, more than 50% recognized that this habit had a detrimental effect on their schoolwork. Moreover, Junco and Cotton (2011) found that using Facebook and texting while doing

THE RESEARCH IS FAIRLY CLEAR THAT THE BELIEF IN OUR ABILITY TO MULTITASK IS MISGUIDED. SIMPLY STATED: YOU CANNOT EFFECTIVELY MULTITASK.

schoolwork were negatively associated with overall college GPA, and Greenfield (2009) reported that multitasking decreases our ability to process and retain information. If you want to be your best in your academic work, take the time to focus on your studies and avoid multitasking.

# Scheduling Tools

Making the most of your time involves focusing and using intentional strategies to organize and track obligations and commitments. Students who have a clear idea of what they need to accomplish in the coming week and who write goals, to-do lists, and schedules at the start of each day have higher GPAs (Britton & Tesser, 1991). It is important to manage your time to support your values, priorities, and goals. There are multiple scheduling tools and methods to help you stay on track and achieve your goals, so you do not have to do it all by yourself.

## *Your Syllabus*

One of the most important tools to help you succeed in your academics and stay organized is the course syllabus. The syllabus provides a holistic understanding of the information to be covered in class and due dates for assignments and tests.

Do not make the mistake of putting the syllabus in your binder (or a trashcan) without reviewing it often. The course syllabus is considered a contract between you and your professor and outlines the expectations he or she has for the course. Be sure to review the syllabus to become familiar with all course expectations, exam and presentation due dates, workload, and policies. However, *knowing* is not the key to success; *doing* something with the information is key! Use your syllabus as a preparation tool to stay abreast of assignments and exams.

In the first few weeks of each semester, take all of your syllabi and complete the Semester at a Glance Worksheet located at the end of the chapter. You can create your own document on your computer or spreadsheet if you prefer. This worksheet will help you compile all major due dates into one document and display it where you will see your

# Jamie's Calendar

| | MONDAY | TUESDAY | WEDNESDAY | THURSDAY | FRIDAY | TO DO LIST: |
|---|---|---|---|---|---|---|
| 7 AM | | | | | | ☐ Go to Dr. Ray's office hours |
| 8 AM | 8 - 9 Biology Class | 8 - 9:30 Exercise | 8 - 9 Biology Class | 8 - 9:30 Exercise | 8 - 9 Biology Class | |
| 9 AM | Study at Colloquium | | Study at Colloquium | | Study at Colloquium | ☐ Sign up for Service Saturday |
| 10 AM | 10 - 11 Music Class | 10 - 11:30 English Class | 10 - 11 Music Class | 10 - 11:30 English Class | 10 - 11 Music Class | ☐ Call Dad on his birthday |
| 11 AM | | | | | | |
| 12 PM | 12 - 4 Work | Lunch | | Lunch | 12 - 4 Work | ☐ Laundry |
| 1 PM | | | 12 - 2 Work | | | |
| 2 PM | | 2 - 3:30 U101 Class | | 2 - 3:30 U101 Class | | |
| 3 PM | | | 2:30 - 4:30 Biology Lab | | | |
| 4 PM | | 3:45 - 6 Study and Read for Class | | 4 - 6:30 Study and Read for Class | | |
| 5 PM | 5 - 6:30 Student Org. Mtg | | | | | |
| 6 PM | | | | | | |
| 7 PM | | | 7 - 8:30 Intramural Game | | 7 Women's Soccer Game | |
| 8 PM | 8 - 10 Study and Read for Class | | | | | |
| 9 PM | | | | | | |
| 10 PM | | | | | | |

upcoming assignments often. Order your assignments by due date, and note the course and assignment description. Looking at your worksheet will help you prepare for the next project, test, or assignment. You may discover that certain weeks will be more demanding than others, so plan ahead to avoid becoming overwhelmed.

## Planner

A planner can be a valuable way to keep track of classes, meetings, co-curricular activities, and guest speakers or special events on campus. You will want to set blocks of time for homework and studying and add any recurring meetings to your schedule (e.g., weekly student organization meetings or intramural practice). With all activities, be sure to schedule extra time to travel to and from each location.

A weekly schedule in your planner is helpful in breaking your semester into more manageable timelines. When using a weekly schedule, start by filling your schedule with your most important weekly commitments first (e.g., classes, work hours). Then, set aside time in your schedule to study and work on assignments, setting aside specific times for each class. This will allow time to review your material even if nothing is due that particular week. Finally, make sure that you schedule time for yourself and your co-curricular activities.

## Digital Calendar

You may find that a mobile device or other digital calendar is more effective than a paper planner when getting organized. Your cell phone or e-mail calendar can be used to record meetings, appointments, or dinner with friends. There are also several apps designed to serve as a digital calendar that you can download on your phone or tablet. Mobile devices can be an effective tool in organizing your schedule, coursework, and co-curricular activities. You can download apps that are designed to help you manage your courses, keep track of your tasks and grades, provide a week by week timeline, and even sync with your other devices. Your student e-mail account has a calendar feature that can send reminders to your phone and/or laptop. Contact University Technology

> **WHEN USING A WEEKLY SCHEDULE, START BY FILLING YOUR SCHEDULE WITH YOUR MOST IMPORTANT WEEKLY COMMITMENTS FIRST (E.G., CLASSES, WORK HOURS).**

# Semester At A Glance

Use this form to help you visualize and organize your syllabi. List all assignments according to due date.

| DUE DATE | CLASS | ASSIGNMENT |
|----------|-------|------------|
|          |       |            |
|          |       |            |
|          |       |            |
|          |       |            |
|          |       |            |
|          |       |            |
|          |       |            |
|          |       |            |
|          |       |            |
|          |       |            |
|          |       |            |
|          |       |            |
|          |       |            |
|          |       |            |
|          |       |            |
|          |       |            |
|          |       |            |
|          |       |            |
|          |       |            |
|          |       |            |
|          |       |            |
|          |       |            |
|          |       |            |
|          |       |            |
|          |       |            |
|          |       |            |
|          |       |            |

Services at 803-777-1800 for assistance in setting this up. The key to using a digital calendar is to find a system or platform that works best for you.

## To-Do Lists

Making to-do lists can also be beneficial in managing and prioritizing your time. Consider breaking your list into categories of what you need to complete today and what you would like to complete within the week. This list can be on scratch paper, a white board in your room, or in your planner. There are also dozens of great apps available that help identify and organize projects. Choose a structuring system that works for you, such as deadline order, color-coded importance, number priority, A-B-C-D-E method, or your own design. It may take you 10 minutes a day to make your list, but it will save you hours in the long run.

## A-B-C-D-E Method

Tracy (2007) suggested a priority system for creating task lists. After making your to-do list, place an *A, B, C, D,* or *E* before each item before you begin your first task.

> *A* = very important, must do. If this task is not completed (e.g., finishing a research paper, completing a presentation), there are serious consequences involved. If you have more than one *A* on your list, prioritize them by using *A-1, A-2, A-3*, and so on.
>
> *B* = important, should do. If this task is not completed (e.g., filling out an application for a travel grant, responding to an e-mail), there are only mild consequences. Someone may be unhappy or inconvenienced if you do not do it, but not as important as *A*. Never work on a *B* task when there is an *A* task left undone.
>
> *C* = would be nice to do. There are no consequences for whether you complete this task (e.g., doing laundry, getting a haircut, having coffee with a friend) or not.

## BACKWARDS PLANNING

10-PAGE RESEARCH PAPER DUE DECEMBER 1

| | |
|---|---|
| IDENTIFY RESEARCH TOPIC | SEPT 15 |
| FIND 3 SOURCES FOR THE PAPER | OCT 1 |
| WRITE FIRST DRAFT | OCT 5 |
| CREATE BIBLIOGRAPHY | OCT 10 |
| TAKE PAPER TO WRITING CENTER | NOV 1 |
| PAPER DUE | NOV 24 |

*D* = can delegate to someone else. Evaluate if you can delegate this task (e.g., buying groceries, picking up a prescription) to help you complete an *A* task.

*E* = can be eliminated altogether. This is often a task you continue to do out of habit or because you enjoy it.

### Backwards Planning

The reality of managing responsibilities is that not all tasks are created equal. Some projects are much smaller and simpler than others. Larger projects should be broken down into smaller chunks. Rather than list "write 10-page research paper" as a to-do list item, you would be better off breaking this project down into its component parts and listing each in your planner at appropriate intervals. Work backwards from the ultimate due date. (One helpful tip is always back up the date by one week to ensure that you have ample time to complete the project. For instance, if the paper is due on December 1, list the entry in your calendar on November 24). The example to the left illustrates this concept.

## Conclusion

Developing effective time management strategies, including the ability to self-regulate, will be important not only for college success, but in all aspects of your adult life. In college, poor time management skills lead to lower quality work, greater stress, and higher incidence of academic integrity violations. Practice is necessary to become more effective in managing your time. Continue to manage your time in a manner that supports your values, priorities, and goals. Notice the changes you see as you make this shift and recognize when you are slipping from these habits. Should you want more help in identifying strategies, meet with an ACE coach in the University Advising Center for 1:1 consultation and assistance. Time management is a commonly requested topic for ACE. Make an appointment today by calling 803-777-1222 or e-mail: ACE@sc.edu.

## REFLECTION QUESTIONS

1. After reading through the chapter, what can you implement or change in terms of managing your time that would be beneficial to you? Describe why a particular method would be effective for you personally.

2. The chapter presents a lot of evidence that multitasking and poor time management result in a lower GPA. Beyond your GPA, what factors do you think multitasking and poor time management could possibly affect?

3. Why do you think that people with more leisure time have lower GPAs? Can you identify a time in your life where you had a lot of leisure time? Were you very productive? Now, think about a time when you had a lot going on and had limited leisure time. Describe how your ability to accomplish tasks in that setting was different.

4. Think about the most productive person you know. What makes that person able to accomplish so much?

5. Have you experienced a shift in your leisure time since you started college? How has that affected your daily life?

6. What are two strategies you can employ to avoid distractions (such as Netflix) and start studying for exams?

7. Do you consider yourself a procrastinator? Why or why not?

8. This chapter discusses that 50% of college students procrastinate regularly and consider it a problem. If these students recognize it is a problem, why do you think they have not changed that habit in their life?

9. The beginning of this chapter talks about goals. How often do you take the time to sit down and write out your goals? Please list two goals you have for the semester and how you plan to achieve these goals.

## RESOURCES

**University Advising Center** . . . . . . . . . . (803) 777-1222
Close-Hipp Building, Suite 102
http://www.sc.edu/advising/

**Student Success Center** . . . . . . . . . . . . . (803) 777-0684
Thomas Cooper Library-- Mezzanine Level
http://www.sa.sc.edu/ssc/

# REFERENCES

Ackerman, D., & Gross, B. (2003). Is time pressure all bad? Measuring the relationship between free time availability and student performance and perceptions. *Marketing Education Review, 13*, 21.

Boice, R. (1996). *Procrastination and blocking: A novel, practical approach*. Westport, CT: Praeger.

Britton, B., & Tesser, A. (1991). Effects of time-management practices on college grades. *Journal of Educational Psychology*, 83, 405-410.)

Burka, J. B., & Yuen, L. M. (2008). *Procrastination: Why you do it, what to do about it now*. Cambridge, MA: Da Capo Life Long.

Cantor, J. (2011). Getting students to turn off digital distractions and tune into lectures and learning. *E-Source for College Transitions, 9*(1), 7.

Chickering, A., & Gamson, Z. (1987, March). Seven principles for good practice in undergraduate education. AAHE Bulletin, 39(7), 3-7.

Covey, S. R. (1989). *The 7 habits of highly effective people.* New York, NY: Simon and Schuster.

Dux, P. (n.d.). *About Queensland Attention and Control Lab*. Retrieved from http://www.paulduxlab.org/

Ferrari, J. R. (2010). *Still procrastinating: The no-regrets guide to getting it done*. Hoboken, NJ: Wiley.

Ferrari, J. R., Johnson J. L., & McCown, W. G. (1995). *Procrastination and task avoidance: Theory, research, and treatment*. New York, NY: Plenum Press.

Gortner Lahmers, A., & Zulauf, C. R. (2000). Factors associated with academic time use and academic performance of college students: A recursive approach. *Journal of College Student Development, 41*, 544-556.

Gladwell, M. (2008). *Outliers: The story of success*. New York, NY: Little, Brown and Co.

Greenfield P. M. (2009). Technology and informal education: What is taught, what is learned. *Science, 323,* 69-71.

Heath, C., & Heath, D. (2010). *Switch: How to change things when change is hard*. New York, NY: Broadway Books.

Junco, R., & Cotten, S. (2011). Perceived academic effects of instant messaging use. *Computers & Education, 56*(2), 370-378.

Kuhl, J., & Fuhrmann, A. (1998). Decomposing self-regulation and self-control: The volitional components inventory. In Heckhausen, J. & Dweck, C. S. (Eds), *Motivation and self-regulation across the life span* (pp. 15-49). New York, NY: Cambridge University Press.

Misra, R., & McKean, M. (2000). College students' academic stress and its relation to their anxiety, time management, and leisure satisfaction. *American Journal of Health Studies, 16*, 41-51.

Mullendore, R. H., & Hatch, C. (2000). *Helping your first-year college student succeed: A guide for parents*. Columbia, SC: University of South Carolina, National Resource Center for The First-Year Experience and Students in Transition.

Owens, R. J. Q., & Pauk, W. (2008). *How to study in college*. Boston, MA: Houghton Mifflin Company.

Steel, P. (2011). *The procrastination equation: How to stop putting things off and start getting stuff done*. New York, NY: Harper Collins.

Tracy, B. (2007). Eat that frog! (2nd ed.). San Francisco, CA: Berrett-Koehler Publishers.

# CHAPTER 4

# Academic Policies, Processes, and Resources

UNIVERSITY OF
# SOUTHCAROLINA

Dear First-Year Student,

Many students find that one of their favorite parts of college is having the chance to make important choices for themselves -- choices about how to spend their time, what to major in, what to do
outside of class, and eventually what to do for a career. What you do in the short term and in the
long term is up to you! This chapter, "Academic Policies, Processes, and Resources," provides some
valuable information about academic resources at Carolina – and responsibilities, too – that are
yours as a college student at USC.

Your academic advisor is your advocate. Find out who your advisor is and how to make the most
of your time together. Do your part to make that relationship a big plus in your college years. Also
familiarize yourself with the academic policies covered in this chapter. Know how many credits you
need each semester, how to drop classes without long-term penalties, what "grade forgiveness" is,
and how best to stay in good standing for on-time graduation. Working closely with your advisor
and knowing Carolina's academic policies help ensure your success.

Finding your path in college and custom-designing your lifetime career is up to you. As members
of the Carolina family we walk a path of discovery together, offering each other lots of help and
information to make sure all of us are successful.  Use your advisor and these academic policies
and resources to make the most of this first year.  I look forward to watching your own personal
Carolina story unfold!

Best wishes,

Helen Doerpinghaus
Deputy Provost, Office of the Provost

**BEFORE** you start to read the information presented in this chapter, it will be beneficial to take a moment to reflect on your previous educational experiences by considering the following questions:

- How much choice did you have in the courses you were required or allowed to take?
- Did you have a scholarship or any financial aid to attend your previous school? If so, what were the requirements you had to meet to keep them?
- Did you belong to any organization or athletic team that required a certain GPA as a condition of participation?
- How did you know what your school's policies were? Where would you go to find them?
- If you wanted to take care of any administrative task, such as changing a class or paying a fee, how many different places did you need to visit to carry that out?
- How complex was the organization of the school? Were there different policies and expectations based on your course of study?
- What kind of academic support did your school offer? How did you know how to access it? When were you required to make use of it, if ever?

It is likely you already have experience with academic policies and expectations prior to coming to college. Members of sports teams, such as the basketball or soccer team, are often required to maintain a certain GPA in order to compete. Some of you may have enrolled in a series of honors-level courses that had certain prerequisites. It's possible you had a scholarship that had academic or other expectations that had to be met in order to keep it.

The University of South Carolina is similar, but presents a much more complex educational environment than many first-year students are often used to. There are many new kinds of programs, departments and offices, and individuals with strange new titles such as registrar, bursar, and provost, among others. Rather than one central office where all administrative tasks are completed, students are now expected

to visit a different office for each one. As an undergraduate student at the University of South Carolina, you may face challenges associated with living and learning in a new environment. You may feel there is too much to learn and that it is virtually impossible to figure out everything that you will need to know. At Carolina, individual colleges and schools (e.g., the College of Arts and Sciences, the Darla Moore School of Business) set college-specific academic policies and procedures that can often be confusing to new students.

Universities like the University of South Carolina are full of academic policies, processes, and resources. Universities have been described as "loosely coupled systems" (Birnbaum, 1988, p. 37). Even though they might appear to be an integrated organization, universities in actuality have many different and loosely connected parts. These loosely coupled entities at USC include academic colleges and departments (such as the College of Engineering, the Arnold School of Public Health, or the International Business Program), programs for special student populations (such as Capstone Scholars, TRIO programs, or International Student Services), student affairs and services departments (such as University Housing, Financial Aid, or Study Abroad), and many other administrative units that exist to manage the functions of a very large multifaceted institution dedicated to inquiry and knowledge production. Institutions like these have been intentionally designed in this way for several reasons, one of which is to provide students the opportunity to explore a wide range of subjects and to ultimately have the choice for their educational path through college.

What many first-year students need to know is that there are policies and procedures that are unique to each aspect of such a complex organization as is the University of South Carolina. There are academic policies that are specific to each major and college or school. Certain on-campus groups require students to meet certain academic standards, such as student athletes, members of the South Carolina Honors College, or students who have joined a fraternity or sorority. Scholarships and financial aid usually carry with them requirements of a minimum GPA and number of credits for students to maintain eligibility.

Most importantly, because these different parts of the university are loosely coupled, your responsibility for understanding the policies, following the procedures, and taking advantage of the resources ultimately falls to you. While it is not expected that you know or interpret the policies for all undergraduate units, you will be expected to understand policies related to your chosen academic college, major, and the general rules that apply to all students, regardless of class level.

Fortunately, the university has provided important support personnel to assist you as you navigate the system. Your academic advisor is a key person to get to know and can provide valuable assistance in guiding you through the maze of choices, policies, and procedures you will encounter. Establishing a working relationship with your advisor should be made a priority, particularly in the first semester. This relationship will continue to pay dividends throughout your college career.

While the advisor is key to charting an academic path, other staff and faculty can also provide valuable assistance. You should not hesitate to share any advising concerns or questions you have with your University 101 instructor, other faculty, staff, or peer or graduate leaders. While they may or may not have the direct answer, they will be able to provide guidance to the right resource. Asking questions now can save time and avoid potential headaches and hassles later.

In University 101, the aim is to foster academic success by helping first-year students identify relevant academic policies, processes, and procedures related to advising, course planning, and major exploration. This chapter is focused on describing how and where to find information related to academic policies, how to complete some essential academic processes, and where to find resources to help you manage the complex standards, expectations, and procedures that are required to be successful at USC. This chapter will address the interconnected topics of major exploration, academic advising, and University academic policies, as well as suggest strategies that you can use to chart your academic path.

# Academic Policies and Procedures

## Undergraduate Bulletin

The University has a number of policies and procedures related to undergraduate education that are important for you to know. The *Undergraduate Studies Bulletin* is an indispensable reference since it contains useful and important information regarding policies and procedures that apply to all students, as well as those for individual colleges. Each academic unit (e.g., College of Nursing, School of Music) lists their faculty, degree and progression requirements, and brief descriptions of their courses.

The extensive set of policies and procedures found in the *Bulletin* includes critical information on class attendance, final exams, the grading system, dropping a class, repetition of course work, academic probation, academic honors, and other campus issues. To avoid costly mistakes (due to being unaware) that could delay degree progress and graduation, you must become familiar with the *Bulletin*.

## Grade Point Average

Perhaps the academic terminology that carries the most weight for most students is the Grade Point Average or GPA. Simply stated, GPA is a numerical representation of the average grade earned in all classes weighted by the number of credits of each course. In other words, the B earned in a 3-credit course will have more of an impact on the overall (or "cumulative") GPA than the A earned in a 1-credit course. The grade point average is computed on the basis of all semester hours attempted for credit, except for credit hours carried under the Pass-Fail or audit options. Courses in which a grade of I, S, AUD, T, or W was earned are not considered in computing the GPA. The policy on grades is explained in more detail in the *Undergraduate Bulletin*.

To calculate the GPA, two things must be known about each course: (a) the grade for the class and (b) the number of credits. Each grade has a corresponding value assigned to it.

Once the grade points for all your classes have been calculated, you would then add them all together to arrive at the total number of grade points. The "Calculate Your GPA" graphic provides an example of this process.

To arrive at the overall GPA, the grand total of grade points from all classes is divided by the total number of credits from all classes.

Knowing how to calculate the Grade Point Average is important for several different reasons. First, you can create a projection of what your end-of-semester GPA would be if your grades today were your final grades. Knowing this can help you determine whether you are meeting the minimum GPA requirements for any scholarship or financial aid you might have, any organizations or leadership positions you are in or to which you might aspire, or a major or professional program to which you plan to apply. Second, this allows you to create "what-if" scenarios to determine how changing a letter grade in one class can influence your overall GPA for a semester. For instance, in the example provided in the "Calculate Your GPA" insert, if the C+ in HIST 107 were changed to a B, the overall GPA rises from 3.44 to 3.53. This change can mean the difference between keeping or losing a scholarship or between making the Dean's List or not. Finally, sometimes knowing where your GPA currently stands can be a sobering wake-up call to redouble your efforts and seek academic support while there is still a chance to improve your grades.

# Academic Planning Processes

The primary outcome of the student experience at the University of South Carolina is earning a baccalaureate degree. This requires an investment of time, energy, and focus over the entire four year course of study. In order to be a successful student at Carolina, you will need to actively engage in academic planning. There are multiple, interrelated processes that you will go through to successfully complete the degree requirements at USC. An understanding of these processes can help you make progress toward the degree in the most

# GPA CALCULATOR

Your grade point average (GPA) is computed on the basis of all semester hours attempted for credit, except for credit hours carried under the Pass-Fail or audit options. The grade points earned in any course carried with a passing grade (A, B+, B, C+, C, D+, D) are computed by multiplying the number of semester hour credits assigned to the course by a factor determined by the grade.

**A** = 4; **B+** = 3.5; **B** = 3; **C+** = 2.5; **C** = 2; **D+** = 1.5; **D** = 1

No grade points are assigned to the symbols F, S, U, WF, W, I, AUD, T, or NR.

The grade point average is determined by dividing the total number of semester grade points earned by the total number of semester hours attempted for credit.

| Course | Grade and (grade points) | x | Credit hours | = | Total grade points |
|--------|--------------------------|---|--------------|---|--------------------|
| English 101 | B          (3 pts) | x | 3 | = | 9 |
| History 111 | C          (2 pts) | x | 3 | = | 6 |
| Geology 103 | B+         (3.5 pts) | x | 4 | = | 14 |
| Mathematics 111 | D      (1 pt) | x | 3 | = | 3 |
| University 101 | A       (4 pts) | x | 3 | = | 12 |
| **TOTAL** | | | 16 hours | | 44 pts |

| GPA TOTAL | 44 pts | ÷ | 16 hours | = | **2.75 GPA** |
|-----------|--------|---|----------|---|--------------|

*(Adapted from http://www.sc.edu/bulletin/ugrad/acadregs.html#course%20credit)*

# CALCULATE YOUR GPA

| Course | Grade and (grade points) | x | Credit hours | = | Total grade points |
|--------|--------------------------|---|--------------|---|--------------------|
| | | x | | = | |
| | | x | | = | |
| | | x | | = | |
| | | x | | = | |
| | | x | | = | |
| | | x | | = | |
| | | x | | = | |
| **TOTAL** | | | | | |

| GPA TOTAL | | ÷ | | = | |
|-----------|--|---|--|---|--|

# UNDERGRADUATE BULLETIN QUICK FACTS

**1** **What is the difference between a "WF" and a "W" on your transcript?**
""W" does not count in GPA computation and "WF" counts as an "F" (0.0). Both are recorded on the transcript. In the first seven weeks a grade of "W" is recorded, and in the second 7 weeks, a grade of "WF" is recorded.

**2** **At what point would a student be placed on Academic Probation?**
When a student's cumulative University of South Carolina GPA at the end of any semester is less than a 2.00, he or she is placed on academic probation.

**3** **What is Grade Forgiveness?**
**How many courses can be retaken under the Grade Forgiveness policy?**
If an undergraduate earns a D, D+, F, or WF in any class, that class may be retaken for a higher grade. Up to two courses can be retaken for grade forgiveness. Both grades will appear on the student's transcript, but only the second grade will calculate into the University of South Carolina GPA.

**4** **What must a student's GPA be in order to graduate with honors (Summa Cum Laude, Magna Cum Laude, and Cum Laude)?**
Summa Cum Laude: 3.95-4.00
Magna Cum Laude: 3.75-3.949
Cum Laude: 3.5-3.749

**5** **When is it mandatory for a student to declare a major?**
Students must declare a major by the time they are a sophomore or have earned 30 hours credit.

**6** **How many hours will be required per semester for my major in order to graduate in a normal period of time?**
Different majors have different requirements as far as hours required. Students should find their college/school and program on this website to see how many hours are needed to complete their degree: http://bulletin.sc.edu/

**7** **What GPA is required to maintain good standing in your major? With the University?**
(Good standing within the major will depend upon the individual student.) Students must maintain a 2.00 cumulative grade point average to remain in good standing with the University of South Carolina.

**8** **What is the maximum credit hour limit within your college?**
Maximum credit hour limit within college is dependent upon the individual student.

**9** **At what times can you add/drop a class during the semester?**
During the first week of classes.

**10** **How much class credit can students earn when auditing a course?**
None

effective and efficient way possible. These interrelated processes include the following:

- General Academic Planning Strategies
- Major Exploration and Selection
- Academic Advising
- Course Planning
- Registration

An overview of each of these processes follow, working from broad to narrow. As goals change and become more focused, the nature of your engagement with them will adapt and evolve. Therefore, it is important not to think of these as steps in a checklist, but rather a set of tools that are useful for making, adjusting, and executing plans for achieving academic goals.

## Academic Planning Strategies

Components involved with successful academic planning include knowing and understanding yourself, the University academic environment, and the requirements of your chosen college or school. The more knowledgeable you are as you plan your undergraduate academic path, the more likely you are to make decisions that will ultimately keep you progressing toward a timely graduation. Successful academic planning strategies include:

*Knowing yourself.* It is important to reflect on how and why you chose to attend the University of South Carolina and where you are in the process of selecting and pursuing an academic major. If you have already made a decision about a major, you should think about what led you to that decision. If you are undecided about your major, you should identify what information you still need to make a good decision.

*Knowing and understanding the University academic environment.* By reviewing the Undergraduate Studies Bulletin, you can learn about the many options for academic majors, minors, and elective courses, as well as the University's academic policies and regulations. Understanding these options will also make the time spent during meetings with the academic advisor more productive and fulfilling.

*Awareness that the central elements of advising will change as you progress through your college career.* Advising for first-year students typically emphasizes Carolina Core requirements and choice of an academic major, whereas advising for sophomores, juniors, and seniors places greater emphasis on the academic major, minor, or cognate requirements and career or graduate school plans. You should discuss possible internship, graduate school, and career plans with your advisor as you advance toward graduation.

*Familiarity with other campus resources.* The University has several offices that support student success and achievement, and it will be your responsibility to take advantage of all that they have to offer. Offices such as the University Advising Center, Career Center, Writing Center, Math Lab, Student Success Center, Office of Fellowships and Scholar Programs, Office of Pre-Professional Advising, and the Office of Counseling and Psychiatry are staffed with professionals and well-trained students ready to help you navigate your academic journey.

*Self-responsibility.* The academic advisor, academic major department office, dean's office, and other campus offices are resources which can provide you with additional information, help prevent and resolve difficulties, give insight into possible alternatives, and suggest new opportunities. However, ultimately, *you* will be responsible for making appropriate and informed decisions about educational plans, career goals, and meeting the requirements for your degree.

## Major Exploration and Selection

The main purpose of undergraduate study is to gain the educational experiences sufficient to earn a bachelor's degree. As degrees are awarded for specific fields of study, the choice of a major will significantly influence any academic plan. This is also true if you are undecided and have not yet declared a major.

The choice of major has a strong connection to a career path. People are working longer for a variety of reasons, chief among them is the fact that people are living longer. As a result, it is entirely reasonable for graduates to work full time for the 50 years following graduation. Therefore, it is

crucial to choose a major that lines up with your interests, aptitudes, personality, goals, values, and desired lifestyle.

If you have decided upon a major or career you can explore your choice further through career-related work experiences such as job shadowing or internships. Major selection and advising go hand-in-hand with your chosen career path. More information about career exploration and preparation is available in chapter 11.

If you are still unsure about a major or career, one helpful resource is the Career Center. They offer a variety of assessment tools to identify career interests, personality type, personal values, and skills/abilities. Information from these tools can be coupled with workshops and one-on-one appointments to help you make informed and intentional career decisions. These assessment tools are not designed to tell you what to be or what major to choose; instead, they indicate how interests, personality, or values relate to various occupations.

If you are unsure about your major you should discuss this with your current advisor. Advisors can help you work through the questions you might have about your current major or one you might be considering. Advisors can help you understand the process for changing your major, particularly if the new major is within your current college or school.

## Academic Advising

The primary goal of academic advising is to assist you in reaching your academic goals. Academic advising involves developing a positive working relationship between you and a faculty or staff member at the university. Ideally, you will meet with your advisor at least once a semester, either individually or in a group setting. Your academic advisor can provide you with information, insight, and direction related to your academic, personal, and social situations.

In an early model of academic advising, author Terry O'Banion (1972) suggested that the key elements in academic advising include:

## MAJORS AND DEGREES

For a full list of degrees offered at the Columbia campus, visit:

sc.edu/study/
majors_and_degrees

## DID YOU KNOW?

About 80% of students in the United States end up changing their major at least once, according to the National Center for Education Statistics.

# UNIVERSITY ADVISING CENTER

The University Advising Center supports the mission of the University of South Carolina by providing undergraduate students, academic advisors, and the campus community with the resources, training, services, and assessment for academic advising in accordance with national best practices. The UAC was created to facilitate consistent student advising of all undergraduates with focus on first-year students and students in transition. Specifically, the UAC supports students through providing the following services:

- MAJOR CHANGE ADVISING
- TRANSFER ADVISING SUPPORT
- ACADEMIC SUCCESS COACHING
- ACADEMIC RECOVERY INITIATIVES
- WITHDRAWAL SERVICES

The University Advising Center assists students from every major to make informed academic decisions. Students considering changing their major between schools/colleges on the Columbia Campus may make an appointment or stop by the Close-Hipp Building to meet with a **Major Change Advisor**.  Students should see their departmental advisor if they are changing majors within their current school or college. Other services provided by the University Advising Center include transfer student advising for students who may not be in their first choice of major or may need to complete requirements for their first choice of major.

Students needing time to discuss long-term goals may make an appointment to meet with an **Academic Success Coach**.  Other students on probation, suspension, or considering withdrawing from USC, may also meet with one of the advising specialists at the UAC for assistance.

For more information or to schedule an appointment with the University Advising Center, call 777-1222 or go online at www.sc.edu/Advising.

 803-777-1222

 sc.edu/advising

 **Located on the first floor of the Close-Hipp building**

## MAJOR CHANGE ADVISING

Major Change Advisors can assist with a variety of advising needs including:

- Determining how classes you have taken would fit into a different major before switching
- Comparing various majors and college/program requirements side-by-side
- Creating a plan to graduate with more than one major and/or experiential learning opportunity
- Preparing for or clarifying information from your departmental advisement appointment
- Helping you find the campus resources and offices that can answer your specific questions

For more information, or to schedule an appointment:

 803-777-1222

 sc.edu/advising

 Find the University Advising Center on the first floor of the Close-Hipp building.

- An exploration of life goals
- An exploration of career goals
- Consideration of options available in program (major) choice
- Choosing courses to fulfill curricular requirements
- Consideration of the options available to you concerning the scheduling of courses

Note the order of the actions outlined. Students sometimes view advisement as simply scheduling classes. O'Banion asserted many years ago, and many academic advisors today believe, that in meeting its potential, academic advising is far more than just scheduling classes for the upcoming term. When students make the most of academic advising, choosing classes is merely an outgrowth of the career and life planning process. It is important to note that academic advising and career counseling are not the same (see chapter on career planning for more information about what career counseling provides). You should be aware of several key concepts related to academic advising: (a) the purpose for meeting with an academic advisor, (b) scheduling an appointment with an advisor, (c) preparing for a productive meeting with an advisor, and (d) understanding the desired outcomes of academic advising.

### Why Meet with an Academic Advisor?

You will meet with academic advisors under one of two general conditions. The first and most common is during what is called the "formal" advising period. This is the time, typically around the middle of the semester, when all students are required to meet with their advisors to go over academic plans, chart out which courses will be taken in the subsequent semester, and make appropriate preparations for the upcoming registration process. The other is when you want to meet with your advisor for general advice that might not fall within the dates of formal advisement. This might happen if you wish to change your major, are considering studying abroad or an internship, or wish to discuss deepening the educational experience by pursuing a minor or engaging in undergraduate research among other reasons.

## How to Schedule an Advising Appointment

While the role of the advisor and the basic structure and outcomes of academic advising are the same for all students at Carolina, there are some differences in the process of how advisors are assigned to students in each college or school and how to set up an academic advising appointment. Fortunately, a format has been created that eases navigating the process to schedule meetings with academic advisors. Students who wish to meet with an advisor can begin by visiting www.sc.edu/advising/ and selecting the corresponding college or school of their declared major. Undeclared students are advised by the College of Arts and Sciences. Once the college or school has been selected, students may be asked to click on a link corresponding to major, year in school, or based on the nature of the meeting with the advisor which will then take them to a form whereby they can schedule a meeting. Other students may be given instructions on how to identify advisors and contact them directly to set up a visit.

## How to Prepare for a Productive Meeting with an Advisor

Developing an academic advising relationship is a shared responsibility between you and your advisor—someone who can be a mentor, confidante, and aide in assisting in major and career planning. To make the most of this opportunity, you should cultivate and develop a significant bond with your advisor by:

- *Taking the initiative to get to know your advisor.* All too frequently, students visit their advisor only when they need something like a signature on a form. It is unrealistic to expect advisors to remember every detail about each student's entire academic situation, but advisors do remember more about students they see frequently. Advisors will also be more helpful to students who take the time to develop a relationship before they need something. The better your advisor knows you, and the more prepared you are for the advising appointment, the more productive the time together will be.
- *Preparing diligently for appointments.* When you initiate a meeting with your advisor, you should be sure to have questions ready. A mental or written

# ADVISOR & ADVISEE RESPONSIBILITIES

## PURPOSE OF ACADEMIC ADVISING

The purpose of Academic Advising is to assist students in reaching their academic goals. Academic Advising helps students understand key requirements of their selected major, formulate and clarify goals related to academics and/or career, develop a four to six year academic plan, and refer to appropriate campus resources.

## ACADEMIC ADVISORS

Academic Advisors are either full-time professional staff or faculty members who are responsible for working with students in creating an academic plan each semester for every student enrolled at USC. While there are many offices where students may seek advice or assistance, Academic Advisors are charged with assisting all students in their academic and curriculum-related decisions. Academic advisors serve as resources and guides. The more information the advisors know about their students' goals, the better they can assist students in meeting those goals. It is important to remind students that they are ultimately responsible for their education and for making decisions that assist in meeting their goals.

Please Note: While the University of South Carolina offers other advising-related services on campus, such as Career Center Advising, Pre-Professional Advising, Cross College Advising, Capstone Advising, etc., THE College or School's Academic Advisor is the official resource related to degree progression.

## MATERIALS NEEDED FOR ADVISING APPOINTMENT:

- Degree program requirements
- Course listing for upcoming semester
- Tentative four-year plan
- Tentative schedule with alternative options
- Appropriate information printed from the Academic Bulletin
- Major check sheet or list of course requirements you have completed and those you still need to complete
- List of questions for your advisor

# STUDENT RESPONSIBLITIES

- **Prepare for advising sessions.**
  - Review the Undergraduate Bulletin at bulletin.sc.edu.
  - Review student handbooks and appropriate web sites within your college.
  - Understand requirements, be prepared to discuss courses/topics of interest, consider study abroad, internships or other opportunities.

- **Schedule and attend academic advising appointment.**
  - Go to www.sc.edu/advising and select your school/college.
  - Follow links to appointment scheduling.
  - Login using your Blackboard username and ID.
  - Visit your school/college website often for information on academic advising dates, policies and procedures.

- **Incorporate in-class and out- of- class learning.**
  - Be prepared to seek information / advice on how to weave the Carolina Core, major requirements, and your class experiences into a unique skill set.
  - Visit the USC Connect web site/office, the Student Affairs web site and other appropriate offices to develop a list of options.

- **Accept responsibility for your decisions and actions that affect your educational programs and goals.**
  - Please understand that the ultimate responsibility of obtaining your degree rests with the student, not the advisor.

# ACADEMIC ADVISOR RESPONSIBLITIES

- **Notification**
  - Each school/college will notify students on advisement dates/times, policies and procedures via the school/college web site.

- **Curriculum & Policy Knowledge**
  - Academic Advisors are knowledgeable of USC degree requirements, policies, and procedures.
  - Academic Advisors clearly communicate student progress towards degree during each advising session.

- **Technology & Preparation**
  - Be prepared for academic advising session by reviewing student academic record.
  - Use technology such as Self Service Carolina and Advising Webportal.
  - Review appropriate notes from the student file.

- **Referral**
  - Be knowledgeable of various campus resources such as the Student Success Center, Cross College Advising, Career Center, and Counseling and Psychiatry.
  - Refer to the appropriate resource and, if needed, help students schedule appointment(s).

- **Honesty & Confidentiality**
  - Be honest and truthful in interactions with students.
  - Maintain accurate and updated record of student academic progress.
  - Seek assistance in answering questions when not certain of the correct answer.

agenda will help you structure the meeting and keep the conversation focused on the questions and discussion points. If the appointment is for a specific purpose, such as scheduling courses for an upcoming term, it is important to have possibilities and alternatives ready for discussion. Prior to the meeting, you should review the curriculum for your major and learn how to access relevant information online. You should also be sure to understand the significance of course numbers, section numbers, schedule codes, and session codes.

Because the responsibility for a productive advising relationship is dependent on both the student and the advisor, each party has their own responsibilities. A list of the responsibilities for advisor and advisee has been included on pages 88-89. As you make preparations to meet with your advisor, it is important to revisit this list to know what you should and should not expect in that meeting. Doing so will set the stage for the meeting to be as productive as possible.

## Academic Advising Student Learning Outcomes

Academic advisors at the University of South Carolina have developed a set of outcomes that describe what they hope students will be able to do as a result of engaging in academic advising. Specifically, students who participate in academic advising should be able to:

- Articulate **degree requirements** for chosen area of study.
- Understand the **registration** process.
- Articulate rationale and requirements for the **Carolina Core** (i.e., general education).
- Articulate **personal, educational, and career goals.**
- Understand **co-curricular opportunities**, such as study abroad, National Student Exchange, and internships.
- Identify appropriate **campus resources**.

These are the things advisees can expect when they take full advantage of the opportunities provided them by preparing for and fully engaging in academic advising.

## Course Planning

With careful planning, most students can graduate in four years. To stay on track for the 120 hours required for graduation for most majors, students must average 15 hours per semester. Changing the major, experiencing academic difficulties, or pursuing a double major may require students to take summer classes or more than 15 hours each semester. Therefore, successful course planning requires students to pay attention to the categories of courses and course sequencing and balancing, all within the framework of an overall four-year plan to earn the bachelor's degree in a four-year timeframe.

### Categories of Courses

As you meet with your advisor to discuss upcoming course scheduling, the complexities of course planning come into play. Planning a four-year degree program is a complicated process that must be executed well and coordinated to produce the desired outcome—graduation from Carolina. Planning a course schedule will require you to consider many different aspects of the undergraduate academic experience. All selected courses should apply toward your degree in one of the following categories:

- *Carolina Core courses.* Each degree program has a group of courses that will fulfill this requirement. These courses usually comprise approximately 31-40 credit hours of coursework. Courses are drawn from many different departments in order to produce graduates who are academically well-rounded.
- *College/school general education courses.* Each college or school has a certain set of courses, usually meeting the requirements of the Carolina Core, which must be completed before a degree is conferred. These courses are specific to each college; students who transfer from one college to another may have to complete additional required coursework to fulfill these requirements.
- *Major courses.* Majors vary in the number of required courses and credits in the discipline (e.g., some majors require as few as 18 credits while music majors take as many as 60 credits of required courses).

CAROLINA CORE

For a list of *Carolina Core* courses visit:

 **sc.edu/carolinacore/ courses.php**

- *Minors and cognates.* In some colleges, a minor is available or even required. Minors usually consist of 18 hours (six 3-credit courses) chosen from a predetermined list of courses. The colleges publish materials outlining the available minors and program course requirements. A cognate is 12 hours of upper-level course work related to your major and approved by your major advisor. When choosing courses for a cognate, advisor approval is key.
- *Electives.* These courses may or may not meet graduation requirements and do not fulfill Carolina Core, major, minor, or cognate requirements. Electives can be a great way to explore other interest areas and possible majors. Even though the course may not count towards graduation, it will still appear on your transcript and may factor into your GPA. For this reason, it is important to check with your advisor about any courses you want to take as electives.

## Course Sequencing and Balancing

After you determine how each of your selected courses fit into your degree requirements, you can get ready for the upcoming semester. Planning a set of courses that will enable you to be successful in a given semester is an important step in schedule preparation. Both course sequencing and course balancing need to be considered.

*Course sequencing* means taking courses in the proper order. Many courses require a prerequisite course that must be completed before enrolling (e.g., PSYC 101 before PSYC 226) or co-requisite courses (courses that are required to be taken together). Knowledge acquired in a lower-level or prerequisite class is frequently needed to understand advanced material and be successful in higher-level courses.

*Course balancing* means selecting a group of courses for a given semester by evaluating the course content, the professor's teaching style, and course type (e.g., reading intensive, product intensive, homework intensive). For example, you would not want to take five art studio classes in one semester because you would have too many production projects to complete. Likewise, you would not want to take five literature and history classes in one semester because all of the classes would require a significant amount of reading.

## Course Planning Framework

Although graduation is several years away, now is the perfect time to begin thinking about how you will meet your educational goals while at Carolina as well as your post-graduation goals. Focusing on this now will allow you to maximize the use of your time and the services at the University in preparing for graduation and your future career.

The Four-Year Curriculum Planner Worksheet included in this chapter serves as a key resource for mapping out coursework so you can properly sequence and balance your undergraduate studies. You should begin by carefully considering all the courses needed for your degree and when you need to take them.

The *Undergraduate Bulletin* is a critical resource for mapping out a four-year plan. First, the basic degree requirements for all undergraduate majors are available there. Second, the courses included in the requirements are linked to information that includes a brief description of the content of the course, the number of credits, any pre- or co-requisites, and whether the course fulfills the requirements of the Carolina Core. Once this information is used to construct a draft of a plan, you can then discuss with your academic advisor about using this plan to develop your course schedule for the upcoming term.

# Registration

It is important to understand the difference between advisement and registration. When you meet with your academic advisor to discuss what courses you should take during the upcoming semester and to see if you have any questions about your major or schedule, you will not actually register for any classes during this time.

Registration refers to the process through which students enroll in a set of classes for the following semester. You will be assigned a specific date and time to log into Self Service Carolina and schedule classes for the upcoming semester. You can find your registration appointment time by following the steps outlined below. It is important to

## PLANNING TO STUDY ABROAD

If you are planning to study abroad in the coming years, you may want to save some of your *Carolina Core* classes for your semester or year abroad to stay on track in meeting your graduation requirements and timeline. Many foreign institutions may not have your major courses available, but, most likely, will have courses that can be used to meet *Carolina Core* requirements. Whenever possible, it is beneficial to take a few major courses overseas in order to get a different perspective on your major field of study and potential careers. Sometimes this can be achieved by taking major elective courses overseas, or by choosing a study abroad program that has been designed specifically for your major.

# Carolina Core Requirements

The *Carolina Core* curriculum provides the common core of knowledge, skill, and academic experience for all Carolina undergraduates. The *Core* begins with *foundational courses* early in the undergraduate experience, followed by an *integrative course* near the end in which selected *Core* learning outcomes are integrated into discipline-specific study. For more information go to http://www.sc.edu/generaleducation/

| CODE | *CAROLINA CORE* COMPONENTS | *CAROLINA CORE* LEARNING OUTCOMES | CREDIT HOURS |
|------|----------------------------|-----------------------------------|--------------|
| | **I. Lower Division: Core Courses** | Learning Outcomes to be met at foundational level of mastery | **28-34 hours** |
| CMW | Effective, Engaged, and Persuasive Communication: Written Component | Identify and analyze issues, develop logical and persuasive arguments, and communicate ideas clearly for a variety of audiences and purposes through writing and speaking. | **6** Written component |
| ARP | Analytical Reasoning and Problem-Solving | Apply the methods of mathematical, statistical, or analytical reasoning to critically evaluate data, solve problems, and effectively communicate findings verbally and graphically. | **6** |
| SCI | Scientific Literacy | Apply the principles and language of the natural sciences and associated technologies to historical and contemporary issues. | **7** |
| GFL | Global Citizenship and Multicultural Understanding: Foreign Language | Communicate effectively in more than one language. | **0-6** *(depending on placement test)* |
| GHS | Global Citizenship and Multicultural Understanding: Historical Thinking | Use the principles of historical thinking to understand past human societies. | **3** |
| GSS | Global Citizenship and Multicultural Understanding: Social Sciences | Use the principles of the social sciences to explore diverse cultural identities and to analyze political and environmental issues. | **3** |
| AIU | Aesthetic and Interpretive Understanding | Create or interpret literary, visual or performing arts. | **3** |
| | **II. Lower Division: Stand-Alone or Overlay-Eligible Courses** | Up to two of these three *Core* requirements may be met in overlay courses that combine learning outcomes from two *Core* courses. | **3-9 hours** *(depending whether these three outcomes are met with stand-alone or up to two overlay courses)* |
| CMS | Effective, Engaged, and Persuasive Communication: Spoken Component | Identify and analyze issues, develop logical and persuasive arguments, and communicate ideas clearly for a variety of audiences and purposes through writing and speaking. | **0-3** Spoken component |
| INF | Information Literacy | Collect, manage and evaluate information using technology, and communicate findings. | **0-3** |
| VSR | Values, Ethics, and Social Responsibility | Examine different kinds of social and personal values, analyzing the ways in which these are manifested in communities as well as individual lives. | **0-3** |
| Integrative | **III. Upper Division: Integrative Course in the Major** | Upper division course in the major program of study includes learning outcomes from the *Carolina Core*. Students should refer to their program major for more information. | **N/A** |
| | **TOTAL Hours in *Carolina Core*** | | **31 – 43 hours** *(depending on language placement tests and use of at most two overlay courses). Minimum 31 hours required.* |

# Schedule Worksheet

**Instructions**: As you plan for next semester, use the Schedule Worksheet to map out your weekly academic calendar.

| MONDAY | TUESDAY | WEDNESDAY | THURSDAY | FRIDAY |
|---|---|---|---|---|
| 8:30am-9:20am | 8:30am-9:45am | 8:30am-9:20am | 8:30am-9:45am | 8:30am-9:20am |
| 9:40am-10:30am | 10:05am-11:20am | 9:40am-10:30am | 10:05am-11:20am | 9:40am-10:30am |
| 10:50am-11:40am | | 10:50am-11:40am | | 10:50am-11:40am |
| | 11:40am-12:55pm | | 11:40am-12:55pm | |
| 12:00pm-12:50pm | | 12:00pm-12:50pm | | 12:00pm-12:50pm |
| 1:10pm-2:00pm | 1:15pm-2:30pm | 1:10pm-2:00pm | 1:15pm-2:30pm | 1:10pm-2:00pm |
| 2:20pm-3:35pm | 2:50pm-4:05pm | 2:20pm-3:35pm | 2:50pm-4:05pm | |
| 3:55pm-5:10pm | 4:25pm-5:40pm | 3:55pm-5:10pm | 4:25pm-5:40pm | |
| 5:30pm-6:45pm | 6:00pm-7:15pm | 5:30pm-6:45pm | 6:00pm-7:15pm | |
| 7:05pm-8:20pm | | 7:05pm-8:20pm | | |

# Four-Year Curriculum Planner

| First Year | Fall Classes | Spring Classes | Summer Classes |
|---|---|---|---|
| | | | |
| | | | |
| | | | |
| | | | |
| | | | |
| | | | |

| Second Year | Fall Classes | Spring Classes | Summer Classes |
|---|---|---|---|
| | | | |
| | | | |
| | | | |
| | | | |
| | | | |
| | | | |

| Third Year | Fall Classes | Spring Classes | Summer Classes |
|---|---|---|---|
| | | | |
| | | | |
| | | | |
| | | | |
| | | | |
| | | | |

| Fourth Year | Fall Classes | Spring Classes | Summer Classes |
|---|---|---|---|
| | | | |
| | | | |
| | | | |
| | | | |
| | | | |
| | | | |

note that you are not required to register at the exact registration appointment time; you may register at any point after it as well.

How to your locate time ticket for registration:

1. Go to my.sc.edu
2. Sign in with VIP ID and password.
3. Select the **Student Menu** – All registration business takes place under the "**Student**" tab. Information about all student records can be found here, too.
4. Click on **Registration** – The dropdown menu provides all the information necessary for a successful registration. After registration, students can review the schedule of courses for which they have registered. This menu can also be used for other registration-related activities, such as looking up all other available courses being taught on campus during the term.
5. Check **Registration Status**. This will display information to students regarding the date and time they may begin to register for courses. Additional information displayed includes any holds (which will prevent registering for courses), academic standing, and current status as a student.

## Best practices and hints for registering.

Students who follow this list of best practices and hints for registering will find the process easier to navigate:

- Be ready to register at your assigned time.
- Have a game plan. Make a schedule that meets your needs and your preferences. Use the *Registration Worksheet* and *Schedule Worksheet* included in this chapter to help you map out your game plan.
- Check to make sure you do not have any registration holds. You can find this information in Self Service Carolina, and it is important to know ahead of time because it could prevent you from being able to register.

### PEER LEADER ADVICE

The registration process can be stressful because so many people are registering at the same time, but have faith in the first week of class if you don't get the class you need. So many people drop classes in the first week, but far too few students remember that and end up thinking they just won't be able to take the class they need. If it's capped, either try for an override or wait until the semester begins and immediately take action to get into the class you need. Spaces will almost always open up.

**Alexis League**
Greenville, SC • Junior
Experimental
Psychology

- Double check the availability of courses just before registration opens. Remember other students are also registering for classes, thus course availability is constantly in flux.
- Because many students will be registering for courses at the same time, it is better to know the CRN (unique code for each course section) for each class before your registration appointment and use that to register. Using the CRN (rather than looking each course up to add it) will make the registration process go much more quickly and will lessen the likelihood the desired course will no longer be available.
- Have several contingency plans. This is especially true for first-year students who have not accumulated enough credits to register earlier than other students. Some sections of courses may not be available. It is possible that a plan B or C schedule is the one a student ends up with.
- Work the most important courses into the plan first. Consider which courses are most important—required courses for a major or minor, prerequisites to required courses should find their way onto the course schedule despite conflicts or less-than-desirable times.
- Be patient and persistent with courses that fill quickly. If a course is full, that does not mean it will remain that way. Sometimes students will register and hold a seat in a course but will change their schedules for a number of reasons, which means seats will open up in that case. It is advisable to regularly check during high peak registration times and just before classes start to see if a course has openings when it was previously full.

# When things don't work out as you planned

Even the best-laid plans do not end up working out. Chances are, this will happen to most college students during their career in one form or another. Examples include: not being

## Calendar of Key Academic Processes

| SEMESTER | THINGS STUDENTS MIGHT CONSIDER DURING THIS TIME FRAME |
|---|---|
| **BEGINNING OF THE SEMESTER** | • What are the key deadlines for the term, such as fee payment, Add/Drop, etc.?<br>• Do I need to drop a class?<br>• I'm thinking about changing my major – what should I do?<br>• What do I need to do to be able to study abroad?<br>• What do I need to do to be able to secure an internship? |
| **MID-SEMESTER** | • How do I make an advising appointment?<br>• How do I prepare for the appointment with my academic advisor?<br>• What are the courses I will need to register for?<br>• How do I access the registration system on Self Service Carolina? |
| **END OF THE SEMESTER** | • How do I calculate my GPA?<br>• What are the requirements for my scholarship/program/major/student organization?<br>• What is probation? What is suspension?<br>• What is grade forgiveness? |

accepted into a professional program (e.g., nursing, pharmacy, engineering), losing a scholarship because of grades lower than the minimum requirements, or simply because it turns out that the major was not what you thought it would be. So, what do you do when this happens to you?

First, and foremost, do not give up on college just because of this setback. Transitions like this are likely to be a very difficult thing to come to terms with, but they also represent the opportunity for deeper self-discovery.

# Registration Worksheet

**Instructions**: Use the Master Schedule to pick out SEVEN courses you would like to register for. For each course, pick three different sections you would be interested in taking, and record the schedule code as well as days/times for each section.

| Course Option #1 | Requirement | Section Number | Schedule Code | Days/Times |
|---|---|---|---|---|
| | | | | |
| | | | | |
| | | | | |

| Course Option #2 | Requirement | Section Number | Schedule Code | Days/Times |
|---|---|---|---|---|
| | | | | |
| | | | | |
| | | | | |

| Course Option #3 | Requirement | Section Number | Schedule Code | Days/Times |
|---|---|---|---|---|
| | | | | |
| | | | | |
| | | | | |

| Course Option #4 | Requirement | Section Number | Schedule Code | Days/Times |
|---|---|---|---|---|
| | | | | |
| | | | | |
| | | | | |

| Course Option #5 | Requirement | Section Number | Schedule Code | Days/Times |
|---|---|---|---|---|
| | | | | |
| | | | | |
| | | | | |

| Course Option #6 | Requirement | Section Number | Schedule Code | Days/Times |
|---|---|---|---|---|
| | | | | |
| | | | | |
| | | | | |

| Course Option #7 | Requirement | Section Number | Schedule Code | Days/Times |
|---|---|---|---|---|
| | | | | |
| | | | | |
| | | | | |

Take advantage of the opportunity to talk this through with the Counseling and Psychiatry staff. These circumstances can represent a great deal of personal disappointment and you might feel down or depressed as a result. In addition, there might be other important people in your life who express disappointment as well. The Counseling and Psychiatry staff can help you manage your feelings and show you how to cope with others who also are important to you.

Visit the Career Center to take advantage of their services designed to help students explore majors and careers. The Career Center has assessments available that can help you understand your strengths and interests and can point you toward a career path. Having a goal in mind can help you make good academic decisions and can get you back on the path to success.

Visit the University Advising Center to compare major requirements side-by-side. This is especially important if you have spent two years in a major and were not admitted into a professional program or if you have decided that your current major is not for you.

Last, and certainly not least, speak with your academic advisor about possible related fields of study where credits will be applicable. Your academic advisor can also help you find related programs that will help take you to where you want to go.

If you are in a situation where you will need to make a change because your first (or second or third) plan did not work out, remember there are resources and people here at Carolina who can help you meet your goals.

# Conclusion

Your academic success at the University of South Carolina will ultimately be up to you. Balancing your social life with your academic life is indeed possible and should be one of your main goals early on. Engaging in major and career exploration from the start, developing a positive relationship with your academic advisor, and familiarizing yourself with the University's academic policies and procedures will position you for an outstanding undergraduate experience and a bright and promising future!

# REFLECTION QUESTIONS

1. Please name one academic policy that is specific to your academic major and college or school (e.g., minimum GPA, number of credits required). What potential impact does this policy have on your academic experience (e.g., taking more credit hours)?

2. Take a moment to evaluate your performance in the classes you are taking this semester and calculate your GPA based on the instructions on page 80. Is your GPA higher or lower than you expected? What happens if you change one grade up by a letter?

3. What are some ways that you can explore "fit" with your academic major?

4. Describe some of the resources offered to students by the University Advising Center. How might these resources be particularly helpful for you?

5. What can you do in preparation for meeting with your advisor that will make your time most productive?

6. Take some time to reflect on the student and academic advisor responsibilities listed on pages 88-89. In your opinion, are there responsibilities that will take more time or effort than others? Why?

7. What is the purpose of the Carolina Core? Why do you think it is important to take these classes?

8. If you are planning to study abroad, what will be important to consider ahead of time or plan for in terms of your academics?

9. What are some of the best practices or hints about registration from the chapter that are (or will be) helpful to you and why?

# RESOURCES

**Academic Calendars**
    http://registrar.sc.edu/html/calendar/
**Master Schedule of Classes**
    http://registrar.sc.edu/html/Course_Listings/
**Office of the University Registrar** . . . . (803) 777-5555
    516 S. Main Street
    http://registrar.sc.edu/
**Undergraduate Bulletin**
    http://bulletin.sc.edu/
**Student Financial Aid and**
    **Scholarships** . . . . . . . . . . . . . . . . . . . . (803) 777-8134
    1714 College Street
    http://www.sc.edu/financialaid/
**Student Success Center** . . . . . . . . . . . . . (803) 777-0684
    Thomas Cooper Library-- Mezzanine Level
    http://www.sa.sc.edu/ssc/
**University Advising Center** . . . . . . . . . . (803) 777-1222
    Close-Hipp Building, Suite 102
    http://www.sc.edu/advising/
**Self-Service Carolina**
    http://my.sc.edu

# REFERENCES

Birnbaum, R. (1988). *How colleges work: The cybernetics of academic organization and leadership*. San Francisco, CA: Jossey-Bass.

O'Banion, T. (1972). An academic advising model. *Junior College Journal, 42*(6), 62-69.

# Involvement and Engagement

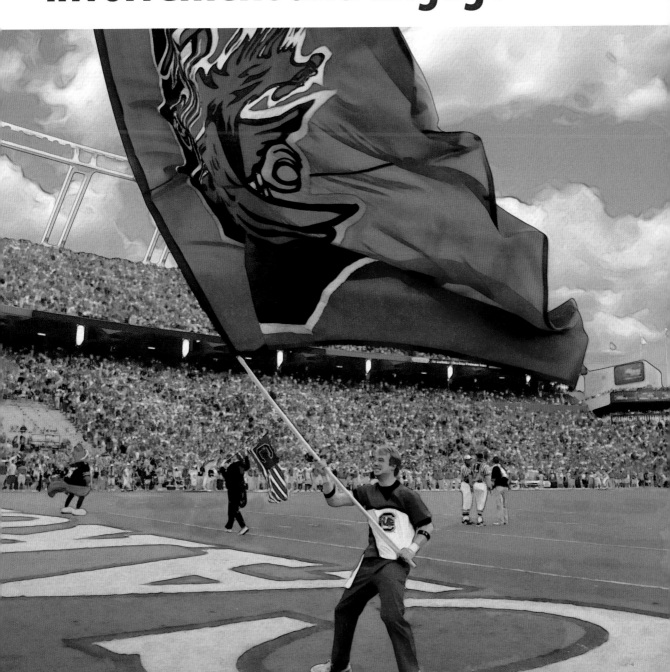

*Dear First-Year Student,*

Welcome to the University of South Carolina! We are thrilled that you have chosen to join us and engage in the Carolina experience, which is something you don't get on just ANY college campus. It is an experience that challenges, entertains, develops, molds, and prepares you. There are many activities and events for students at USC. I encourage you to take advantage of them all and make the most out of being a Gamecock.

As a new student at Carolina, consider your journey here. What will you learn? How will you be challenged as a student, community citizen, student athlete, or student leader? Your final destination (e.g., a degree, a career, a new life direction) is important, but your path toward that goal is equally important. By selecting University 101, you have chosen to be active in this journey and get as much as you can out of your experience. The course will provide you with opportunities to learn about the University and what it takes to be a successful student.

This chapter covers the many ways to become involved and engaged as a Carolina student. Possibilities are available at every turn on our campus from joining a student organization to pledging a fraternity or sorority to attending athletic events to writing for The Daily Gamecock. Involvement is participating, attending, and making a difference. It might be a conversation you have during a Diversity Dialogue or an opportunity to study abroad or explore a research idea through Undergraduate Research. Whatever it may be, make the most of it, and connect with the Carolina experience.

As you plan your career path, consider how student involvement and leadership opportunities can give you the experiences you will need to be competitive for internships, co-ops and full-time positions. Think about the impact you want to make on the Carolina community—what will you do to make a difference? Challenge yourself. Explore new things. Step outside of your comfort zone. Soak it all in. Change the community.

Sincerely,

Anna Edwards
Director of Student Services, Student Life

**THE** University of South Carolina provides you a wealth of opportunities to get involved, meet new people, take on leadership roles, and enhance your learning beyond the classroom. Research has shown that students who get involved in college do better in school, enjoy campus life more, and are more likely to find employment after college (Astin, 1993; Kuh, 2003; Pascarella & Terenzini, 2005). Finding ways to engage with the campus life can help you develop new skills and develop a network of friends and mentors. The university wants you to take full advantage of the resources and opportunities available to you so that you can maximize your Carolina experience.

Throughout your college search, admission, and orientation process you were probably told countless times to "get involved." Involvement is not a complex process and can start with an act as simple as going to a varsity athletic event, participating in a program at your residence hall, or watching a movie at the Russell House. These kinds of activities will help you step out of your comfort zone and connect with others and the university.

## Involvement Versus Engagement

Involvement implies some degree of participation or occupation. It is different than engagement which conveys attachment, donating attention to, and carrying out an enterprise or activity (Merriam-Webster, 2015). In your first semester, you will likely attend a number of events or programs and your level of participation may vary. Likely, you will participate in these activities in an effort to meet new people and experience what Carolina has to offer. But being involved does not necessarily mean you are engaged. Engagement indicates a higher level of commitment and attention devoted to the activity or experience. True engagement synthesizes classroom knowledge with out-of-classroom experiences, enhancing your overall learning experience and reinforcing important information. Later in this chapter, you will learn more about USC Connect, including Graduation with Leadership Distinction. USC Connect is all

## HOW AND WHEN CAN I REQUEST A FOOTBALL TICKET?

Ticket requests generally begin at 9 a.m. on the Monday before a Saturday game. There is no advantage to being first to request a ticket. Once you have requested your ticket, the students who are awarded are notified via email. Students receiving tickets have two days to claim their ticket. After that, students who were not awarded tickets will be able to claim any unclaimed tickets until 4 p.m. on the day prior to the game. When the number of student tickets requested exceeds the amount of student tickets available, tickets are awarded to students based on loyalty point totals. For a step by step guide on requesting your ticket or for more information, you can visit the Student Athletic Ticketing webpage.

 sa.sc.edu/studenttickets/ football-2

about helping you move beyond involvement so that you can become engaged and think about your experiences on a deeper level. Graduation with Leadership Distinction prepares you to be a strong leader and set yourself apart.

The first part of this chapter provides you with a wealth of resources on ways to get involved on and around campus. These opportunities will help you meet new people and learn more about the university and surrounding community. Be sure to check out the sidebar resources for more information on offices and services that can help you in this process. The latter part of the chapter focuses on ways to engage and connect your experiences beyond the classroom to what you are learning through your academics.

# Athletics

As a new student at the University of South Carolina, you can show your support for the Gamecock athletic program by attending sporting events for 19 varsity athletic teams. You are also likely to make new friends as you cheer for the Gamecock athletes. By attending sporting events, you can earn reward points through the Gamecock Student Rewards program that count towards USC football tickets and reward prizes. Attendance at sporting events is free for all students; however, tickets are not guaranteed. In order to attend home football, men's and women's basketball, and baseball, you must claim a student ticket. You can gain entrance to all other sporting events by using your Carolina Card. The more athletic events you attend, the more points you accumulate, and the more likely you are to get tickets to football games. Make sure you familiarize yourself with both the Gamecock Student Rewards program and Student Ticketing to get the most out of your experience with athletics.

## Intramural Sports

Leagues, tournaments and special events are offered throughout the year in men's, women's, and CoRec divisions for sports, including but not limited to flag football, volleyball, softball, and bowling. The program emphasizes social opportunities through athletics in a fun and safe environment. Consider getting together a team of students from your floor, U101 class, Greek organization, or student group. Register your team in the Intramural Sport Office, located in the Strom Wellness and Fitness Center.

## Athletic Team Schedules

| MEN | SEASON | HOME VENUE |
|---|---|---|
| Baseball | February–May | Carolina Stadium |
| Basketball | November–February | Colonial Center |
| Football | August–November | Williams-Brice Stadium |
| Golf | September–April | Cobblestone Park |
| Soccer | August–November | Eugene Stone III Stadium |
| Swimming & Diving | October–February | Carolina Natatorium |
| Tennis | September–April | Carolina Tennis Center |
| Track & Field | November–May | USC Fieldhouse |
| WOMEN | SEASON | HOME VENUE |
| Basketball | November–February | Colonial Center |
| Cross Country | August–November | Owens Field |
| Equestrian | September–April | One Wood Farm |
| Golf | September–April | Cobblestone Park |
| Beach Volleyball | March–May | Sand Volleyball Courts |
| Soccer | August–November | Eugene Stone III Stadium |
| Softball | February–May | Beckham Field |
| Swimming & Diving | October–February | Carolina Natatorium |
| Tennis | January–April | Carolina Tennis Center |
| Track & Field | November–May | USC Fieldhouse |
| Volleyball | August–November | Volleyball Competition Facility |

Students playing intramural soccer on the Blatt PE field.

# Student Life

## *Carolina Productions*

Carolina Productions is the student programming board responsible for coordinating free events in the Russell House University Union and other venues around campus for the entire USC community. Events include weekly movies in the Russell House Theater, student talent showcases (such as USC's Got Talent), speakers, comedians, and concerts. In the past, Carolina Productions has brought Seth Meyers, Young the Giant, Nick Offerman, and Hoodie Allen. They also offer other great acts, including Inside *The Onion* with Scott Dikkers.

## *Outdoor Recreation*

There are also many opportunities to get outside and enjoy South Carolina. Outdoor Recreation helps students engage with the environment through a variety of activities, including adventure trips, skiing, climbing, backpacking, and mountain biking; wilderness first aid courses; sustainability clinics; and weekly events, such as tubing and slacklining. They also offer free bike shop services.

## *Service to the Community*

Service Saturdays is a program offered once a month where students can volunteer and partner with various non-profit agencies to serve the local community. Students engage in activities such as working with the homeless at the Salvation Army, aiding the Red Cross, renovating a Boy Scout camp, and learning about environmental problems in South Carolina. In the fall, Service Saturdays are offered on non-home football game weekends and typically held between the hours of 10 a.m. and 3:30 p.m.

Cocky's Reading Express is an on-the-road program that serves to eliminate illiteracy in South Carolina one school child at a time. Since the project began in 2005, Carolina students have volunteered to visit elementary schools in every corner of the state, reading books aloud to children and sharing the importance of learning to read. Cocky makes an appearance at the end of each story time.

Hip Hop star Hoodie Allen performed at Carolina in fall 2015.

### Residence Hall Involvement

Your residence hall provides you with more than a place to eat and sleep. You can become part of the community and engage in personal growth by taking advantage of events planned by the resident mentors and hall government. Your living and learning community can help you feel more connected to others as well as grow personally. In the residence hall you will find a number of individuals dedicated to making your experience worthwhile, including the resident mentors (RMs) or peer coordinators (PCs), assistant residence life coordinator (ARLC), residence life coordinator (RLC), residence hall director (RHD), and assistant director (AD). The residence hall positions that are staffed by students are excellent opportunities for involvement and leadership.

# Discover Columbia

To maximize your involvement at the University of South Carolina, dedicate some time to familiarize yourself with the Columbia area and all it has to offer. After all, Columbia is going to be your home for the next few years!

Ready for something different? The city of Columbia has it all: films, symphony concerts, jazz, theater, museums, Renaissance art, ballet, avant-garde performance art, stand-up comedy, and even a puppet theater. In addition to these offerings, Columbia also boasts a wide variety of other cultural, historical, educational, and recreational activities and attractions—many within a short walk from campus. The following are just a sample of what Columbia has to offer.

Gervais Street Bridge

### Music

If you are a music lover, no matter what your taste, Columbia has it. The local bands and great food can be found in the Vista almost every weekend. The **Music Farm** hosts a full calendar ranging from comedy, rock, hip hop, EDM, bluegrass, country, jam, and alternative rock. Past shows include Corey Smith, Cherub, Moon Taxi, and Sam Hunt. The **Colonial Life Arena** is one of the largest venues in Columbia and features musical artists such as Taylor Swift, Kenny Chesney, and the Zac Brown Band. The **Township**

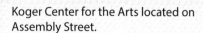

Koger Center for the Arts located on Assembly Street.

**Auditorium** is another place to check out great entertainment. Past shows have included Pretty Lights, R. Kelly, and Kevin Hart. Columbia also has its own symphony orchestra, the **South Carolina Philharmonic**, which performs regularly at the Koger Center and often features guest artists.

One of the real advantages to being a student on a campus with a first-rate School of Music is that almost every week there are free recitals and mini concerts on campus. Do not pass them up. The **University of South Carolina Symphony Orchestra** performs regularly at the Koger Center and often features guest artists. **Carolina Alive**, the University's internationally renowned vocal performance company, presents lively and exciting productions of modern popular music. The **University Opera Theatre** produces two operas a year from the best in classical and modern opera.

## Local Theater

Columbia is a great theater town and showcase for professional and amateur artists. With 13 theaters in the area producing live shows, there is something exciting for almost everyone. All the theaters have special student prices. During the fall and spring semesters, three to four plays are concurrently performed within two miles of campus. The best part is that you can be either an audience member or artist. Every company is looking for actors, stage managers, and crew members. Opportunities abound for those who have experience or who just want to get a taste of what it is like to be there when the curtain goes up.

The **Ira and Nancy Koger Center for the Arts** is located on the Columbia campus. This 2,250 seat, state of the art theater provides opportunities for students to see traveling Broadway productions of musicals (e.g., Hairspray and The Producers), musical performers (e.g., Colbie Callat, John Legend), comedians (e.g., Jim Gaffigan, Tracy Morgan), and even see live shows such as the Blue Man Group.

**Trustus Theatre**, located in the Vista, features big comfortable audience chairs with productions that range from classical to innovative theater. Past productions include *The Rocky Horror Picture Show*, and *Anatomy of a Hug*. **Workshop Theatre** presents a wide variety of productions throughout the year, from big musicals to dramatic New York hits. **Town Theatre** is the nation's oldest continuing community theater and specializes in musicals and traditional American comedies. The **South Carolina Shakespeare Company** produces Shakespearian plays in Columbia parks and throughout the state during the spring and summer months.

While Columbia's community is rich with theater opportunities, you do not have to leave campus to get involved. **Theatre South Carolina**, the production arm of the Department of Theatre and Dance, presents a full season of productions that vary from the ancient to the contemporary and experimental. Many of these productions include guest artists from professional companies across the country. These actors and artists give students an opportunity to learn from the best. Each semester, there are a number of student-directed projects and other opportunities to break in as an actor, director, designer, or techie. In addition to Theatre South Carolina, the University hosts several student performance groups. **Puppet Regime** is not about puppets; it is the student production company of the University and produces four shows a year, some of which are original plays by students. **Toast** is an improv comedy troupe that performs on campus and throughout the nation. Once a month, they do a Toast and Jam show on campus that combines outrageous improv with sketch comedy and bands or other kinds of performances.

## Dance

Is dance your thing? If so, you will find a wealth of opportunities here in Columbia. The **University of South Carolina Dance Company** presents some of the most exciting work in the region. Each year, this student company presents two productions that combine classical pieces with student-choreographed work in a variety of styles. The company always is looking for dancers and choreographers. **Columbia City Ballet** specializes in classical ballet, but also creates new works, as does **Columbia Classical Ballet**. The **Columbia City Jazz Dance Company** and the **Eboni Dance Theatre**, in contrast, specialize in the production of contemporary works.

## INTERESTED IN LEARNING MORE?

Visit these websites for more information, show dates, and times:

**Koger Center**

 sc.edu/koger

**Trustus Theatre**

 trustus.org

**Workshop Theatre**

 workshoptheatre.com/home.html

**PEER LEADER ADVICE**

One of my favorite places in Columbia is the
river walk. It's a great place if you want to
get a run in, walk with some friends, sit on
the rocks, or even hang up your Eno.

*Gilly Levy*
Atlanta, GA • Junior
Chemistry

## Film

Columbia has a number of movie theaters across town. If,
however, you want an occasional break from the endless
stream of action-packed thrillers and broad comedies coming
out of Hollywood, try the **Nickelodeon Theatre,** Columbia's
home for classic and experimental films. Bringing back the
best of the past and exploring the new, the intellectual, or
the innovative, the "Nick" is a great place to learn about
film and meet interesting people, including faculty. You
can become a regular member at a low student rate or just
attend an occasional flick.

## Visual Arts

If you are interested in the visual arts, start with the **Columbia Museum of Art**, located on the corner of Hampton and
Main Streets. This museum has a marvelous collection of
Renaissance religious art and exciting contemporary works.
The museum additionally hosts new exhibitions several times
a year. You also can visit **McKissick Museum**, located on
the Horseshoe, which not only houses the geology museum
and the Movietone News archives but also features traveling
exhibitions of special collections of graphic and other visual
arts. The **University of South Carolina Department of
Art** has a small museum of outstanding works created by its
students. There are also several small galleries downtown and
in Five Points where you can see what is new and innovative
in the world of art. Columbia has more than 40 art galleries
with something for every taste.

## Parks

For you outdoor enthusiasts, consider visiting one of Columbia's many parks. Several parks are located in or near
downtown. **Finlay Park**, a 17.5-acre park in the heart of
Columbia's Congaree Vista at Laurel and Assembly streets,
features a 1.5-acre man-made lake, a 40-foot cascading
waterfall, an amphitheater, and several walking paths. The
park hosts many outdoor concerts throughout the year.
**Columbia Riverfront Park and Historic Canal**, off Laurel
Street, is planned around the city's original waterworks
and hydroelectric plant. The park offers jogging, bicycling,
and walking paths. The **West Columbia Riverwalk** is part

of a joint effort by the City of West Columbia and the River Alliance to protect our regions' rivers and provide recreational benefits to collective communities. Riverwalk hosts 4.5 acres of the **Three Rivers Greenway**, and is located between Gervais Street and Knox Abbott Drive.

Other parks, further from campus, also offer opportunities for outdoor relaxation and recreation. **Saluda Shoals Park**, a 300-acre park located along the banks of the Saluda River, provides visitors paved and unpaved trails for hiking, biking, and horseback riding; boat, canoe, and kayak launch areas; picnic shelters; and an observation deck overlooking the river. **Congaree National Park,** located 20 miles from Columbia, offers over 20 miles of marked hiking trails, a 2.3-mile boardwalk loop, 8 miles of marked canoe trails, and picnic areas. The 22,000 acre park is home of the largest intact tract of old-growth bottomland hardwood forest remaining in the United States. You can visit most of these parks free of charge; however, some (e.g., Saluda Shoals Park) require small entrance fees that you might want to know about before venturing out!

## Historical Sites

Four **Historic Columbia House Museums** are managed by Historic Columbia, a preservation and education foundation dedicated to the cultural heritage of Columbia and its environs. The historic house museums include **Hampton-Preston Mansion and Gardens, Mann-Simons Site, Robert Mills House and Gardens,** and the **Woodrow Wilson Family Home**. Historic Columbia offers tours of the homes as well as educational activities, lecture series, and special exhibitions. You can also find out more about South Carolina and its history at the **South Carolina State Museum**, located at 301 Gervais Street. In this renovated textile mill, you will find exhibits of art, history, natural history, science, and technology unique to South Carolina. The museum also offers educational programs, demonstration theaters, and an art gallery. General admission is only $1 per person on the first Sunday of every month.

Kayaking on the Congaree River

## SOUTH CAROLINA STATE MUSEUM

For more information about the history of South Carolina, visit the South Carolina State Museum! Admission is only $1 on the first Sunday of every month. They also have a planetarium and 4D shows! Find out admission and exhibit information on their website:

 scmuseum.org

South Carolina State Fair

Koala at Riverbanks Zoo and Gardens

## Festivals and Fairs

The Columbia area hosts multiple festivals and community celebrations throughout the year. The **Columbia Greek Festival** is held downtown every September at Holy Trinity Greek Orthodox Church. The four-day festival showcases traditional Greek dancers, ceremonies, music, theater, and delicious food. The **South Carolina State Fair** is held each year in October at the South Carolina State Fairgrounds located near Williams-Brice Stadium. This statewide celebration features homemade crafts, demonstrations, livestock shows, rides, games, live entertainment, and a variety of eats (including fried Oreos). Columbia is also home to the annual **South Carolina Pride Festival**. Held in September, this statewide celebration of sexual orientation and gender identity is sponsored by the Gay and Lesbian Pride Movement and hosts a variety of local and celebrity entertainment. In the spring, festivals continue with the **South Carolina Cornbread Festival** in March and the **Rosewood Crawfish Festival** in May.

## Other Opportunities for Fun

Columbia really does have something for everyone: performing and visual arts, parks, historical landmarks, and seasonal festivals and fairs. If you still are looking for more to do, consider checking out the **Riverbanks Zoo and Gardens**. The zoo and gardens, located 10 minutes from campus, are home to more than 2,000 animals and 70 acres of scenic overlooks and spectacular gardens. Special events such as Boo at the Zoo and Lights Before Christmas are fun opportunities to visit the zoo during the evening hours. The Zoo was the 2002 winner of the Governor's Cup for the Most Outstanding Tourist Attraction in South Carolina.

As you can see, there are a vast number of opportunities for Carolina students. If you hope to take advantage of all of the things that interest you, start by considering how you can get involved while still leaving time for your academics.

# Going Deeper

An important part of making the most of your Carolina experience is taking advantage of opportunities to work in groups and build your leadership skills. USC has hundreds of student organizations and leadership positions available to students. There are a variety of strategies to find these kinds of opportunities at USC, including attending the Get Connected Fair, Student Organization Fair, and/or Community Service Opportunity Fair. You can search for ways to engage through the USC Connect website including an activities calendar, the opportunities database, and recommendations by major. Most organizations offer interest meetings early in the fall semester and these are often posted on their websites or on social media. In addition to hearing more about student organizations at the fairs, you can do your own research by searching the Leadership and Service Center website or the USC Connect database. By joining an organization, typically you are expected to attend meetings and participate in events or programs. Organization involvement contributes to your sense of belonging at the institution and provides you outlets for getting to know your peers. These experiences also provide opportunities for formal and informal leadership.

## Developing a Plan

One challenge many new students face at USC is having too many options to choose from. It is important to consider which co-curricular opportunities make the most sense for you, and when might be the best time for you to engage in those opportunities. Planning is important to ensure you accomplish everything you want to do before you graduate. Developing a plan is also easier when you have someone to help you through the process. The Leadership and Service Center offers professional leadership coaches who will sit down with you one-on-one to discuss next steps. Whether you are looking to start your involvement journey, looking to do something new, trying to make sense of what you have already done, or just want to bounce some ideas off someone, they are here to help you chart your own course and have meaningful experiences that will help you achieve your after-graduation goals.

## LEADERSHIP OPPORTUNITIES

For a complete listing of leadership opportunities, you can explore the following websites:

**Leadership and Service Center**

sa.sc.edu/
leadershipandservice

**USC Connect database**

sc.edu/uscconnect

Ideally, your involvement will provide opportunities for you to gain valuable leaderships skills. The University of South Carolina provides a very wide range of programs and opportunities for developing leadership skills. This includes taking advantage of meaningful beyond-the-classroom opportunities such as community service, global learning, research, or professional and civic engagement. These experiences will provide an opportunity to grow in your leadership and ultimately communicate *why* these engagements are important. It involves sustained commitment, but provides unique, real-world opportunities to apply what you are learning in the classroom and develop meaningful transferable skills.

University 101 students volunteer with Habitat for Humanity.

## USCCONNECT — Integrating learning within and beyond the classroom

In order to make the most of your education, it is important to think about the experiences that you'd like to gain during your time at the university. Now, think about how those experiences can influence your academics, how your academics can enhance your experiences and how both can impact your long-term goals. This interweaving of learning inside and beyond the classroom is called integrative learning. At the University of South Carolina we call it USC Connect. By following the steps of USC Connect, you can create your plan so that your experiences can be applied in a purposeful way. Faculty and staff across the university can show you how to choose your experiences and engage in the ones that are right for you, reflect on what you've learned, and then share what you have learned with others to demonstrate your leadership skills.

One way to choose experiences that work for you is to focus on a *pathway* that leads to Graduation with Leadership Distinction. Graduation with Leadership Distinction recognizes students who have completed specific leadership requirements. Whether or not you ultimately choose to complete requirements for earning the distinction for your degree, all students can use the framework of integrating learning within and beyond the classroom to make the most of their educational experiences. The pathways for Graduation with

Leadership Distinction relate to all majors. Within each pathway, students are encouraged to engage in a variety of experiences and learning activities.

## Community Service

Community service and service-learning allow students to apply skills and knowledge gained in the classroom to real-world issues. By engaging in service, students develop character and a sense of civic responsibility, and make a positive impact on the community. Students who participate in community service and service-learning often feel more connected to the community as a result of their involvement. Additionally, students gain confidence in their abilities to make a difference in the world and are energized by the opportunity to use their talents and resources to help others in need. Students who serve in areas related to personal- or career-related interests also have the opportunity for real-world experiences that may impact their long-term life goals.

The Leadership and Service Center promotes opportunities for students to become engaged in service in and around the Columbia area. The office supports and develops projects and services that address unmet needs and issues in the community; maintains a database of primary community, nonprofit agencies in the Columbia area; serves as a resource for student service organizations; and acts as an advocate for community agencies and social issues. There are several service opportunities for students to engage in and develop their servant leadership skills:

### Alternative Break Program

Through this program, South Carolina students travel together to different locations, most of which are in the United States, to provide service to people in need during fall, winter, and spring breaks. Alternative Breaks have included trips to Mississippi, Georgia, Tennessee, Washington, DC, Philadelphia, Florida, and Costa Rica to address problems including homelessness, poverty, and improving the environment. This program provides a fun and meaningful way to meet and work with other passionate students who share a desire and commitment to make a positive difference in the lives of others.

**GARNET GATE**

Find a student organization, event, or track your involvement through Garnet Gate.

 garnetgate.sa.sc.edu

Students volunteer with a service-learning course.

## Service-Learning Courses

These courses intentionally integrate academic coursework and service experiences in ways that are mutually beneficial to both students and the community. These are not classes where students simply clock hours of service; rather, students take what they learn in the classroom and apply it in a real-world setting to address a specific community need. Intentional opportunities for reflection and discussion are built into the course experience and provide mutually beneficial experiences for the students and community members.

## EcoReps

EcoReps is a peer leadership program educating and engaging students in sustainable living. The EcoReps work in the residence halls to make connections between individual behaviors and environmental stewardship through fun, interactive programs and campus-wide campaigns.

# *Global Learning*

Even first-year students can begin thinking about incorporating international study abroad or domestic study away into their academic curriculum. You can also begin to explore international connections through local opportunities. Studying away internationally or domestically can provide you with experience that you cannot gain in the traditional classroom through immersion in a new culture. The Study Abroad Office facilitates study abroad programs and other opportunities for students to gain leadership skills through cross-cultural collaboration. An overseas experience can give you a competitive edge in the job market as you gain a breadth of knowledge about other cultures, languages, politics, and practices, both across oceans and across the country. You also learn to think critically and problem solve while becoming more self-reliant; these are skills employers look for. Additionally, it is possible to earn credits that will count toward your major, minor, or elective requirements without delaying graduation. Further, you can improve your foreign language skills by taking courses in another language or taking courses in English while living among non-English speakers.

## Study Abroad

Many students begin planning nine months to a year in advance of studying abroad. Allowing sufficient time to plan will enable you to apply for scholarships and financial aid and incorporate your experience into your curriculum to earn credits while studying abroad so you can stay on track for graduation.

Typically, students embark upon a study abroad experience during their sophomore or junior year, but you are eligible to apply for the program as early as the spring break of your first year. If you wish to go during your senior year, you will need special permission from your department. Long-term programs, such as those lasting an entire semester, may be best if you are trying to increase your foreign language proficiency. Students with very structured degree programs may find a summer session more suitable for their academic needs, though this is not always the case.

In choosing an international study abroad program, there several options, including Global Exchange, Direct, Partner, and Classroom Programs, which vary in tuition and fee requirements, structure, and institution sponsorship. For the student who would like an international experience, but not necessarily study at another school, there are also teaching, volunteering, working, researching, or interning opportunities.

## Domestic Experiences

There are also many options for studying away domestically, including the United States, Canada, or the U.S. territories. While Carolina students can participate in a number of independent domestic study programs, the most popular choice is the National Student Exchange. Through this program, students pay their tuition directly to the University of South Carolina but they spend a semester, summer, or year studying at one of approximately 200 schools that participate in the program. More often than not, all financial aid will apply to the program. Students can also enhance their experience by adding an internship in their area, serving as a peer leader on the host campus, or engaging in undergraduate research.

Students study abroad in Iceland.

### PEER LEADER ADVICE

I studied abroad for the past year in Bishkek, Kyrgyzstan, and gained a deeper understanding of the challenges and differences present in a developing country versus the United States. Much of the culture, especially in regard to women's rights, seemed backwards to me as a Westerner. I used to think rather cynically about problems facing the U.S., and while plenty of problems do exist, I feel like I have a greater understanding of the struggles that stem from living in an impoverished non-Western nation.

*Laura Tarbox*
Richmond, VA • Senior
Russian and
International Studies

Students can also enroll in courses taught by USC faculty that have a domestic travel component as part of the course. By traveling to Washington, D.C. to learn about governmental policy or to the South Carolina coast to learn about marine life, students have the opportunity to learn beyond the typical classroom setting. Domestic courses are typically offered in the spring semester, Maymester, or summer.

## Local Opportunities

You can take advantage of international opportunities right here on campus and in the surrounding community. There is an ever growing population of international students at USC. If you love learning about other cultures and meeting new people, become a "buddy" through Buddies Beyond Borders (a program sponsored by International Student Services); be a conversation partner through English Programs for Internationals; or check out a program at the International House at Maxcy College. Be on the lookout for cultural events from music performances to International Education Week to community festivals.

# Research

Students who get involved in research are willing to ask questions and are committed to finding answers. Undergraduate research provides students with opportunities to:

- Gain real-world experience for future graduate study or employment
- Build relationships with faculty that are valuable when applying to graduate school or seeking employment
- Explore a new major or minor and learn about potential career options
- Improve skills and abilities (e.g., communication, critical and creative thinking)
- Earn money and gain valuable experience in your field

The earlier you start, the better. You can attend one of the introductory workshops or advising sessions with the Office of Undergraduate Research (OUR). These interactive sessions allow you to learn about research, identify potential faculty mentors, and discuss funding opportunities. OUR

A student swims with dolphins during a semester studying in Hawaii through the National Student Exchange.

can help you explore research opportunities through a variety of programs including Magellan Embark, Magellan Grants, Discovery Day, and the *Caravel* journal.

## Magellan Embark

This program encourages and promotes undergraduate research during the first year. This four-week, not-for-credit seminar meets once a week for an hour. You will learn how to take the initial steps to develop relationships with faculty, learn about opportunities for funding and showcasing research, and create a plan for research during your college experience.

## Magellan Grants

There are several grants through OUR that can help fund your project. From the "Scholar" to the "Mini-Grant," there is something for everyone. Each program has different application deadlines and requirements, but all require working with a project mentor and presenting at Discovery Day.

## Discovery Day

Discovery Day is held at the end of every April for students to share any and all scholarly pursuits in and out of the classroom, including study abroad, internships, leadership activities, research/scholarship, service-learning and community service, and national fellowship competitions. Presentations can be poster, oral, or creative (e.g., art, theater, music, creative writing).

## Caravel

*Caravel* is USC's undergraduate research journal, chronicling student research and creativity. The journal highlights all disciplines and includes articles, poems, videos, and music. See what students have researched and accomplished at http://caravel.sc.edu/.

## *Professional and Civic Engagement*

Professional and civic engagement is about preparing to lead in any work (professional) or community context. At Carolina, there are countless opportunities to develop your skills as a leader. Building on a 200-year tradition of educating leaders at the University, President Harris Pastides formed the Carolina Leadership Initiative in 2010 in an effort to provide coordination, support, and vision for the numerous programs on campus that develop leadership skills among our students. The Carolina Leadership Initiative is about:

- Inspiring change
- Recognizing individual strengths and opportunities for improvement
- Learning effective communication and interpersonal skills
- Developing integrity and putting ethics into practice
- Valuing diversity and teamwork
- Increasing self-awareness
- Promoting creativity and thoughtful risk-taking
- Developing strategic visions to benefit our communities

Academic opportunities related to leadership include completing a minor in Leadership Studies, becoming a Leadership Scholar, and Graduating with Leadership Distinction. A wealth of opportunities that can help you develop leadership skills are also available through the Leadership and Service Center. These include the Emerging Leaders program, Student Leadership in the Workplace, and Skill Builders Workshops.

## Internships

Internships and other work-based experiences (e.g., job shadowing, externships, part-time employment) provide important opportunities for you to be able to apply what you are learning in a context beyond the classroom. Many academic programs integrate internships into their courses or provide support for finding internships in their areas. Students interested in a government internship can check out opportunities offered in Washington, DC or in South Carolina. The Career Center's online resources will help you explore work-based opportunities, and chapter 11 will offer more information about how these experiences strengthen your employability.

## Peer Leaders

A peer leader is a "student who has been selected and trained to offer educational services to their peers. Each peer leader service is intentionally designed to assist in the adjustment, satisfaction, and persistence of students toward the attainment of their educational goals" (Ender & Kay, 2001, p. 1). In general, peer leaders work one-on-one with students to share specific information regarding a certain topic or interest area. Often these positions require an application and interview to be selected. Competitive applicants are students who have gotten involved on campus in some way, achieved academic success, and demonstrated responsible behavior. There are nearly 60 different peer leadership opportunities available on campus that range from academic support to diversity or wellness education. Below, you will find several examples of peer leaders on the USC Campus.

**Student Government Members and Leaders** respond to student needs and concerns on a variety of topics and define student powers and responsibilities by taking issues that affect student life directly. Students are then able to present these concerns to the University administration and various state governing bodies. Student members serve the student body by managing organizations' registration and renewal and by distributing student activities funds to registered campus organizations. More than 400 students currently hold leadership positions on Freshman Council, Student Senate, and as Executive Officers.

**University 101 Peer Leaders** support the successful transition of new students to the University of South Carolina by serving as role models, mentors, and resources within and outside of the UNIV101 classroom.

**University Ambassadors** are the official tour guides for USC, serving thousands of prospective students and parents each year. Through very specific training and skill development, they serve USC while developing the professional skills needed for the world of work.

**Orientation Team Leaders** are an essential part of the orientation experience at the University of South Carolina. Each year, exceptional students are selected to help guide incoming first-year and transfer students, as well as their parents through the Orientation process and introduce them to the vast resources available at University of South Carolina.

**EMPOWER Peer Educators** are a group of students committed to creating a more inclusive Carolina through education, inspiration and encouragement. These peer leaders are active and informed individuals who develop an appreciation for multicultural ideals and help guide other Carolinians to learn about these ideas as well.

**Supplemental Instruction Leaders** have previously taken a course where they excelled. SI leaders attend class and facilitate three study sessions per week throughout the semester in order to help their peers improve their understanding of content and earn higher course grades.

**Resident Mentors (RMs)** are upper-class students who are selected because they demonstrate a desire to help first-year students in their transition to college. Resident Mentors (RMs) live and work with a diverse group of people and the goal is to maintain and continually improve the quality of the students' experiences within the residence halls.

## Graduation with Leadership Distinction

YOU could graduate with distinction! This honor recognizes the scope of achievements for students engaged in experiences like community service, research, leadership, internships, and peer leadership. You receive graduation cords and the distinction appears on your transcript and diploma (an advantage that will help with graduate school and future employers). Most importantly, completing Graduation with Leadership Distinction helps you make sense of how your experiences fit together to prepare you for the future. You will learn how to tell your story as you develop your final presentation and e-porfolio.

### Make the Most of Your Carolina Education: USC Connect including Graduation with Leadership Distinction by Class Year

**First Year**
- Search the USC Connect database to find opportunities
- Talk with people who can help: advisor, faculty, peer leader, leadership or career coaches

- Attend the meeting of a student organization that interests you
- Do a Service Saturday
- Attend opportunity fairs: Get Connected, Study Abroad, and more
- Check out the Study Abroad Student Blogs

**Second Year**
- Attend welcome back events to re-engage with campus
- Focus on your greatest areas of interest so you can dig deeper
- Attend workshops to learn about funding and opportunities (Study Abroad, internships, research, leadership)
- Document what you are doing in class and beyond by uploading pictures, videos, papers and presentations to the cloud (Dropbox, Google Drive, iCloud)

**Third Year**
- As you continue to be engaged and document your work, think carefully about what you have been doing and why it is important to you
  - What has been most valuable?
  - How do your activities relate to your future goals?
- Take opportunities to lead in your areas of interest
- Meet with a coach in the Career Center
- Visit Discovery Day to see what others are presenting
- Complete the orientation for Graduation with Leadership Distinction and think about how you can fit UNIV 401 or a similar seminar into your senior year

Students who graduate with Leadership Distinction are given distinctive cords to wear at graduation.

**Fourth Year**
- Learn to tell your story. Be ready for job interviews and graduate school applications
- Take UNIV 401 (or major specific seminar) to help you articulate how your educational experiences have prepared you for the future
- Participate in a Mock Interview in the Career Center
- Present at Discovery Day
- Complete requirements for Graduation with Leadership Distinction

## Conclusion

As this chapter indicates, there are numerous ways to get involved and make the most of your experience at USC. It is important for you to explore what is available to you, and then make informed choices about which opportunities are best for you and your personal, academic, and professional goals. If you ever have questions, reach out to the leaders of an organization or visit the Leadership and Service Center in the Russell House University Union to talk to one of the Leadership Coaches. There is always someone willing to help you get connected.

# REFLECTION QUESTIONS

1. The beginning of this chapter discusses the difference in involvement versus engagement in college. Can you think of an example of an activity that you were only involved with instead of being engaged in? Why was your involvement different than truly being engaged in an activity? What could you have done differently to become more engaged with the activity?

2. Which of the co-curricular opportunities stood out the most to you? Why? In what ways could you actively pursue these?

3. Are you already involved in any of the activities listed in the chapter? What have you enjoyed most about this experience or opportunity?

4. What role does motivation play in getting involved on campus? What can you do to increase your motivation?

5. Which of the opportunities within the Columbia community interested you most? In what ways could these opportunities enhance your college experience?

6. What resources have you identified that could help you engage with different co-curricular activities?

7. What connections can you make between co-curricular engagement and employability?

# RESOURCES

**Campus Recreation**
Intramural Sports . . . . . . . . . . . . . . . (803) 576-9387
Outdoor Recreation . . . . . . . . . . . . . (803) 576-9397
Solomon Blatt Physical Education
Center . . . . . . . . . . . . . . . . . . . . . . . . . (803) 777-5261
Strom Thurmond Wellness & Fitness
Center . . . . . . . . . . . . . . . . . . . . . . . . . (803) 576-9376
http://campusrec.sc.edu/

**Carolina Productions** . . . . . . . . . . . . . . (803) 777-7130
Campus Life Center, Russell House 318
http://www.cp.sc.edu

**Fraternity and Sorority Life** . . . . . . . . . . (803) 777-3506
Russell House
http://www.sa.sc.edu/fsl

**Gamecock Athletics** . . . . . . . . . . . . . . . . . (803) 777-4202
http://gamecocksonline.cstv.com

**Garnet Gate**
**(Database for student**
**organizations and events)**
https://garnetgate.sa.sc.edu/

**Graduation with Leadership**
**Distinction** . . . . . . . . . . . . . . . . . . . . . (803) 777-3272
Thomas Cooper Library, Level 1
http://sc.edu/about/initiatives/usc_connect/

**Leadership and Service Center** . . . . . . (803) 777-7130
Campus Life Center, Russell House 227
http://www.sa.sc.edu/leaders

**Office of Undergraduate Research** . . . (803) 777-1141
Legare College 223
http://www.sc.edu/our/

**Peer Leadership/Education**
Student Success Center
Complete list of opportunities available at:
http://www.housing.sc.edu/
studentengagement/pl.html

**Residence Hall Involvement** . . . . . . . . . (803) 777-4283
http://www.housing.sc.edu

**Student Government** . . . . . . . . . . . . . . . . (803) 777-2654
Campus Life Center, Russell House 227
http://www.sg.sc.edu

**Student Media** . . . . . . . . . . . . . . . . . . . . . (803) 777-3888
Russell House 343
http://www.sa.sc.edu/studentmedia

**Student Organizations** . . . . . . . . . . . . . . (803) 777-2654
Campus Life Center, Russell House 227
http://www.sa.sc.edu/studentorgs

**Study Abroad** . . . . . . . . . . . . . . . . . . . . . . (803) 777-7557
Close-Hipp Building, Suite 453
http://www.studyabroad.sc.edu

**USC Connect** . . . . . . . . . . . . . . . . . . . . . . . (803) 777-3272
Thomas Cooper Library, Level 1
http://sc.edu/about/initiatives/usc_connect/

# REFERENCES

Astin, A.W. (1993). *What matters in college? Four critical years revisited.* San Francisco, CA: Jossey-Bass.

Ender, S. C., & Kay, K. (2001). Peer leadership programs: A rationale and review of the literature. In S. L. Hamid (Ed.), *Peer leadership: A primer on program essentials* (Monograph No. 32, pp. 1-12). Columbia, SC: University of South Carolina, National Resource Center for The First-Year Experience and Students in Transition.

Kuh, G. D. (2003). *The National Survey of Student Engagement: Conceptual framework and overview of psychometric properties.* Bloomington, IN: Indiana University Center for Postsecondary Research and Planning.

Merriam-Webster. (2015). Retrieved from: http://www.merriam-webster.com/dictionary/engagement

Pascarella, E. T., & Terenzini, P.T. (2005). *How college affects students: A third decade of research* (2nd ed.). San Francisco, CA: Jossey-Bass.

# CHAPTER 6

# Positive Relationships

# UNIVERSITY OF
# SOUTH CAROLINA

*Dear First-Year Student,*

Welcome to the University of South Carolina! You join a wonderful family of over 30,000 students, faculty, and staff and have the ability to take advantage of numerous opportunities to expand your knowledge and leadership. One of the initial questions you may have is, "How do I get started, especially on a campus this large?" Trying to find your way and make your mark may seem like a daunting task but, fortunately, this chapter can help provide insight and advice.

Building and maintaining positive relationships provides a fantastic life lesson and is a skill you should acquire early and continue to develop throughout your Carolina experience. In fact, one of the fundamental aspects of leadership is developing positive relationships with other people, so recognize that as you reach out and expand your personal network you are also increasing your leadership potential.

It is important to consider when building and maintaining positive relationships that it does not only mean meeting new friends. Yes, your network of peers is extremely important and therefore something you should focus upon. But, this also means developing positive relationships with your professors. Many students overlook this opportunity, and it is unfortunate because professors not only provide instruction in the classroom, they also can become vital mentors who guide you and offer important advice beyond your courses. Several studies indicate that identifying a mentor and developing that relationship is one of the most important factors for success. Yet, these same studies note that only a small proportion of students take the time to find mentors and build these relationships.

Building and maintaining positive relationships with both peers and faculty who can serve as potential mentors helps shrink a campus of 30,000 individuals to a smaller community. This community of people will likely support you throughout life while also challenging you to broaden your horizons and grow as an individual. They will introduce you to new experiences, present you with new information to consider, and assist in identifying opportunities that you can pursue.

I wish you the very best and hope to see you either in class or somewhere on campus!

Sincerely,

Kirk Randazzo
Professor of Political Science
Director of the Carolina Leadership Initiative

**WHEN** you arrived at the University of South Carolina, you came with a "clean slate" and the opportunity to become the person you want to be. You've heard the old adage, "You only get one chance to make a first impression." Beginning college is a fresh start. For the majority of people you will meet, your reputation has no history, there are no teachers who know what kind of student you were, and no friends who knew you when you were in middle school. What an exciting time! Carolina is a place where you can become who you want to be and there are, indeed, "no limits" to the opportunities ahead of you in this new environment. Making new friends and establishing new relationships throughout the University community are among the most important aspects of developing a sense of belonging and finding your niche in college. At no other time in your life will you again have the opportunity to be surrounded by so many people your same age, same educational level, with similar interests, and in the same situation as you. Making the most of this unique situation is an opportunity not to be taken lightly. Relationships made and nurtured in college—both positive and negative—can have a lifelong impact on your development and success.

This chapter, and the way in which you focus on relationships in your University 101 class, will help you better understand the importance of relationships and learn skills that can help you develop and nurture new relationships. You will consider how positive and healthy relationships differ from unhealthy ones. We will look at relationships as a broad topic, including making friends in the new environment of college and the importance of developing relationships with staff, faculty, and your peers. We will also consider the challenges you may have with changing relationships with your family and high school friends. And finally, we will consider how to manage the inevitable interpersonal conflict that all people experience in life.

Relationships are important in many facets of life. Humans are social beings, and leading a fulfilling life is dependent upon relationships of many kinds and impacts many areas of our lives. Optimal health and wellbeing depend on many things, among them are relationships. This book devotes

ACCORDING TO SCHREINER, LEWIS, AND NELSON (2012), "THRIVING IMPLIES THAT SUCCESS INVOLVES MORE THAN SURVIVING A FOUR YEAR OBSTACLE COURSE. WHEN THEY ARE THRIVING, STUDENTS ARE CONNECTED TO OTHERS IN HEALTHY AND MEANINGFUL WAYS, AND THEY DESIRE TO MAKE A DIFFERENCE IN THE WORLD."

considerable attention to developing and maintaining positive relationships. In addition to what you will find in this chapter, there are several other chapters with this focus. Chapter 8, "Values and Identity," emphasizes the importance of knowing and understanding your own values and identity as a prerequisite to understanding your relationships with others. This is even more essential as you get to know and interact with people who are different from you. Chapter 9, "The Carolinian Creed," is about Carolina's aspirational code of behavior and conduct which is based on the fact that we live in community and are in relationship with each other. It addresses integrity, diversity, interpersonal relationships, and mutual support. As a student at Carolina, you are expected to strive to live in accordance with the creed. Chapter 10, "Wellbeing," describes the seven dimensions of wellness, including the social dimension. This dimension emphasizes the creation and maintenance of healthy relationships and encourages positive contribution to the welfare of the community. Finally, relationships are one of the six pillars in the University of South Carolina's newly developed Employability Model, described in detail in chapter 11.

# Making Friends in a New Environment

Developing and maintaining positive relationships with your peers is critical to your sense of belonging and first-year success. A sense of belonging also is a significant factor in student success and persistence. Finding your niche at the University of South Carolina is a key accomplishment for the first year of college, as is diversifying your associations and groups.

Perhaps the most influential associations you will have are with the friends you choose. It is natural to choose friends who share your values, goals, and interests. So, knowing yourself is critical. Knowing the difference between your true self and the self that others expect you to be or that you expect of yourself can be a challenge to understand. Understanding your values and how your core values shape your interests and behaviors is addressed in chapter 8.

In this fast-paced world, we have to intentionally take the time to reflect on who we are, what we value, and what we want in life. There are many tools available to help us better understand our personalities and how we naturally interact with others in the world. True Colors and StrengthsFinder are quick and easy assessments to start, or extend, the process of self-understanding. Other tools include FOCUS, the Strong Interest Inventory (SII), and the Myers-Briggs Type Indicator (MBTI).

The friends you make in college are likely to last a lifetime. These friendships will also influence the behavioral patterns of how you relate to other people throughout your life. The great thing about student life at Carolina is that there are so many ways to make new friends. You now have the best opportunity you have ever had to develop a diverse and wide-ranging group of new friends. Diversifying your networks can be a very enriching experience, as you learn from people who are different from you and who have had very different life experiences! You have others on your hall, you have classmates, and you have 300+ student organizations you can choose to join. Connecting with others is a very easy thing to do if you take the initiative to do so. New friends will not always come to you; you have to go to them sometimes. Getting out of your room and into campus life is the first step.

Finding your niche at Carolina is something every first-year student needs to do. There are many ways to get connected and find a group with similar interests. Among the hundreds of student organizations offered through Student Life, are topical interest groups, sports clubs, political and student government organizations, honor societies, Greek life organizations, leadership and service organizations, and religious and faith-based groups. If, in for some reason you cannot find a group on a topic of your interest, there is a process for creating a new organization, and the Leadership and Service Center in the Russell House can guide you in this process.

The University of South Carolina has created rich networks to help students find their niches. But you also don't have to depend on programs like this to help you. There are things you can do every day to put yourself in the position to make

> **NEW FRIENDS WILL NOT ALWAYS COME TO YOU; YOU HAVE TO GO TO THEM SOMETIMES. GETTING OUT OF YOUR ROOM AND INTO CAMPUS LIFE IS THE FIRST STEP.**

### PEER LEADER ADVICE

I tried to develop a "yes" attitude, in that whenever I was invited to go on an adventure or go out for a dinner I would say yes. This helped me meet people I may have never met if I just stayed in my comfort zone.

*Carolyn Jouben*
Burke, VA • Junior
Public Health

new friends. First, get your eyes off your phone screen and put your phone in your pocket! See what is around you, see people you are passing as you walk across campus. Make eye contact and say hello. Start conversations in the elevators or in line at the Grand Marketplace. Take the initiative to meet new people. When you are in your room in the residence hall, leave your door open so people will know you are there and available for socializing. Start conversations with your classmates that sit near you before class begins or after it ends. Talk about the homework or an upcoming test.

Making new friends comes naturally to some and takes more of an effort for others. One thing is for certain, if you stay in your room or in your apartment all the time, you are not putting yourself in a situation to meet new people. Don't assume that everyone else is busy with school work or doing exciting things. Everyone is in the same situation as you. If you are having a hard time making new friends, ask for help! Take the initiative to intentionally step out of your comfort zone and make a new friend.

# Relationships with University Faculty

One of the most significant transitions from high school to college is the change in relationships between students and instructors. You may have been told the myth that professors in college won't care as much, or they won't care in the same way that your high school teachers did. You may also feel intimidated by large classes and might need some encouragement to visit faculty during office hours for help. Visiting during office hours can also help you get to know your professors and form a more personal relationship with them. Not only will it help you, it will help them get to know you.

In high school, your teacher's primary role was just that, to teach. Understanding the various roles and responsibilities that faculty have beyond teaching is important in helping you better understand faculty. In addition to teaching the class you are in, your faculty may teach additional courses, engage in scholarly research, contribute to their field by writing and publishing journal articles and books, serve on university committees, participate in faculty governance in the University's Faculty Senate, serve on theses and dissertation committees for graduate and undergraduate students, and serve as an academic advisor in their department. Needless to say, faculty are busy people with competing pressure in their work lives. And their advancement in their careers depends on more than just good teaching evaluations each year.

College is a learning environment in which you take responsibility for thinking through and applying what you have learned. Taking the initiative to pursue your college professors is critical, and getting to class early and staying late can give you a way to interact with your professors. In addition to helping you get focused for the class, it can also let your professor see you and hopefully recognize you outside of class. Sitting near the front of the room is always a good strategy for engaging with the instructor and the course material.

Utilizing office hours to meet with your instructor is one way to get to know them better. Office hours are listed on every syllabus at the University so that you will know when your instructor is available for consultation and meetings. Making an appointment in advance is advisable, but not always necessary. You can use office hours to get help understanding material that you find difficult, to seek advice on how to study for an upcoming test if there has been no guidance in class, and other individual questions that are not appropriate to ask in the class setting.

Another fun way is to participate is through the Out to Lunch program that the Student Success Center sponsors. This program allows you to take an instructor out to lunch using a free lunch ticket available for this purpose. You use your meal plan, but the instructor's meal is free. Sharing conversation over a meal is one of the best ways to get to know someone better! You can prepare in advance for the conversation you will have to avoid any awkwardness. Topics might include class assignments and projects, the broader discipline of the course, and academic advice for

# HIGH SCHOOL TEACHERS VERSUS COLLEGE PROFESSORS

| HIGH SCHOOL TEACHERS | COLLEGE PROFESSORS |
| --- | --- |
| Teachers check your completed homework. | Professors may not always check completed homework, but they will assume you can perform the same tasks on test. If not, you will ask for help. |
| Teachers remind you of your incomplete work. | Professors may not remind you of incomplete work. |
| Teachers are often available for conversation before, during, or after class. | Professors expect and want you to attend their scheduled office hours. |
| Teachers have been trained in teaching methods to assist in imparting knowledge to students. | Professors have been trained as experts in their particular discipline. |
| Teachers provide you with information you missed when you were absent. | Professors expect you to get from classmates any notes from classes you missed. |
| Teachers present material to help you understand the material in the textbook. | Professors may not follow a textbook. Instead, to amplify the text, they may give illustrations, provide background information, or discuss research about the topic you are studying. Or they may expect you to relate the classes to the textbook readings. |
| Teachers often write information on the board to be copied in your notes. | Professors may lecture nonstop, expecting you to identify the important points in your notes. When professors write on the board, it may be to amplify the lecture, not to summarize it. Good notes are a must. |
| Teachers impart knowledge and facts, sometimes drawing direct connections and leading you through the thinking process. | Professors expect you to think about and synthesize seemingly unrelated topics. |
| Teachers often take time to remind you of assignments and due dates. | Professors expect you to read, save, and consult the course syllabus; the syllabus spells out exactly what is expected of you, when it is due, and how you will be graded. |
| Teachers carefully monitor class attendance. | Professors may not formally take roll, but they are still likely to know whether or not you attended, and it leaves an impression. |

*Source*: Muskingum College, Department of Academic Affairs.

being successful in the course and discipline. You might also ask other questions about the professor's background and their academic path, their research interests, and their interests outside of their job. Consider some of the following questions as conversation starters over lunch:

- How did you decide to become a professor?
- What is your favorite thing about your discipline?
- What is your specialty in the field?
- What is it about the subject that attracted you?
- What were you like when you were a freshman?
- Where did you go to school?
- What characteristics do students who are successful in your class/your discipline have?
- What should I do to be successful in your course?
- What do you like most about the University of South Carolina?
- What do you enjoy doing when you are not working?

## A Word about your Digital Identity

In addition to the way you interact with others in person and in written communication, there is another way in which you are in relationship with others - your digital identity is also a factor. Social media is ubiquitous in society today and it can be useful in making and developing friendships. It can also impact others' perceptions of you - positively, negatively, professionally, and personally. The way you present yourself through various social media like Facebook, Snapchat, Instagram, Twitter, and the many other platforms is as much a part of your identity as is what you say and do in person. Once something is on the Internet, it is there forever. Not only are your friends and acquaintances influenced by your online persona, but so are future employers, graduate school admissions committees, and scholarship selection committees. So remember, what goes on the Internet, stays on the Internet.

### OUT TO LUNCH PROGRAM

Another great way to meet your professors in a more casual setting is through the Student Success Center (SSC) Out-to-Lunch Program. With this program, you are given a voucher that will cover a professor's meal at any dining location on campus. All you have to do is invite them to lunch. If this intimidates you, consider asking another classmate to come along as well. You can pick up an Out-to-Lunch ticket at any SSC office and the campus offices for University Housing, including:

- Patterson Hall SSC satellite office
- Columbia Hall SSC satellite office
- Bates House SSC satellite office
- Student Success Center, Thomas Cooper Library
- Capstone Scholars Office (behind Gibbs)

There is no limit to the number of times you can use the Out-to-Lunch program!

# EMAIL ETIQUETTE

It is important to consider how to craft professional email communication to various individuals – faculty, staff, friends, and current or future employers. Take a look at the emails below and discuss both the positive and negative implications of each.

To: futureinternshipsupervisor@companyname.com

Subject:

From: student@email.sc.edu    Signature

When will I know if I got the internship?

Katie

---

To: faculty@email.sc.edu

Subject: Monday's quiz

From: partygurlxoxo@hotmail.com    Signature: None

Dr. Dan,
Why do I have a 0 for the quiz on Monday, I was in class and took the quiz?!
Katie

---

To: studentsuccess@mailbox.sc.edu

Subject: SI sessions

From: student@email.sc.edu    Signature: None

What times r the SI sessions 4 this class? Im rly confused about the stuff we covered 2day.
Katie

---

To: SGpresident@email.sc.edu

Subject: SG elections

From: student@email.sc.edu    Signature: None

Dear Name,
I'm the SG representative from the DMSB, I was wondering what I should do to prepare for my first SG meeting. Would it be possible for us to meet in advance of the first meeting?
Thank you I look forward to meeting with you,
Katie

# Changing Relationships

After being away from home for six or seven weeks, returning home for fall break or later for Thanksgiving holiday can be strange and wonderful at the same time. It will be wonderful to be in a familiar and comfortable environment at home again with family. But, it is also likely that there may be tensions that arise unexpectedly. You are not the only one for whom this visit may be uncomfortable or tense. You have been away and on your own for weeks, making your own decisions and managing your own life. When you return home, you are returning to a place that is primarily the same as it was when you left it.

The changing relationships that result from your new status as a college student may be eye-opening for all involved – you, your parents, and your other family members. Keeping in mind that good and open communication is the best way to resolve differences may be helpful. Talking about your experiences and hearing about theirs is useful. Your family has basically continued in their daily patterns while you have had transformative experiences. Sharing them is important to those who love you.

Cocky and Parents

Make sure that you communicate in advance about their expectations of you for the time at home. Are you expected to participate in family routines? Is there an expectation for certain events? What are the expectations about curfews, times to get out of bed in the mornings, and family meals? Comparing expectations in advance is better than having to deal with conflict that may arise if expectations are not communicated in advance.

A good resource for you to share with your parents is the University's Parents Program. Not only do they plan and present Parents Weekend each fall, but they have a newsletter and other resources that help parents support you in your education and better understand your student experience. Signing up with the program is free for USC parents!

Seeing your high school friends can also be both wonderful and strained at the same time. The long-time friends with whom you shared much of your experience before college will be as excited to see you as you will be excited to see them. Keep in mind that they have had new experiences, made new friends, and grown in new ways as much as you have, but in a totally different environment. Remembering this will provide interesting conversations. Even those friends who are at Carolina, but in different circles of experience, will be different.

Patience, understanding, and communication are all needed as you head home after the exciting and life-changing experience of the beginning of your college career. Being aware that things have changed and are likely to be different can be helpful at that time.

## Managing Conflict

Conflict is natural. Every relationship of any depth at all has conflicts. No matter how close, how understanding, how compatible you are, there will be times when your ideas, actions, needs, and goals won't match those of others around you. There's no end to the number and kinds of disagreements possible. Even though conflict is part of a meaningful relationship, you can change the way you deal with it. There are typically five ways in which people respond to conflict.

- **Accommodation** - agreement through yielding or conforming to the positions of others. This is a non-assertive, highly cooperative technique for handling conflict.
- **Avoidance** - simply ignore the conflict. This may be a good option when the time is not right for dealing with the situation. However, on major issues, avoidance can lead to frustration and misunderstanding with no final resolution.
- **Collaboration** - tries to blend all the positive aspects of the difference in a conflict into a solution. Giving and taking is seen on both sides and everyone seems to come out a winner.
- **Competition** - ignores the wants and needs of the other person involved. Competing can be a useful strategy in an emergency when a decision is needed,

although frequent misuse of this approach can leave others feeling neglected.

- **Compromise** - involves searching for solutions and making sacrifices. It may not be the best outcome because people are settling for "the best they can get." Conflict is sure to arise again when everyone tries, once again, to get what they could not before.

Because conflict can't be controlled, but only managed, there are strategies for dealing with conflict that are productive and produce more positive results.

# Five Step Process of Dealing with Conflict

The foundation for dealing with conflict rests with accurate listening. Hear what is being said. This is especially important in diagnosing conflict. Listening plays a significant role when dealing with your own conflict – listen to what you are saying. Avoid factors that impede listening. Some of these include: distractions, emotions, preconceived thoughts, and thinking about your response rather than what is being said.

## 1. Diagnose the conflict

Objectively consider what, why, and where the conflict is coming from. After you have done this, consider your feelings about the conflict.

## 2. Decide on an appropriate response to the conflict

Consider the consequences of avoiding the conflict. Consider the consequences of dealing with the conflict. When making this decision, ask: "Is there really a conflict?" "Is it worth dealing with?" "Is it long-term conflict or will it go away?"

## 3. Initiate a plan of action

Formulate a plan or strategy by yourself or with someone acting as a sounding board. List possible alternatives and their consequences and make a choice. Select an appropriate time and setting. Select a style of approach, direct or indirect.

### 4. Problem-solving

Carry through with the chosen plan of action. If the chosen plan of action involved confrontation, talk slowly, remain calm, and try to be objective in your presentation. If the plan of action does not work, be prepared to compromise or go back to the list of alternatives in step 3 and formulate a different plan of action.

### 5. Follow-up

Sometime later, check the following: Is the plan of action working successfully? How do you feel about the results? Is further action necessary? Is the conflict resolved? If not, go back to step 3.

Make sure to use statements such as "I feel...," "I don't understand why...," and "When you...I feel...." Do *not* use statements such as "You make me feel...," "You aren't fair...," "Why do you always...," and "Everyone else knows..."

If you find that you are in a conflict situation that you cannot manage even after using the suggestions here, do not fail to reach out for assistance. There are many resources available to you on campus to help such as your residence hall staff, a UNIV 101 peer leader, or the USC Student Ombudsman. Managing conflict is a life-long experience. With time and intention you can get better at it, but the need to manage conflict will exist as long as you are in community with other humans. Work at it and do your best, but always be willing to seek help when appropriate.

# Conclusion

Our world today is connected, and all career fields need people that can develop and maintain positive relationships. For better or worse, the relationships you develop during college can have a profound impact on how you see yourself. Learning now what makes a relationship healthy or unhealthy also can help you make decisions about how you relate to others and give you more tools to develop a positive self-image. Much of what you can learn about relationships

# WHAT TO DO WHEN YOU DON'T GET ALONG WITH YOUR ROOMMATE

At the University of South Carolina, incoming students have the opportunity to choose their own roommate, live with someone who is paired with them based on a questionnaire each incoming student fills out, or utilize RoomSync to interact with potential roommates via social media. Many students also choose to use the Facebook page for their incoming class to find a roommate with similar likes and dislikes.

Living with a roommate isn't always easy, especially if you are not used to sharing a space. It can be stressful and conflicts can arise. University Housing encourages students to work on their conflicts themselves before involving their resident mentors (RMs). In addition, room changes are not granted until students try to address the issue and work through it. These room changes also do not occur until the second or third week of September, to allow time for students to discuss expectations of living with one another and to learn more about one another.

Prior to completing roommate agreements (a document created by roommates to hold one another accountable for mutual expectations), RMs hold a community gathering (or a floor meeting) where all of the residents come together and discuss communication styles and go over a few scenarios of how to address someone in a specific situation. For example, you and your roommate(s)/suite-mate(s) may have opposite schedules where one of you prefers to stay up late and sleep late but the other person wants to go to bed early and get up early. If you are not quiet while getting ready in the mornings when your roommate tries to sleep or if your roommate comes in late, turns on the light, and makes noise while you are trying to sleep, conflict is likely to rise. Your RM can talk you through your situation and give you tips on how they have dealt with roommate conflicts before. Below are some tips that will be helpful in addressing issues that may arise:

- Approach your roommate in private.
- Confirm that this is a good time for both of you to talk. If one of you feels rushed or blindsided, they will be less able to communicate effectively.
- Be direct. Discuss the issue with regard to behaviors rather than personality traits. This tactic is less likely to put your roommate on the defensive.

- Be patient. Listen to your roommate and remember that there are two sides to every story.
- Each person should be given a chance to present what they feel the problem really is.
- Revisit your roommate agreement. You should have it posted in the room. Which of your guidelines are working and which of them needs to be reconsidered?
- Remember that a solution will probably involve each person giving something and getting something. The solution may not be your ideal scenario, but it should be an improvement on the current state of things.
- If you feel as if the conversation isn't productive, you may involve your resident mentor, who can help mediate the conversation.

Most roommate conflicts are the result of miscommunication or, in some cases, a total lack of communication. If you can communicate effectively, it will be much easier to develop a comfortable living environment for yourself and your roommates. Keep the following in mind in order to communicate in a healthy way with your roommate:

- Talk to your roommate directly when something is bothering you. Don't discuss it behind their back because this can cause a breakdown in trust between you. Also keep in mind, passive communication such as text messages and post-it notes are not effective ways to communicate issues.
- Be direct and clear about what is bothering you. If you don't tell your roommate that there is a problem they won't be able to do anything about it.
- Remember that communication works two ways: talking and listening. Neither one is effective without the other.
- Respect each other's differences. Everyone has different values, lifestyles, expectations, and communication styles. Get to know each other and establish common ground. It is easier to solve a problem with a friend than a stranger.

*Source*: University Housing, University of South Carolina

can apply in any type of relationship you have – with friends, with staff and faculty, and with parents/family.

In conclusion, if you think about it, you are the hub of the many relationships you have with others. Some of the people you know may know one another, but you are the center of your web. You have relationships from before you came to the University of South Carolina. You have high school friends, high school teachers and counselors, and family. You may also have teammates from the sports you played, friends from church or a faith community, co-workers and supervisors if you had an afterschool or summer job, and others you know from your extracurricular activities. Now that you are in a new environment, you will make new friends and meet new people. You will have roommates, suitemates, teammates, advisors, instructors, supervisors, and fellow club and organization members. And this network of people will continue to grow throughout your life. Knowing how to develop positive relationships, find your niche on campus, interact appropriately with faculty and staff, and manage the conflict that will inevitably occur from time to time will help you to have a bright future at Carolina!

In the figure to the right, fill in the names of people in your network of relationships. Draw lines to represent how well you know each of these individuals (e.g., a solid line represents a strong relationship and a dotted line represents a weaker relationship). Are any people connected to each other? Use this activity to reflect on the relationships you have with others at Carolina.

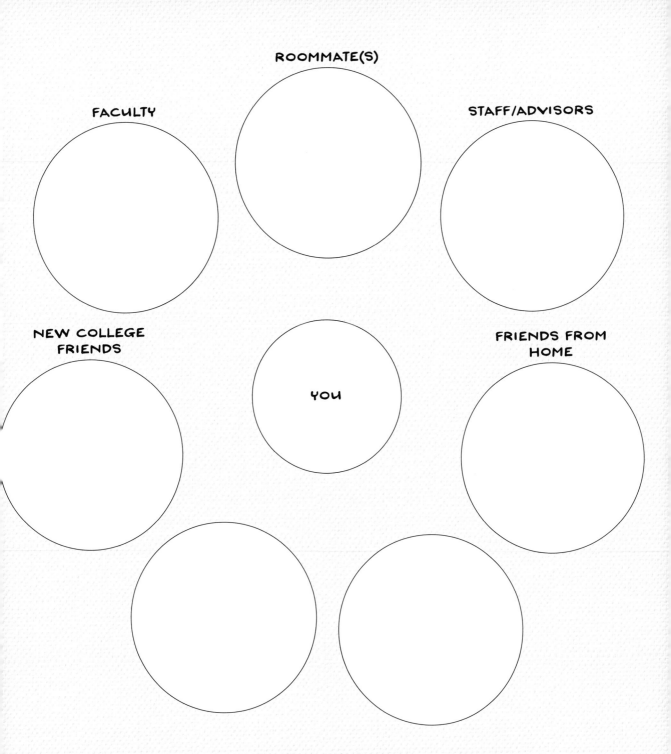

ROOMMATE(S)

FACULTY

STAFF/ADVISORS

NEW COLLEGE
FRIENDS

YOU

FRIENDS FROM
HOME

## REFLECTION QUESTIONS

1. What was the last situation where you had to make new friends (before coming to college)? Was that a challenge or did it come naturally to you? Why do you think this is?

2. To what extent are you comfortable taking the initiative to meet new people? What are some things you can do to make this process less intimidating for you?

3. This chapter discusses your relationships with professors. What are some of the benefits to developing positive relationships with faculty and staff? What suggestions from the chapter will you utilize throughout your college career?

4. Think about the last time you had a conflict with a roommate, friend, family member. How did you resolve that conflict? Did you use any of the suggestions listed in this chapter? Which of the strategies for managing conflict do you think will be most helpful in your future relationships?

5. The chapter suggests that the key to dealing with conflict is accurate listening. What impedes people from being able to listen to others and what can be done to avoid worsening the conflict?

6. Consider your relationships with others since you arrived at Carolina. How have these relationships affected you positively (or negatively)? What are one or two goals that you have set for yourself in terms of improving your relationships with others?

## RESOURCES

**Counseling and Psychiatry- Student Health Services**
Counseling Services . . . . . . . . . . . . . (803) 777-5223
Close-Hipp Building, 5th Floor
https://www.sa.sc.edu/shs/cp/

**Counseling and Psychiatry- Student Health Services**
Psychiatry Services . . . . . . . . . . . . . . (803) 777-1833
Thomson Student Health Center, 3rd Floor
https://www.sa.sc.edu/shs/cp/

**Sexual Assault and Violence Intervention and Prevention** . . . . . . . . . . . . . . . . . . . . . . (803) 777-8248
Thomson Student Health Center
https://www.sa.sc.edu/shs/savip/

**Student Success Center** . . . . . . . . . . . . . (803) 777-0684
Thomas Cooper Library-- Mezzanine Level
http://www.sa.sc.edu/ssc/

**University Housing** . . . . . . . . . . . . . . . . . . (803) 777-4283
Patterson Hall, Garden Level
http://www.housing.sc.edu

## REFERENCES

Muskingum College, Department of Academic Affairs. (n.d.) Retrieved from: http://www.muskingum.edu/academicaffairs/downloads/RealityCheckHSvCollege.pdf

Schreiner, L.A., Louis, M.C., & Nelson, D.D. (Eds). (2012) *Thriving in transition: A research-based approach to college student success*. Columbia, SC: National Resource Center for The First-Year Experience and Students in Transition.

Tagg, J. (2003) The learning paradigm college. Boston, MA: Anker.

# CHAPTER 7

# History and Traditions

Dear First-Year Student,

"Carolina feels like home." That is the message we hear from many of our incoming students, some of whom made their decisions to apply to and enroll in the University of South Carolina the moment they first stepped onto the historic Horseshoe. With its tree-lined brick pathways, lush lawn, and federal architecture, there is no denying it is a beautiful spot. But there is more to that feeling of home than simply appearance. There are 200 years of history and tradition that have shaped Carolina into the premier place of learning and living it is today.

Though the students who came before you followed different fashion trends and never imagined sending text messages to celebrate a Gamecocks victory, you have a lot in common. Just like you, generations of Carolinians have studied on the Horseshoe grass, raised a "health" during the singing of the alma mater, pored over The Daily Gamecock, and cheered on the Garnet and Black.

This is not to say, however, that we are stuck in the past. Every day at the University of South Carolina, we are generating innovative ideas through research, scholarship, and leadership endeavors. We are forging new traditions, like Alternative Break Service Trips, Parents Weekend, and Graduation with Leadership Distinction.

There are infinite possibilities for you—in your own way—to contribute to Carolina's great legacy by participating in these time-honored traditions and by creating new ones to enhance our vibrant campus culture. Learn about where the University has been and where it is going, then decide how you will be a part of it—how you can be a model for future Carolinians.

Start by reading the Carolinian Creed. Written by a group of our students, faculty, and staff, it describes the principles that guide our lives as members of the Carolina community, the attributes that distinguish us from all others. The Creed, quite simply, is what it means to be a Carolinian.

I wish you, a new Carolinian, all the best.

Dennis A. Pruitt
Vice President for Student Affairs and Academic Support
Vice Provost and Dean of Students

**YOU** chose Carolina and Carolina chose you! Through the presentation of the University's rich history and an introduction to the traditions that are unique to the South Carolina community, this chapter will help you begin to understand what it means to be a Carolinian. Your journey of discovery will continue as you explore the wealth of opportunities available to Carolina students, take advantage of many learning experiences, and make Carolina your home.

As a student at Carolina, it is important to understand and appreciate the University of South Carolina's history so that you can better understand your role as a member of the community and determine the impact that you want to have on the University's future. There are many traditions at Carolina that are rooted in the past, and as you explore its history, you will begin to understand the culture of your campus and feel a growing connection as you become a true Carolinian!

## Keeping It Cocky Since 1801: A Chronological History

*(Adapted from http://www.sc.edu/about/our_history/ and used with permission.)*

The University of South Carolina, chartered on December 19, 1801 as South Carolina College, was a part of an effort to unite South Carolinians in the wake of the American Revolution. South Carolina's leaders saw the new college as a way to promote "the good order and harmony" of the state. The founding of South Carolina College was also a part of the Southern public college movement spurred by Thomas Jefferson. In the antebellum era, South Carolina College was the first university in the United States to be supported continuously by annual state appropriations.

In the years before the Civil War, South Carolina College rapidly achieved a reputation for academic excellence and was known as one of the best endowed and most distinguished colleges in the country. The institution featured impressive faculty, including such noted European scholars as Francis Lieber, editor of the *Encyclopedia Americana;* nationally

Governor John Drayton delivers a message to the South Carolina General Assembly recommending the establishment of a state-supported college. With little opposition, the South Carolina General Assembly approved the legislation that established South Carolina College.

known scientists John and Joseph LeConte; chemist William Ellet, who produced some of the first daguerreotype photographs (e.g., images made on light-sensitive, silver-coated, metallic plates) in the United States; and Thomas Cooper, a man Thomas Jefferson referred to as "the greatest man in America, in the powers of mind, and in acquired information" (Honeywell, 1931, pp. 90-91). By the 1830s, almost all of the state's General Assembly members were distinguished alumni of the University. James H. Hammond and Wade Hampton III were the most prominent of the future governors, senators, judges, and generals who graduated during the pre-Civil War period.

Offering a traditional classical curriculum, South Carolina College became one of the most influential colleges in the South before 1861, earning a reputation as the training ground for South Carolina's antebellum elite. The pre-Civil War campus included Longstreet Theatre and all of the buildings (with the exception of the McKissick Museum) in the area known today as the Horseshoe. When the voluntary enlistment of all its students into Confederate service forced the College to close in June 1862, the buildings were confiscated by the Confederate government for use as hospital facilities. By the time Sherman's army reached Columbia in February 1865, the campus buildings contained several wounded Union soldiers. A fire soon destroyed most of the city, but federal troops helped save the historic Horseshoe from the flames.

State leaders revived the institution in 1866 as the University of South Carolina with ambitious plans for a diverse university that included the first African-American students admitted in 1873. While politically controversial, this development was an extraordinary opportunity for South Carolinians at a time when opportunities for higher education were rare. The University of South Carolina became the only Southern state university to admit and grant degrees to African-American students. The leaders of the university were very conservative and, as a result, closed the university once again in 1877. When they reopened the doors in 1880, the college was an all-white agricultural college and was called South Carolina College of Agriculture and Mechanical Arts. The University faced additional challenges in the 1890s adjusting to the arrival of women and intercollegiate athletics on campus.

Longstreet Theatre, 1875

In 1894, USC agreed to admit women as students, becoming the first collegiate institute in the state to allow coeducation.

Over the next 25 years, the institution became enmeshed in the upheaval of late 19th century South Carolina politics. Carolina went through several reorganizations in which the curriculum frequently changed and its status shifted from college to university and back again. In 1906, the institution was rechartered for the final time as the University of South Carolina. In the early decades of the 20th century, Carolina made strides toward becoming a comprehensive university, and in 1917 it became the first state-supported college or university in South Carolina to earn regional accreditation.

The 1920s witnessed further progress and growth with the introduction of new colleges and degree programs, including the doctorate. The Great Depression temporarily stalled this progress, but the outbreak of World War II launched an era that transformed the university. Carolina hosted U.S. Navy training programs during the war and enrollment more than doubled in the post war era as veterans took advantage of the G.I. Bill. In sharp contrast to South Carolina College's antebellum elitist philosophy, President William Davis Melton in 1925 expressed a far-reaching principle that emerged in the first quarter of the century saying, "Education is not a special privilege to be enjoyed by a special few." Thus, in its final reorganization, the University of South Carolina developed the institutional objective to provide both liberal and professional education to the people of South Carolina.

The General Assembly approves legislation converting the South Carolina College into the University of South Carolina, once and for all.

In the 1950s, the university began recruiting national-caliber faculty and extended its presence beyond Columbia with the establishment of campuses in communities across South Carolina. On Sept. 11, 1963, Henrie D. Monteith, Robert Anderson, and James Solomon became the first African-American students to enroll at the university in the 20th century; in 1965, Monteith became the first African-American graduate, earning a Bachelor of Science degree in biochemistry.

In the ensuing years, Carolina underwent explosive growth as enrollment stood at 5,660 in 1960, but by 1979 had reached nearly 26,000 students on the Columbia campus alone. To meet the needs of these students and South Carolina's changing economy, the university put a new emphasis on research and introduced innovative degree programs as well as a number of new schools and colleges. Carolina had become a true research university.

Since then, dynamic academic expansion and the development of a statewide network of campuses produced highly diverse and innovative educational programs. An increasing commitment to graduate education, along with involvement in major research programs, attracted an outstanding faculty. Moreover, an intense building program resulted in the construction of excellent modern physical facilities as well as the preservation of historic pre-Civil War buildings.

Today, the University of South Carolina, Columbia is not only the state's flagship university but also a rising national star. USC is increasingly an institution of choice among the best and brightest students in the nation. Carolina is one of 40 public universities to receive the Carnegie Foundation's highest research designation. The University system serves the entire state and includes, in addition to the Columbia campus, three four-year campuses (Aiken, Beaufort, and Upstate) and four regional campuses (Sumter, Lancaster, Salkehatchie, and Union). In keeping with its 19th- and 20th-century heritage, the University continues to promote academic excellence while offering progressive educational opportunities to the citizens of South Carolina. With 45,000 students on eight campuses, nationally respected faculty and nearly 260,000 alumni, the University of South Carolina has a bright future to match its rich history.

# Noteworthy Moments in University History

The history of the University of South Carolina is rich with events and stories that have significantly impacted campus identity today. Ranging from important steps to providing opportunities for any citizen to attend college, to oddities like Barefoot Day and the infamous student duel between A. Govan Roach and James G. Adams, these events help tell the story of how South Carolina College became the University of South Carolina.

# The History of the Horseshoe

The buildings on the Horseshoe form the original campus and are now the heart of the University. Listed on the National Register of Historic Places, this modified quadrangle was the next major building project in Columbia after completion of the state capital. Most of these buildings reflect the federal style of architecture common in the early 1800s.

As in all architecture, climate was the dominant influence in the college's design. Fires were always a threat to the buildings in the winter because fireplaces in each room were the only available means of heating. The buildings were made of brick, which was locally available and inexpensive. Also, the main floors, designed as faculty residences, were above ground level, which promoted air circulation during South Carolina's infamous long, hot summers. Robert Mills, the nation's first federal architect and the designer of the Washington Monument, greatly influenced the architecture of South Carolina College. Mills was involved in the design of Rutledge College, the South Caroliniana Library, and the Maxcy Monument in the center of the Horseshoe, named for the first president of the college, Jonathan Maxcy.

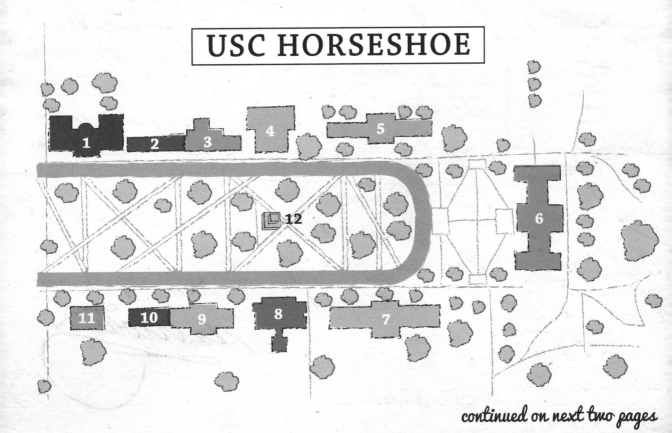

## USC HORSESHOE

*continued on next two pages*

## SOUTH CAROLINIANA LIBRARY (1840)

**Then:** South Caroliniana served as the main library on campus until the construction of McKissick Memorial Library (now McKissick Museum) in 1940.

**Now:** The library houses extensive collections concentrating on South Carolina.

**Fun Facts:** Landmarked as the first freestanding college library in the United States, the South Caroliniana Library is the most architecturally distinctive building on the Horseshoe. The grave in front is that of J. Rion McKissick, president of the University, 1936-1944.

## ELLIOTT COLLEGE (1837)

**Then:** Constructed to accommodate the growing campus, Elliott College served as a dormitory.

**Now:** Today this building houses students of the South Carolina Honors College.

**Fun Facts:** It is named for Stephen Elliott (1777-1830), the first president of the Bank of the State of South Carolina. Along with Harper College, Elliott mirrors the Pinckney and Legare buildings across the lawn.

## HARPER COLLEGE (1848)

**Then:** Built to be used as a dormitory, when classes were suspended in March 1862, Harper, along with other campus buildings, was used as a hospital. In 1865, the Federal army used four interior rooms as a military prison.

**Now:** Now it is home to the Office of Fellowships and Scholar Programs. Elliott and Harper serve as housing for upper-level students in the South Carolina Honors College.

**Fun Facts:** The building is named for William Harper, Class of 1808, a noted South Carolina judge and U.S. senator. One of the two original student organizations, the Euphradian Literary Society, held its meetings in Harper. The societies died out by the 1980s, but Euphradian Hall, located on the third floor, has been restored.

## MCCUTCHEN HOUSE (1813)

**Then:** McCutchen, Formerly the Second Professors House, was built to house two faculty families.

**Now:** Home of the Hotel, Restaurant, and Tourism Management Program's student-run restaurant.

**Fun Facts:** Professor George McCutchen, for whom the building is named, lived in the house with his family from 1915 until World War II. McCutchen was a professor at the University of South Carolina for 48 years.

## DESAUSSURE COLLEGE (1809)

**Then:** During the Civil War, DeSaussure College was part of the general hospital. Through the years, DeSaussure was used as a federal military prison and later as the home of the Normal School for the training of secondary teachers.

**Now:** Departmental and administrative offices as well as student residences.

**Fun Facts:** Named for Henry William DeSaussure (1763-1839), director of the U.S. Mint and chancellor of the state of South Carolina, this building is the second oldest on campus.

## MCKISSICK MUSEUM (1940)

**Then:** McKissick Memorial Library served as the primary library until the construction of Thomas Cooper Library (1959).

**Now:** McKissick is home of the University's Visitor Center and offers outstanding collections, exhibitions, and educational activities in history, natural science, and art.

**Fun Facts:** Named for J. Rion McKissick, president from 1936 to 1944, and his wife, Caroline McKissick.

## RUTLEDGE COLLEGE (1805)

**Then:** Rutledge College contained all college facilities, including faculty and student housing, classrooms, library, chapel, and labs. Gutted by fire in 1855, it was rebuilt immediately.

**Now:** Home to the Department of Religious Studies, student residences, and a chapel, often used for weddings and funerals.

**Fun Facts:** The first building to be erected at South Carolina College. Formerly referred to as South Building, Old South Building, Old South, or simply South, it is named for John Rutledge (1739-1800), governor of South Carolina, and his brother Edward (1749-1800), also a governor and a signer of the Declaration of Independence.

## PRESIDENT'S HOUSE (1810, REBUILT 1854)

**Then:** A faculty residence until the 1940s, it was later converted to a women's residence hall.

**Now:** In 1952, it was transformed into the official President's House, enhanced by the beautiful downstairs library and the splendid reception room on the second floor. The latest renovation was completed in 2003.

**Fun Facts:** The home of the president of the University is the most elegant building on the Horseshoe. The second floor contains several public rooms one of which features wallpaper with an oriental theme that dates from 1832. There also includes an alcove with a chair that was specially made for the visit of Pope John Paul II in September, 1987.

## LEGARE COLLEGE (1848)

**Then:** This building once housed the Clariosophic Literary Society, one of the original student organizations.

**Now:** Legare houses the Office of Undergraduate Research, Office of Fellowships and Scholar Programs, student residences, and departmental or administrative offices.

**Fun Facts:** Pronounced "Luh-gree", the building was named for Hugh Swinton Legare, Class of 1814, a U.S. attorney general and founder of the Southern Review.

## PINCKNEY COLLEGE (1837)

**Then:** Built as a residence hall and a twin to Elliott College across the Horseshoe.

**Now:** Now serves as a coed, apartment-style residence hall.

**Fun Facts:** It is named for a family long prominent in South Carolina, one of whom, Charles Cotesworth Pinckney (1757-1824), authored the Pinckney Draft of the U.S. Constitution. A statesman and diplomat, Charles Cotesworth Pinckney also fought with General George Washington during the Revolutionary War and was the first elected board member of the South Carolina College.

## LIEBER COLLEGE (1837)

**Then:** The Third Professors House, now known as Lieber College, was a duplex home that accommodated two faculty families.

**Now:** Home to the Office of Undergraduate Admissions.

**Fun Facts:** The three stories of exposed brick, white trim, austere lines, and small windowpanes are the embodiment of the early architecture of the campus. It was named for Francis Lieber (1800-1872), an illustrious faculty member and editor of the Encyclopedia Americana.

## 12  MAXCY MONUMENT (1827)

**Then:** The Maxcy Monument in the center of the Horseshoe was built by the Clariosophic Society to honor Reverend Jonathan Maxcy, first president of the South Carolina College, from 1805 to 1820.

**Now:** The Maxcy Monument still serves as a focal point of the historic Horseshoe.

**Fun Facts:** The Maxcy Monument cost $873 to build and was designed by Robert Mills, the nation's first federal architect and the designer of the Washington Monument. Mills was involved in the design of Rutledge, South Caroliniana Library, and the Maxcy Monument.

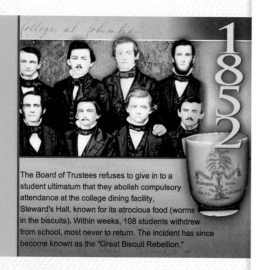

The Board of Trustees refuses to give in to a student ultimatum that they abolish compulsory attendance at the college dining facility, Steward's Hall, known for its atrocious food (worms in the biscuits). Within weeks, 108 students withdrew from school, most never to return. The incident has since become known as the "Great Biscuit Rebellion."

The Great Biscuit Rebellion

## Student Duel

College students have historically engaged in playing pranks or mischievous behavior. Common student misbehaviors on the University campus during the 1800s included throwing rocks through the windows of the President's residence (this behavior prompted the administration to enforce a glass tax to help supplement the cost of replacing broken glass) or stealing livestock from the surrounding neighborhoods. Fortunately, typical student misconduct did not result in much harm; however, the shenanigans of an infamous student duo, best friends A. Govan Roach and James G. Adams, met a fatal end in 1833. The tradition of the steward's, or dining hall, was that when a man got hold of a dish of bread, or any other dish, it was his. Unfortunately, Roach and Govan both caught hold of a dish of trout at the same moment. Adams did not let go and neither did Roach. Finally, Roach let go of the dish and glared fiercely at Adams and said, "I will see you after supper." Roach left the dining hall first and Adams immediately followed him. A battle between the two friends outside ensued and Adams was killed. Roach was left permanently lame and drank himself to death two years later (Geiger, 2000, pp. 100-101).

## Campus Dining and the Great Biscuit Rebellion

*(Reprinted with permission from Carolinian [April, 2003])*

The subject of campus food is seasoned throughout Carolina's history, starting in December 1806 when the first college dining hall was completed and all 56 students ate their meals there for $2.50 per week.

Things might have gotten off to a good start at the old steward's hall, as it was then known, but it did not last long. A massive case of indigestion plagued the campus for years, characterized by strikes, civil disturbances, mass disobedience, and declining enrollment, which all were linked to Carolina's poor-quality food in the 19th century. It did not help that dining in steward's hall was mandatory.

The first outright rebellion against campus food occurred in 1827 when a boycott by students led to the expulsion of

41 scholars. Before the action, students had broken into the home of the campus steward and thrown his silver, plates, and furniture into the college well. President Jonathan Maxcy complained that the college "was in yearly jeopardy of being destroyed because of disputes about eating."

Perhaps the most notorious campus unrest happened in 1852 during what came to be known as the Great Biscuit Rebellion. One hundred eight students who were required to eat on campus demanded that they be allowed to eat off campus because they found worms in their biscuits. Trustees were displeased by the ultimatum, but before the impasse could be resolved, the students withdrew from the college, with only a few returning to campus.

The mass withdrawal reduced the junior class in 1852 from 56 to 11 and only 11 seniors graduated in 1853, the smallest class since 1823. The next year the trustees abolished the compulsory dining system.

## Integration

The University of South Carolina has been racially integrated twice. In 1873, the Radical Republicans demanded the University accept black students, making it the only state-supported Southern university to integrate fully during the Reconstruction Period. When the Democrats came to power again in 1877, the University was closed, reorganized, and reopened in 1880 as an all-white institution. The University integrated for a second and final time in 1963.

One of the most influential names associated with the first integration of the University of South Carolina is Richard T. Greener, a professor during the 1870s. Richard Greener earned a degree from Harvard College and pursued a faculty position at the University of South Carolina at a time in American history when it was unheard of to have an African-American professor in the South. Greener broke through these stereotypes and become the first African-American professor at USC. He taught mental and moral philosophy as well as constitutional history, served as a librarian, and provided assistance in the Latin, Greek, and Mathematics Departments. He was not only the first African-American professor at USC, but he was also the

Richard Greener, the first African-American professor at USC.

only African-American professor to be employed by the University of South Carolina for decades.

After integration of African-American students occurred in 1873, the push for equality in education heightened and was extended to women. Female students were not allowed to enroll at the University until 1895, and the first women graduated in 1898. Most of the students and faculty members did not want women attending the University. One faculty member referred to them as "that monstrous regiment of women" (Monstrous Regiment, 1998, para. 2). However, female students soon proved themselves to be fully capable of competing academically with their male counterparts. Every year since 1981, the University of South Carolina has enrolled more women than men.

## Barefoot Day

In the early 1900s, it was customary for upper-level students to haze the newest students on campus. One notable tradition was that first-year students were required to purchase and wear a beanie style cap, known as a rat cap, at all times up until a day late in spring known as Barefoot Day. On Barefoot Day, first-year students were allowed to remove their caps but had to walk barefoot throughout the day. Only the male students were expected to participate in the barefoot activity as it was considered improper during this time period for women to be seen without shoes. In addition to a campus of bare feet, on Barefoot Day upper-level students spent the day hazing the first-year males by ordering them to perform silly or outlandish tasks.

Wednesday, April 6, 1938, marked the end of the Barefoot Day tradition when some upper-level students told a group of first-year male students to kiss the female students as they passed them on campus. Many of the female students were disturbed by this behavior and fled from the men as they chased them in pursuit of a kiss. One first-year student, Hugh Tarte, was credited as the student responsible for much of the chaos that ensued that day. Although he seemed to be the leader of the commotion, Tarte was not the only first-year student that behaved poorly; complaints flooded the administration offices and several female students took legal action against the male students and the University. President

Rat Cap

Ron McKissick was deeply disturbed by the behavior of these students and, in an address to the student body said:

> In the years past there have sometime been gross disorder and misconduct here, but I say to you that nothing in all our long past has been so disgraceful, so contemptible, so cowardly, so brutal, so unworthy of gentlemen and so outrageous as what took place in our campus yesterday. (McKissick records, 1938)

As a result of the events of that day, Hugh Tarte was expelled from the University, most of the other male students involved were suspended for the remainder of the semester, and the hazing tradition of Barefoot Day was abolished, although students continued to wear rat caps until the early 1960s.

# Current Carolina Traditions

From Carolina Welcome to the Carolina-Clemson rivalry, from Creed Week to Service Saturdays, from the 2001: A Space Odyssey Entrance to Chicken Finger Wednesday, your time at Carolina will be steeped in traditions. As a student at the University of South Carolina, you have an opportunity to participate in many campus traditions that unite the student body and pay tribute to Carolina's history.

## First Night Carolina

First Night Carolina is one of many Carolina Welcome events planned for first-year students. It is a night of food, fun, and noise as the entire first-year class travels to the Colonial Life Arena for an introduction to campus traditions. An all-star lineup of campus athletes and student leaders are present and provides an excellent opportunity to meet fellow students.

## Convocation

Convocation is an event held each fall before the start of classes. Sponsored by the Office of the Provost and Undergraduate Admissions, the program introduces students to academics on campus by bringing everyone together before the first day of classes to focus on history and traditions at the University of South Carolina.

# OTHER NOTEWORTHY MOMENTS IN UNIVERSITY OF SOUTH CAROLINA HISTORY

## 1896

On November 12 at 11:00 a.m., a rainy Thursday, a football team from Clemson Agricultural College kicks off to a team from South Carolina College on the state fairgrounds in front of a crowd of 2,000. This began the famed Big Thursday football series between South Carolina's two largest public colleges. Carolina won this meeting 12-6.

## 1909

President William Howard Taft becomes the first sitting president to visit the USC campus.

## 1957

Senator John F. Kennedy delivered the commencement address at USC.

## 1963

Henri Dobbins Monteith files suit in federal court seeking to become the first African-American to attend USC since 1877. Her suit was ultimately successful, and she and two other students broke the University's 84-year color barrier.

## 1972

In response to the student riots against the Vietnam War, University 101 was created to build trust, understanding, and open lines of communication between students, faculty, staff, and administrators.

## 1980

USC's Longstreet Theater plays host to a debate between candidates for the Republican presidential nomination. Future presidents Ronald Reagan and George Bush participated, along with Tennessee Senator Howard Baker and former Texas Governor John Connally.

# OTHER NOTEWORTHY MOMENTS IN UNIVERSITY OF SOUTH CAROLINA HISTORY

## 1987

Pope John Paul speaks to a crowd of 8,000 gathered in front of the President's Home, declaring, "It is wonderful to be young, it is wonderful to be a student, it is wonderful to be a student at the University of South Carolina."

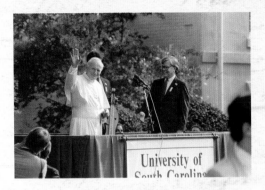

## 1991

Archbishop Desmond Tutu gives the commencement address in Columbia and receives the honorary degree of Doctor of Human Letters. Tutu won the Nobel Peace Prize in 1984 for his work against apartheid in South Africa.

## 1998

The National Advocacy Center opens on campus. Located on Pendleton Street, the Center is operated by the United States Department of Justice and is used to train federal, state, and local prosecutors and litigators in advocacy skills and management of legal operations.

## 2001

USC celebrates the 200th anniversary of its charter and concludes its bicentennial year.

## 2010 & 2011

USC wins back-to-back National Championships in baseball!

## 2012

The hit heard around the world. Jadeveon Clowney delivers an impressive tackle in the Outback Bowl. This was also the year that the South Carolina Honors College was ranked #1.

## 2014

Vice President Joe Biden delivers the commencement address in Columbia.

## *First-Year Reading Experience*

Introduced in 1993, the First-Year Reading Experience (FYRE) is a longstanding tradition at Carolina. The FYRE takes place in September and provides an opportunity for first-year students to focus on a common reading and participate in programming based on themes from the book.

## *Tiger Burn*

The tradition of Tiger Burn grew from the 1902 feud between the University of South Carolina and Clemson University. That year, USC upset Clemson, and Carolina students paraded through the streets near campus carrying a transparency, drawn by USC mathematics Professor F. Horton Colcock, of a gamecock standing over a fallen tiger. Feeling offended, Clemson cadets lined up in a battle formation in front of the brick wall on Sumter Street. Mr. Benet, who led the Carolina students in the victory parade earlier that day, intervened and formed a group of students from Carolina and Clemson to find a resolve. While they were meeting, J. Rion McKissick, a sophomore at Carolina, occupied a spot in the front of the wall. A senior approached McKissick and asked him solemnly, "McKissick, are you armed?"

The sophomore showed him his revolver.

"How many bullets do you have?"

"Five."

"McKissick!" The senior's hand grasped his shoulder in fervent appeal. "Make every shot count!"

Luckily no shots were fired by McKissick, and the committees finally reached the agreement that since the transparency bore an emblem of each team, they would burn the transparency. As the emblem burned, each body of students gave three cheers for the other, and the Clemson cadets retreated. J. Rion McKissick later served as the 19th President of the University.

Each year, students design and construct a nearly 30-foot tiger that is burned at a pep rally before the South Carolina-Clemson football game. Until 1959, this annual gridiron brawl was known as Big Thursday and was always played during the week of the South Carolina State Fair in Columbia. Currently, the annual event is held the week of Thanksgiving. Students from the College of Engineering work all semester to design and construct the large tiger as a project for their classes. In recent years, the tiger has been built so that its arms and mouth actually move. The annual event culminates in a mass gathering of students and community members torching the tiger to signify an anticipated win for the Gamecocks.

## Mascot and Garnet and Black

*(Adapted from http://www.sc.edu/usc/gamecock.html and printed with permission.)*

The origins of the University's moniker, Gamecocks, are unknown. A possible link is to one of South Carolina's colorful military figures, Thomas Sumter. During the War of Independence, Sumter energized South Carolina in its fight against the British. He was known for his fearlessness in battle as well as for the flashy gamecock colors of his hat, coat, and epaulettes-garnet and black; the British referred to this as the South Carolina Game Cock. Another link is to the 1902 South Carolina-Clemson football game. Two weeks after the game and the riots that followed, the state newspaper began referring to the team as the Game Cocks. By 1904, the two words had been joined, and the name stuck.

Tiger Burn

Cocky first took action at USC events in 1980 and soon won the hearts of Gamecock fans all over and now is one of the most recognizable figures to young and old at USC. One of Cocky's trademarks is his 2001 Magic Box entrance. The spectacular performance can be seen at every home football game when the Gamecocks take the field. The Magic Box entrance is one of many things that Cocky does to get the crowd pumped up and cheering. Cocky can be seen pepping the crowd up not only at football games, but at men's and women's basketball, volleyball, men's and women's soccer, baseball, softball, swimming, golf, track, and tennis events as well. Cocky also brings his parents to the football game on Parents Weekend!

### Fight Song: "The Fighting Gamecocks Lead the Way"

When you attend an athletic event, you will often hear one of the University's talented bands playing the fight song. The music, chosen by former football coach and athletic director, Paul Dietzel, is from the 1967 Broadway musical *How Now, Dow Jones*. Dietzel also wrote the lyrics of the song. Learn the fight song and show your school spirit the next time you hear it played.

HEY, LET'S GIVE A CHEER,
CAROLINA IS HERE,

THE FIGHTING GAMECOCKS
LEAD THE WAY.

WHO GIVES A CARE, IF THE
GOING GETS TOUGH,

AND WHEN IT IS ROUGH, THAT'S
WHEN THE 'COCKS GET GOING.

HAIL TO OUR COLORS OF
GARNET AND BLACK,

IN CAROLINA PRIDE HAVE WE.

SO, GO GAMECOCKS GO - FIGHT!

DRIVE FOR THE GOAL - FIGHT!

USC WILL WIN TODAY - GO COCKS!

SO, LET'S GIVE A CHEER,
CAROLINA IS HERE.

THE FIGHTING GAMECOCKS
ALL THE WAY!

## Alma Mater: "We Hail Thee Carolina"

The University's alma mater was written in 1911 by George A. Wauchope, an English professor, and set to the music of Robert Burns' "Flow Gently, Sweet Afton." A March 1911 issue of *The Daily Gamecock* reported that a year or two earlier, the faculty, "realizing we should have a soul-stirring alma mater," offered a prize of $50 for the writing of an alma mater. Of the songs that were submitted, this one became the most popular and, after several years, became known as the official University alma mater. At each Commencement exercise following the awarding of degrees, the audience is asked to rise and sing our alma mater. It is also often sung during athletic events. The custom has arisen over the years of raising the right hand, with the fingers cupped (as if offering a toast), when the phrase "Here's a health, Carolina" is sung. To many alumni, the toast is synonymous with watching the Fighting Gamecocks compete in major athletic events.

*We hail thee, Carolina, and sing thy high praise*
*With loyal devotion, remembering the days*
*When proudly we sought thee, thy children to be:*
*Here's a health, Carolina, forever to thee!*

*Since pilgrims of learning, we entered thy walls*
*And found dearest comrades in thy classic halls,*
*We've honored and loved thee as sons faithfully;*
*Here's a health, Carolina, forever to thee!*

*Generations of sons have rejoiced to proclaim*
*Thy watchword of service, thy beauty and fame;*
*For ages to come shall their rallying cry be:*
*Here's a health, Carolina, forever to thee!*

*Fair shrine of high honor and truth, thou shalt still*
*Blaze forth as a beacon, thy mission fulfill,*
*And crowned by all hearts in a new jubilee:*
*Here's a health, Carolina, forever to thee!*

### USC Official Seal

The seal of the University was adopted on April 26, 1803. The University seal quotes the Latin poet Ovid, "Emollit Mores Nec Sinit Esse Feros," which translated means "Learning humanizes character and does not permit it to be cruel."

Beneath the words stand the figures of Minerva, the goddess of wisdom, and Liberty. Minerva's shield is decorated with the South Carolina state seal. The words and image are designed to remind us that a university education builds not only intellect, but also character. The Latin inscription below the figures is the school name and founding year, 1801.

### Class Ring

One of the University's most prestigious traditions, the official University of South Carolina ring, is a time-honored expression of South Carolina pride and is recognized worldwide by University alumni. Designed by students and alumni, the ring forever symbolizes the history and tradition of the University of South Carolina. The design displays the seal of the University, which should be worn to face the wearer while a student at the University. Once a graduate, the ring should be turned so that the seal faces the world. Students with 60 or more credit hours are eligible to purchase a ring through the University of South Carolina Alumni Association. Each semester a Ring Ceremony is held for students who have purchased their ring.

## Conclusion

The history and traditions presented in this chapter will be the foundation for the legacy that you will create while at Carolina. Your challenge as a member of the Carolina community is to continue to explore the history of this remarkable institution while also contributing to its future.

# OUTSTANDING ALUMNI

South Carolina has a long history of graduating successful individuals—and employing them too! Many alumni have become TV personalities, corporate executives, star athletes, artists and musicians, and pioneers in research and health care. Take a look below and see how these notable Gamecocks made their mark on the world.

**Millie Jean Adams** (1898) was the first female graduate of the University of South Carolina.

**John Swearingen** (1938, chemical engineering) retired chairman, Standard Oil Company, Indiana; namesake of USC's engineering center.

**W.W. Hootie Johnson** (1953, finance) was the chairman of the executive committee of Bank of America Corporation and chairman of the Augusta National Golf Club.

**Robert McNair** (1958, psychology) was founder, chairman, and CEO of NFL's Houston Texans, chairman of McNair Foundation, and founder of McNair Scholar Program.

**Andrew Card** (1971, engineering) was the White House Chief of Staff under President George W. Bush, 2001-2006; served in the administrations of Presidents Ronald Reagan and George H. Bush; former U.S. Secretary of Transportation; former vice president for government relations, General Motors Corp.

**Darla Moore** (1975, political science) is a financier and partner in Rainwater Incorporated as well as one of the first female members inducted into the August National Golf Club.

**Kaye G. Hearn** (1977, law) was the first woman elected chief judge of the South Carolina Court of Appeals.

**Cliff Hollingsworth** (1977, journalism; 1979, master's in education) is a screenwriter for "Cinderella Man," starring Russell Crowe and Renee Zellweger.

**Leeza Gibbons** (1978, broadcast journalism) is a television celebrity and radio personality; three-time Emmy winner for former talk show "Leeza;" created the Leeza Gibbons Memory Foundation to support victims of Alzheimer's disease and their families.

**Gary Parsons** (1978, Master of business administration) is the founder XM Satellite Radio; former executive vice president of MCI Communications.

**David King** (1983, mechanical engineering) was the director of NASA's Marshall Space Flight Center, Huntsville, Ala.; recipient of Presidential Rank Award for Distinguished Executives, the highest honor a government employee can receive; former Space Shuttle launch director and director of Shuttle Processing.

**Rita Cosby** (1989, journalism and spanish) is a television news anchor and correspondent, radio host, and best selling author. She is currently a Special Correspondent for Inside Edition.

**George Rogers** (1989, interdisciplinary studies) was the 1980 Heisman Trophy winner and former NFL number one draft pick.

**Charlie Weis** (1989, master of education) is the offensive coordinator for the Kansas City Chiefs; former football coach of Notre Dame; and a former NFL assistant coach, winning three Super Bowl rings with the New England Patriots and one with the New York Giants.

**Amos Lee** (1995, English) is an American singer-songwriter known for his folk, rock, and soul musical style.

**Tonique Williams-Darling** (1999, business administration) is the University's first Olympic gold medalist, as the 400-meter champion for her native Bahamas in the 2004 Games.

**Hootie and the Blowfish** (aka Dean Felber, Mark Bryan, Jim Sonefeld, and Darius Rucker) are Grammy award-winning musicians and founders of the philanthropic Monday After the Masters Celebrity Pro-Am Golf Tournament and Hootie and the Blowfish Foundation.

DARLA MOORE

LEEZA GIBBONS

DAVID A. KING

AMOS LEE

HOOTIE AND THE BLOWFISH

## REFLECTION QUESTIONS

1. After reading this chapter, what are the most surprising or interesting historical facts/traditions that you learned about the University of South Carolina?
2. What University of South Carolina traditions did you know about prior to coming here? Did any of these play a role in your decision to attend Carolina?
3. Name one historical figure referenced in the chapter and the impact that they made on Carolina. How does his or her impact affect your experience as a student at the University of South Carolina?
4. Why do you think it is important to learn about the history and traditions of South Carolina as a first-year student? How might the culture of USC be different if we did not teach the history and traditions?

## RESOURCES

**Bicentennial Timeline of University of South Carolina**
http://www.sc.edu/bicentennial/pages/timeline.html

**Board of Trustees**
http://trustees.sc.edu/

**Gamecock Traditions**
http://www.gamecocksonline.com/trads/scar-trads.html

**My Carolina Alumni Association** . . . . . (803) 777-4111
http://www.mycarolina.org/

**Office of the President** . . . . . . . . . . . . . . . (803) 777-2001
http://president.sc.edu/

**Slavery at South Carolina College**
http://library.sc.edu/digital/slaveryscc/

**University of South Carolina Archives** (803) 777-5158
http://www.sc.edu/library/socar/archives/

**University of South Carolina Mission Statement**
http://www.sc.edu/about/south_carolina_at_a_glance/our_mission.php

## REFERENCES

Barefoot Day. (1938). McKissick records, Box 1, 1938-39. Retrieved from http://library.sc.edu/socar/archives/finding_aids/mckissick_1938-1939.htm

Geiger, R. (Ed.). (2000). *The American college in the nineteenth century*. Nashville, TN: Vanderbilt University Press.

Honeywell, R. J. (1931). *The educational work of Thomas Jefferson*. Cambridge, MA: Harvard University Press Language.

Monstrous regiment: Establishment of coeducation at USC. (1998, spring). *Caroliniana Columns*. Retrieved from http://www.sc.edu/library/socar/uscs/98spr/coeds.html

Wormy salt meat and no steaks for breakfast: Campus dining in the 1800s. (2003, April). *Carolinian*. Retrieved from http://www.sc.edu/carolinian/features/fea_03apr_01.html

# CHAPTER 8

# Values and Identity

UNIVERSITY OF
SOUTH CAROLINA

Dear First-Year Student,

At the University of South Carolina, the diversity of our students, faculty, and staff is the defining characteristic of our institutional success. Yet, the diversity of our community means little without interactions across the range of social identities that will enhance your own learning experiences, or our collective learning, research, and scholarship.

Simply put, your success at Carolina and beyond is based on your interactions with, understanding of, and respect for all of the students, faculty, and staff identities that are represented in our community. My hope for you is that you don't waste these four years by remaining in your comfort zone and failing to make friends or develop relationships with people who may at first seem very different from you. Rather, I hope that you take every opportunity to explore all that the university has to offer. Taking time to understand your personal values is an important part of getting to know others around you. The "Values and Identity" chapter will help you to better understand yourself, your classmates and their cultures, viewpoints, and motivations.

As Carolinians, we ascribe to a statement of shared values that guides our discourse and treatment of each other. The Carolinian Creed does not suggest that we suspend our personal beliefs and values. Rather, it requires that we bring our beliefs and values to the university as a means of learning from one another and growing while respecting and honoring the uniqueness that each of us brings to making this a high functioning learning environment. Using the Carolinian Creed as our beacon, the University of South Carolina will continue to encourage and support an environment that is both diverse and inclusive.

However you identify yourself, you are a welcome member of our university community. Best wishes for a productive and engaging first year!

John Dozier
Chief Diversity Officer
Director of Community Engagement

# Understanding Your Values

Values represent an important aspect of self-awareness and, thus, a foundational piece of understanding of others. Values are defined as the attitudes and beliefs that determine what is important to you. Your University 101 class provides the perfect environment to explore your values and get to know yourself and others better. This chapter and the activities you will do in class are designed to help you reflect on how well you know yourself and others around you. It is important to keep in mind that you will only get out of your experience as much as you are willing to put in. Therefore, challenging yourself to be open to learning more about yourself and others is the most important part of this process.

While similar to elements of your identity, values typically reflect an ideal state of being. For example, *middle class* is an identity element describing socioeconomic status while *economic security* or *wealth* represents a value. Similarly, describing oneself as Baptist or Muslim is part of an identity, whereas, *spirituality* is a value. It is important to keep in mind that your values can impact your overall experience at USC. For example, if you value time with your family, but you live 12 hours away and do not get home very often, you will need to find creative ways to spend time with them (e.g., daily phone calls, Facetime/Skype). Or, if you value being financially independent, you may need to get a job which means potentially forfeiting time with friends or making more effort to balance academic responsibilities. Exploring what is most important to you early in your college career will help maximize your college experience.

Life is much easier to navigate when you have a good understanding of your values. Barrett (2006) found that people who use their values (as opposed to relying on past experiences, habits, or traditions) to make decisions had an easier time making tough decisions within complex situations. During your college career, you will experience challenging classes, interactions with peers who may have different beliefs than you, and personal dilemmas. Your current values and beliefs will impact how you react in these situations. The more you know ahead of time, the easier it will be down the road.

### *How do you Determine Your Values?*

Most people have about five to seven values that determine who they are at their core. These values can range in scope from people to things. The most important part of understanding your values is creating space for reflection. Taking time to actively think about what is most important to you will help you better understand where your priorities lie. Consider the categories below as you reflect on what is most important to you:

- *Family members.* Your family could be those who are related to you (e.g., parents, grandparents, siblings) or it could even be a pet.
- *Non-family members.* There are likely people in your life who you may not consider family, but they still hold high importance for you (e.g., friends, significant other/partner).
- *Experiences.* There are often experiences in your life that shape who you are. The experiences can be in the past or current experiences (e.g., death of a family member).
- *Places.* The places you have lived, visited, are currently at, or plan to go can hold high importance for you. These places can be tangible or even metaphysical (e.g., the house/town you grew up in, a place you consider when you pray or meditate).
- *Things.* A "thing" you value might be a material object, or it may include beliefs, ideas, or principles (e.g., your car, your faith).
- *Goals.* A goal is something that is most important for you to achieve (e.g., making friends, maintaining your scholarship, finishing your degree, getting married).

## Clarifying Your Identity

Identity is the combination of personal elements that create your understanding of who you are as a person and, within the context of the University, who you are as a student. Identity elements are the characteristics you use to understand

# PERSONAL VALUES

There are 15 personal values listed in the chart below. Place an X next to your top five values and bottom five values. Once you have completed this, take a moment to consider some of the following questions: Why did you select the top five values you chose? Are there any connections between the ones you chose? Do you think your friends and family would have a similar or different set of values?

| PERSONAL VALUE | TOP 5 | BOTTOM 5 |
|---|---|---|
| Being physically healthy | | |
| Being emotionally healthy | | |
| Being there for my family | | |
| Completing my education | | |
| Being wealthy | | |
| Working to promote equality and justice in our society | | |
| Being in a healthy and satisfying romantic relationship | | |
| Living according to my religious beliefs | | |
| Being in a career that I enjoy | | |
| Traveling and exploring the world | | |
| Being respected by others | | |
| Having a close group of friends | | |
| Being able to support myself financially | | |
| Making a positive contribution to my community | | |
| Having fun and enjoying my life | | |
| Other: | | |

*Source*: Adapted from "My Personal Values Activity." Retrieved from www.wire.wisc.edu

and articulate your individuality and include both *internal* dimensions and *external* dimensions.

- *Internal dimensions* are aspects over which you have no control or are not easily altered. Examples include: race, age, and physical abilities.
- *External dimensions* are aspects of our identity "which we have some control over, which might change over time, and which usually form the basis for" life decisions (Amelio, 2008, pp. 6-7). Examples include gender, relationship status, income, work experience, appearance, and personal habits.

Throughout your college experience and in your life, your sense of identity will shift and adapt. At certain points or in certain situations, aspects of your identity may become more or less important. For instance, if you are transitioning from a religiously affiliated high school to Carolina, you may find that your religion is a particularly critical aspect of your identity as a first-year college student. Similarly, if you are one of only a few women in a course or a major, your gender may be the primary element of your identity in that environment. Further, you may find that your connection to particular traditions may strengthen or lessen as you separate from your family and cultural community and become part of new communities on campus.

Regardless of the identity elements that are important to you, the building blocks of identity are also typically the elements of diversity. For example, internal elements are often used to describe ourselves as well as to identify aspects of similarity or difference with other individuals or groups. Similarly, external dimensions are also used to describe who we are as well as to identify diversity in a student population.

Identity elements generally do not exist in a vacuum. It is rare that people describe themselves using only one term or considering only one aspect. People generally combine multiple aspects of identity into their awareness (e.g., Italian-Catholic, Black man, urban youth). As such, it is helpful to have a firm understanding of the identity elements that are important to you because they represent the viewpoint from which you perceive the similar and different identity elements in others. Your ability to understand and embrace a multifaceted sense of self is a valuable skill both with respect to your own development as well as for your ability to accept and embrace the complex identities of the people with whom you interact.

## My Multifaceted Self

Each of us have several different dimensions of identity that define who we are. Examining the various dimensions (and challenging stereotypes if necessary) will help you become more aware of yourself and others around you. The following diagram highlights these multiple dimensions. You can start by placing your name in the center circle in the structure to the right. In each of the satellite circles, write an aspect of your identity that you feel defines you. This could be anything (e.g., athlete, biology major, female, African American, member of a Greek organization).

Once you have identified four factors, reflect on a time you felt *included* or *respected* in relation to the descriptors listed below. Now, take a moment to reflect on a time you felt *excluded* or *disrespected*. Considering both the positive and challenging aspects of identity are an important part of understanding yourself and others; you can take this a step further by filling in the blanks below and thinking of ways you identify that is not consistent with the stereotypes around you. For example, you might say, "I am a <u>Christian</u>, but I am not <u>judgmental/radical.</u> Or, I am <u>Asian</u>, but I am not a <u>mathematician</u>.

I AM A _____ ,

BUT I AM NOT A _____ .

I AM A _____ ,

BUT I AM NOT A _____ .

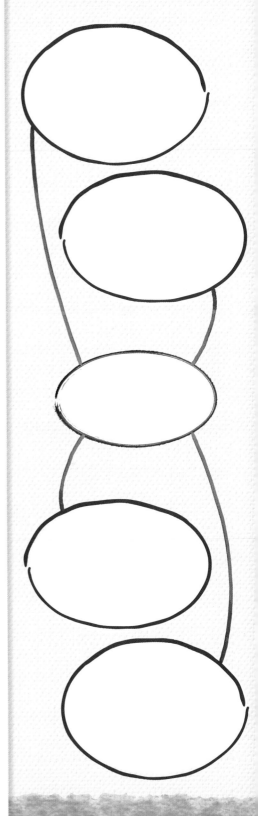

# Understanding Others

Once you have taken the time to reflect on who you are and what is most important to you, you are better prepared to understand the many different people on our campus. Your values and how they differ from your peers represent yet another important aspect of thriving within our complex and dynamic Carolina community.

Each student at the University of South Carolina has a unique personal history, characteristics, beliefs, and pathway to the University. Research suggests that students benefit from studying at a college or university that has a significant number of students from different backgrounds than their own (Gurin, Nagda, & Lopez, 2003) and for many students, attending Carolina is the first opportunity they have had to be exposed to so many different kinds of people in one place.

You have probably already met many people at the University of South Carolina who are different from you, your family, and your friends at home in a number of ways, such as ethnicity, religion, sexual orientation, gender, culture, age, physical ability, income, social class, hometown, native language, learning style, family status, or major. The variety in the student population of the Carolina community is one of the things that will make your college years such a rewarding learning experience.

## Educational Value of Diversity

Research has pinpointed three good practices that promote students' learning: (a) academic challenge and high expectations, (b) good teaching and high quality interactions with educators, and (c) experiences with diversity (Goodman, Magolda, Siefert, & King, 2011). The individuals you are surrounded by in your learning environment are just as important as where you receive your education (Gurin, Nagda, & Lopez, 2003). Interactions with a diverse range of people provide opportunities to develop skills related to learning *effective communication* and fostering *mutual respect* and *teamwork*—skills that will enhance your employability. Major corporations have stated that the skills needed in today's global market can only be obtained through exposure to widely diverse people, ideas, and cultures. The qualities

> MAJOR CORPORATIONS HAVE STATED THAT THE SKILLS NEEDED IN TODAY'S GLOBAL MARKET CAN ONLY BE OBTAINED THROUGH EXPOSURE TO WIDELY DIVERSE PEOPLE, IDEAS, AND CULTURES.

# RESEARCH TELLS US DIVERSITY WORKS

In 2006 Margaret Neale of Stanford University, Gregory Northcraft of the University of Illinois at Urbana-Champaign and I set out to examine the impact of racial diversity on small decision-making groups in an experiment where sharing information was a requirement for success. Our subjects were undergraduate students taking business courses at the University of Illinois. We put together three-person groups—some consisting of all white members, others with two whites and one nonwhite member—and had them perform a murder mystery exercise. We made sure that all group members shared a common set of information, but we also gave each member important clues that only he or she knew. To find out who committed the murder, the group members would have to share all the information they collectively possessed during discussion. The groups with racial diversity significantly outperformed the groups with no racial diversity. Being with similar others leads us to think we all hold the same information and share the same perspective. This perspective, which stopped the all-white groups from effectively processing the information, is what hinders creativity and innovation.

This effect is not limited to race. For example, last year professors of management Denise Lewin Loyd of the University of Illinois, Cynthia Wang of Oklahoma State University, Robert B. Lount, Jr., of Ohio State University and I asked 186 people whether they identified as a Democrat or a Republican, then had them read a murder mystery and decide who they thought committed the crime. Next, we asked the subjects to prepare for a meeting with another group member by writing an essay communicating their perspective. More important, in all cases, we told the participants that their partner disagreed with their opinion but that they would need to come to an agreement with the other person. Everyone was told to prepare to convince their meeting partner to come around to their side; half of the subjects, however, were told to prepare to make their case to a member of the opposing political party, and half were told to make their case to a member of their own party.

The result: Democrats who were told that a fellow Democrat disagreed with them prepared less well for the discussion than Democrats who were told that a Republican disagreed with them. Republicans showed the same pattern. When disagreement comes from a socially different person, we are prompted to work harder.

---

*Except from:* Phillips, K. W. (2014, September 16). How diversity makes us smarter. *Scientific American, 311*(4). Retrieved from: http://www.scientificameri-can.com/article/how-diversity-makes-us-smarter/. Used with permission.

that you can develop through contact with diversity require a conscious effort on your part to be open and willing to explore the differences you may experience in your interactions.

It is important to remember when interacting with and "learning from people with different backgrounds, college offers a fundamentally different opportunity from most other environments, [which] arises precisely because all incoming students are likely to share certain values" (Light, 2001, p. 240) that drew them to South Carolina.

# Microaggressions

Microaggressions are the everyday verbal, nonverbal, and environmental slights, snubs, or insults, whether intentional or unintentional, that communicate hostile, derogatory, or negative messages to target persons based solely upon their marginalized group membership (Garibay, 2014). The first step in addressing microaggressions is to recognize when a microaggression has occurred and what message it may be sending. The context of the relationship and situation is critical. Below are common themes to which microaggressions attach. The microaggressions table on the following page provides examples as well as the messages often received as a result of the statement.

# Carolina Community

Communities are often born out of similarities between individuals rather than in ways that celebrate differences. Your high school was most likely comprised of students who were from the same geographic area and/or who shared a similar religious or personal history. If you are from a small town or rural region, you might have been in classes with many of the same people since elementary school. Your closest friends are probably from your neighborhood and share similar characteristics and personal histories.

Learning about, accepting, and valuing others who are different from you is an ongoing process toward intercultural competence and maturity. The more you interact with and talk with people from a variety of backgrounds, the easier it will

# MICROAGGRESSIONS

| THEMES | MICROAGGRESSION EXAMPLES | MESSAGE |
|---|---|---|
| **Alien in One's Own Land**<br><br>When Asian Americans, Latino Americans and others who look different or are named differently from the dominant culture are assumed to be foreign-born. | "Where are you from or where were you born?" | You are not a true American. |
| | Asking an Asian American or Latino American to teach you words in their native language.<br><br>Continuing to mispronounce your peers' names after they have corrected you time and time again. Not being willing to listen closely and learn the pronunciation of a non-English based name. | You are a perpetual foreigner in your own country. |
| | "What are you? You're so interesting looking!" "You speak English very well." | Your ethnic/racial identity makes you exotic. |
| **Ascription of Intelligence**<br><br>Assigning intelligence to a person of color or a woman based upon their race/gender. | "You are a credit to your race." | People of color are generally not as intelligent as Whites. |
| | "Wow, you're so liberal and open-minded for an Arab girl." | Arab women are submissive and do not have their own thoughts or opinions. |
| | To an Asian person, "You must be good in math; can you help me with this problem?" | All Asians are intelligent and good in math/science. |
| | To a student of color: "I would have never guessed that you were a scientist." | I wouldn't have thought you were smart enough. |
| **Color Blindness**<br><br>Statements that indicate that a White person does not want to or need to acknowledge race. | "When I look at you, I don't see color." | Denying the significance of a person of color's racial/ethnic experience and history. |
| | "There is only one race, the human race." | You need to assimilate to the dominant culture. |
| | "He is the whitest Black guy I know." | Referring to a person of color who doesn't fit the "Black" stereotype. |

continued on next page

continued from previous page

# MICROAGGRESSIONS

| THEMES | MICROAGGRESSION EXAMPLES | MESSAGE |
|---|---|---|
| **Criminality/Assumption of Criminal Status**<br><br>A person of color is presumed to be dangerous, criminal, or deviant based on his/her race. | A White man or woman clutches his/her purse or checks wallet as a Black or Latino person approaches. | You are a criminal. |
| | A store owner following a customer of color around the store. | You are going to steal/you are poor, you do not belong. |
| | Someone crosses to the other side of the street to avoid a person of color. | You are dangerous. |
| | While walking through the halls of the Chemistry building, a professor approaches a student of color to ask if she/he is lost, making the assumption that the person is trying to break into one of the labs. | |
| **Denial of Individual Racism/Sexism/Heterosexism**<br><br>A statement made when bias is denied. | "I'm not racist. I have several Black friends." | I could never be racist because I have friends of color. |
| | "As a woman, I know what you go through as a racial minority." | Your racial oppression is no different than my gender oppression. I can't be a racist. I'm like you. |
| | "Dude, I totally forgot you were gay when we were playing basketball earlier." | Denying the person the ability to be anything outside of the stereotype. |
| **Myth of Meritocracy**<br><br>Statements which assert that race or gender does not play a role in life successes, for example in issues like faculty demographics. | "I believe the most qualified person should get the job." | People of color are given extra unfair benefits because of their race. |
| | "You're lucky to be Black…it makes it easier to get into college." | People of color are lazy and/or incompetent and need to work harder. |
| | "Men and women have equal opportunities for achievement."<br><br>"America is the land of opportunity."<br><br>"Everyone can succeed in this society, if they work hard enough." | The playing field is even so if women cannot make it, the problem is with them. |

become to accept and respond appropriately to differences and the more you will gain from your college experience. Ultimately, the knowledge you gain from diverse experiences will help build communities where members are judged by the quality of their character and contributions, not by their external appearance or other stereotypical attributes.

Chapter 9 focuses on the Carolinian Creed which establishes a set of shared values, including personal and academic integrity, respect, concern for others, and regard for human dignity. Students agree to "respect the dignity of all persons (and) discourage bigotry, while striving to learn from differences in people." Students who adhere to this principle recognize that differences among students present positive learning opportunities.

An appreciation of those who are different from you is impossible without engaging yourself within a community; full appreciation comes with the ability for an individual to interact effectively and meaningfully with others. Ultimately, this involves the process of forming relationships with people you may have never imagined you would when you first arrived on campus.

Fellow students are not the only members of the campus community. Professors, academic administrators, instructors, student affairs staff, and administrative support staff are also community members that you will have many opportunities to interact with throughout your time at Carolina. These faculty and staff, like your peers, represent a broad spectrum of backgrounds, cultures, interests, experiences, and personal characteristics that can add to your understanding of others. For example, you may be in a class taught by an instructor who has lived or studied in a country outside of the United States. They can offer a rich perspective on course content based on their life experience.

As you engage in discussions in your University 101 class, in other classes, in your living environment, and with friends, consider both the commonalities and differences that you share with your peers and faculty and staff and how these similarities and differences will affect your understanding of one another.

# Communicating with Others

To fully engage in relationships and be a participating member of your new community, you must communicate. Communication skills—both talking and listening—are critical to your understanding and appreciation for people who see the world from a different lens. It may not always be easy to communicate with someone who is different from you or to talk about those aspects of difference. As mentioned earlier, elements of diversity are tightly connected to the very fundamental aspects of our identity and values. As such, they can represent personal and perhaps sensitive dimensions of our personalities. You may or may not feel comfortable talking about your experiences or identity or hearing about these same issues from others, but these situations provide excellent opportunities to grow and learn. Use the following communication strategies in your daily interactions within the campus community.

## The Power of Words

Be aware of the power of language and what you mean when you use diversity terms. In situations where you are introducing yourself using value and identity labels, be aware that others in the group may associate different meanings to these same words—and vice versa. For example, many of us immediately think of race when diversity is mentioned, but we often confuse race with ethnicity. *Race* is associated with shared biological characteristics, while *ethnicity* is associated with the environment into which you were born and specifies membership in a group historically connected by a common national origin or language.

## It Is All in a Name

When you are unsure of the appropriate title (any title) to use when addressing or discussing an individual, it is important to ask for clarification. Does that person prefer the long version of his or her name or a nickname; the term African American or Black to describe race; Hispanic, or Latina/o to refer to ethnicity; Republican or Conservative to identify political views; the name of his or her homeland (e.g., Canada) or a slang term (e.g. Canuck) for national origin?

Using the right gender pronouns is also important. Asking and correctly using someone's personal pronoun is one of the most basic ways to show your respect for their gender identity. When someone is referred to with the wrong pronoun, it can make them feel disrespected, dismissed, or alienated. While it may feel awkward at first, a respectful inquiry of someone's preferences will go a long way to help facilitate communication across and about areas of difference.

## Beware of Assumptions

Everyday language is a function of our identity and values. Consider how the words you use in conversation suggest your assumptions about gender, sexuality, culture, religion, or power. Is there a way to choose other words that are more inclusive or more sensitive? For example, it may be more inclusive to reference the end-of-semester break as Winter Break instead of Christmas Break. Similarly, it avoids assumptions about sexuality if you refer to someone's significant other as "partner" instead of their boyfriend or girlfriend.

In addition to viewpoints, be aware of potential differences in communication styles. Certain cultures may be more direct or more passive in their verbal expressions and body language; others may prioritize written communication over the spoken word. Accents and different word pronunciation or word order can be especially challenging and require you to think of tactful ways to ask for information to be repeated that do not place the speaker in an awkward, embarrassing, or frustrated position. For instance, if you have difficulty understanding a professor's accent, ask for clarification in class by paraphrasing the instructor's comments and prefacing the question with a comment such as, "so if I understand you correctly, are you saying...." Or, you may need to explain slang or lingo that is unique to the United States or your region of the country to an international student. It is important to be aware of cultural differences in communication patterns and protocol and be as patient and as inclusive as possible in your discussions.

## Awareness Is Key

It is important to maintain an awareness of issues of representation and privilege in discussions of diversity. If you are the only person of a certain viewpoint, particularly if it is one that is widely perceived as being historically underrepresented or a minority position, it can be especially uncomfortable to have open and honest discussions about difference. Gently make others aware of this aspect of the conversation and be open about what that means for the discussion. You should never feel that you are being forced to speak as a representative for a larger group or that you are in a defensive position with respect to your personal history or experiences. Conversely, if you are in the majority position in a particular discussion, do not make the assumption that this equates to being right. Be open to alternate viewpoints.

## Do Not Take it Personally

Try not to personalize remarks that are made in discussions of diversity and difference. Although it may be difficult when it feels like someone is attacking who you are or what you believe, it may be healthy to separate yourself from the role being discussed in order to see what the other person is saying. By doing your best to balance your personal experiences with an objective viewpoint, you may be better able to explore and explain your view on an issue than if you adopt a defensive position.

## Be Willing to Share

Everything you have encountered in life, including your family history and cultural heritage, contributes to the person you are today. Share with others how your background influenced you. Be proud of the identity elements and values that are important to you and make you unique, and be willing to share them with others. Your participation will likely encourage others—your roommate, hallmates, classmates, and new friends—to share how their backgrounds have influenced them.

## Explore Outside the Box

In addition to your classroom and residence hall experiences, there are other opportunities to explore diversity on campus, including joining student organizations and attending multicultural events and celebrations. You can also explore diversity on your own by visiting websites, reading magazines and books written by and about people different than you, attending workshops on diversity, reading newspapers from other countries, traveling abroad, or participating in service activities. As you look for experiences that will enrich your college experience, consider opportunities, both on and off campus, that will provide new perspectives and increase your awareness about the various ways our campus, community, and world are so richly diverse.

Getting to know others who come from different backgrounds or experiences will benefit you throughout your life. As a student at Carolina, consider taking part in one of the following opportunities:

- Reading the newspaper regularly to stay current with local, national, and international issues
- Learning a second language
- Asking a student who has studied abroad to share about their experiences and consider taking part in international travel before you graduate
- Asking a nontraditional-age student in your class to study or serve with you on a group project
- Promoting international programming and events in your groups and organizations
- Reading biographies of human rights and social activists
- Seeking out a faculty or staff member who has an academic interest in international issues and learn how they entered their field or discipline
- Introducing yourself to international students in your classes. They, too, may be new to campus and often enjoy meeting American students
- Studying history other than American history
- Researching a particular social, ethnic, cultural, religious, or political group
- Attending an event that supports those with various disabilities, or volunteering to aid students with impairments through note taking or proctoring individualized exams
- Taking classes in a wide variety of subjects, such as political science, humanities, women's studies, African American studies, Latino and immigrant studies, or Asian studies

International students taking a selfie on the Horseshoe.

- Getting to know international students through the Buddies Beyond Borders or Conversation Partners programs
- Asking questions during class discussions if you do not understand the viewpoints of the professor, guest speaker, or another classmate
- Volunteering to participate in activities sponsored by or involving international organizations in the community
- Accepting invitations to hear professional speakers through one of the University's many student organizations, academic departments, or other venues

## Campus Offices

There are a number of offices and departments at Carolina that are focused on promoting diversity and inclusion. Whether you are a student who is curious to learn more about others or if you are looking for support due to feeling like an outsider, these resources provide a great springboard to understanding yourself and others better.

**The Office of Diversity and Inclusion** focuses on ways to create the most positive and supportive environment possible for students, faculty and staff. The Office provides research support and collaboration with campus partners and provides a venue to report a bias or hate incident.

**The Office of Multicultural Student Affairs (OMSA)** works with students, faculty, and staff to help promote an accepting environment and to assist in fostering an appreciation for our unique human differences. The Office provides programs, services, and initiatives for the multicultural development of all students at South Carolina. Lesbian, Gay, Bisexual, and Transgender (LGBTQ) Programs in the Office of Multicultural Student Affairs, uses outreach, education, advocacy, and collaborative relationships to foster a fair, safe, and receptive climate in which all Carolinians, regardless of sexual orientation or gender identity, are treated with dignity and respect.

**International Student Services** provides support to international students by offering pre-arrival information,

## WHEN VALUES CLASH

USC celebrates the diversity of backgrounds, cultures, and values of the members of our community; however, the reality of differing values also presents the possibility of conflict and bias. There is a difference in bias and illegal bias. Illegal bias is a violation of Federal law, State law, or University policy. It is for this reason that the University of South Carolina has created the following resources such as the Office of Equal Opportunity Programs. To file a complaint or report an incident of illegal discrimination, please contact us!

## POLICY TO PROTECT STUDENTS: STAF 6.24 STUDENT NON DISCRIMINATION POLICY

 803-777-3854

 sc.edu/eop

orientation programs, immigration advising, and personal assistance. They also seek to connect internationals with American students through programs such as Buddies Beyond Borders and Conversation Partners.

**The Leadership and Service Center** works to build alliances with campus and community groups in order to educate, empower, and mentor female students at the University. Women's Student Services, a program through the Leadership and Service Center educates female students on issues related to personal development, leadership, health and wellness, and safety. Additionally, the Leadership and Service Center provides mentoring to students through the Women's Mentor Network, which pairs faculty and staff women on campus with undergraduate women interested in the same academic area or career path.

**Carolina Campus Ministries** is an association of ministers and advisors. These USC affiliate staff serve as registered religious workers at Carolina, representing a variety of religious traditions. Each chaplain is available to University students for crisis counseling and spiritual direction.

**The Office of Student Disability Services** provides support for students with documented learning, physical, and psychological disabilities. Students registered with the Office may be eligible for a wide range of support services and accommodations, including priority registration, classroom adaptations, test proctors, and note takers. Accommodations are based on the nature and extent of each student's disability.

## Around Campus

You can attend forums and panels, hear nationally renowned speakers, attend screenings of films, and participate in cultural discussions. Events usually are open to the public and free for South Carolina students. Observances, such as Creed & Diversity Week or LGBTQ History Month Programs, offer a variety of events and activities focused on raising awareness and celebrating differences in our campus community. The International Student Association sponsors World Night, a festival hosted by the international student community that showcases international food, traditional dress, music, and dance from the many countries and cultures represented at the University. International Education Week, also held annually, celebrates opportunities for and benefits of international education and international awareness.

## Community Opportunities

Carolina students are fortunate to be located in a vibrant metropolitan city that is also the state capital. As such, there are many opportunities in the community to become engaged with and appreciate difference. These include cultural events and festivals, visual and performing arts shows, and community organizations. While many of the campus diversity programs collaborate with community partners, it is valuable to also learn what is available in Columbia to complement your experience at the University.

One specific form of community involvement is through service. Many community service experiences offer an opportunity to work with individuals who come from different backgrounds than your own. Engaging in service in the community allows you yet another opportunity to experience new ideas, cultures, people, and backgrounds. As you consider your choices for service outlets, it may also be useful to think of it as an opportunity to expand your exposure to diversity, as well.

## Conclusion

While you are a student at South Carolina, actively seek opportunities to learn more about the people with whom you live, learn, and interact—both on campus and in the surrounding community. There are many areas of diversity to explore during your college years. Opportunities abound to learn about other cultures, observe how others behave, and, most importantly, learn more about yourself. You have already taken on the challenge to better yourself by enrolling in the University of South Carolina. You took the first step towards promoting a more unified campus community and humane respect for diversity when you signed the *Carolinian Creed*. Continue to challenge yourself to create and maintain an unwavering respect for and understanding of diversity while you are a student and after you leave the University.

---

### CELEBRATIONS AND AWARENESS EVENTS

Each year, the University hosts several cultural celebrations and awareness events, such as:

- Hispanic Heritage Month (September)
- Lesbian, Gay, Bisexual, Transgender and Questioning History Month (October)
- International Education Week (November)
- Native American Heritage Month (November)
- Black History Month (February)
- Women's History Month (March)

# REFLECTION QUESTIONS

1. This chapter lists family members, non-family members, experiences, places, things, and goals as categories of what you value most in your life. Which of these categories do you think is most important to you? Least important? Why?

2. In what ways have your values and identity shifted since coming to college? In what ways are you different than the student you were when you first arrived?

3. What kinds of stereotypes or labels have others used to describe you? Do you agree with these stereotypes? Why or why not?

4. Take time to reflect on the table describing microaggressions. Which of these microaggressions have you seen or heard since you have been here at USC?

5. Diversity is a sensitive topic, and one that many people feel uncomfortable discussing. Why do you think this is the case? What measures can the university take to create a welcoming environment for all students?

6. Which suggestion under the "Try Something New" section in the chapter interested you most? Why?

# RESOURCES

**Carolina Campus Ministries**
http://www.carolinafaith.com/

**Diversity and Inclusion**
Osborne Administration, Room 107B
http://www.sc.edu/about/offices_and_divisions/diversity_and_inclusion/

**Equal Opportunity Programs** ........ (803) 777-3854
http://www.sc.edu/eop

**Garnet Gate**
**(Database for student organizations and events)**
https://garnetgate.sa.sc.edu/

**International Student Services** ...... (803) 777-7461
Close-Hipp Building, Suite 650
http://www.sc.edu/about/offices_and_divisions/international_student_services/

**Leadership and Service Center** ...... (803) 777-7130
Russell House, Suite 227

https://www.sa.sc.edu/leadershipandservice/community-service/

**Multicultural Student Affairs** ........ (803) 777-7716
Russell House, Suite 115
https://www.sa.sc.edu/omsa/

**SafeZone Ally Training** ............... (803) 777-8248
https://www.sa.sc.edu/omsa/safezone

**Student Disability Services** .......... (803) 777-6142
TDD ............................. (803) 777-6744
1523 Greene St.
http://www.sa.sc.edu/sds/

**Student Organizations** ............... (803) 777-7130
http://www.sa.sc.edu/studentorgs/

**Study Abroad Programs** ............. (803) 777-7557
Close-Hipp, Suite 453
http://studyabroad.sc.edu/

**Women's Student Services** ........... (803) 777-7130
Leadership and Service Center
Russell House, Suite 227
http://www.sa.sc.edu/wss/

# REFERENCES

Amelio, R. (2008). The four layers of diversity [Electronic version]. *Color Magazine, 1*(18), 6-7.

Barrett, R. (2006). Building a values-driven organization. New York: Taylor and Francis.

Garibay, J. C. (2014). *Diversity in the classroom*. Retrieved from University of California–Los Angeles, Office of Faculty & Diversity Development website: https://faculty.diversity.ucla.edu/publications/diversity-in-the-classroom

Goodman, K. M., Magolda, M. B., Seifert, T. A., & King, P. M. (2011), Good practices for student learning: Mixed-method evidence from the Wabash National Study. *About Campus, 16*, 2–9.

Gurin, P., Nagda, B. A., & Lopez, G. E. (2003). The benefits of diversity in education for democratic citizenship. *Journal of Social Issues, 60*, 17–34.

Light, R. J. (2001). *Making the most of college: Students speak their minds*. Cambridge, MA: Harvard University Press.

Phillips, K. W. (2014, September 16). How diversity makes us smarter. Scientific American, 311(4). Retrieved from: http://www.scientificamerican.com/article/how-diversity-makes-us-smarter/

# CHAPTER 9

# The Carolinian Creed

# UNIVERSITY OF
# SOUTH CAROLINA

*Dear First-Year Student,*

I am happy to join my administrative team in welcoming you to the University of South Carolina. By choosing Carolina, you have made one of the most important decisions of your life. We are a University on the move and as we continue to make gains in national attention, we've become a destination of choice, attracting an impressive community of scholars—including you. Our faculty and staff are all here to make sure your transition is smooth and successful.

This chapter, "The Carolinian Creed," provides a deeper understanding of the inspirational tenets of our Creed and reflects our rich generosity of spirit. As always, we remain "dedicated to personal and academic excellence" while embracing a code of "civilized behavior."

The Carolinian Creed, thoughtfully crafted more than 25 years ago by a diverse group of University of South Carolina students, faculty and staff, was designed to foster a new age of civility at Carolina as we continually celebrate and learn from our differences. Its powerful message is evergreen and gives all of us an opportunity to pause, reflect, and evaluate our willingness to create conditions that support each other's work and development.

Our Creed also suggests that our campus community is wide enough to embrace inclusiveness, wise enough to listen to opposing views and strong enough to discourage bigotry. We agree to respect the dignity of all persons. Indeed, the Carolinian Creed offers the essence of a university life. Living up to these high expectations enhances the Carolina experience for all.

I cherish this university and remain steadfastly committed to improving our institution for the benefit of all members of the Carolina family. Every day, I witness a rich generosity of spirit and I want that to be the experience of every member of our community. I hope you'll join us in demonstrating concern for others as we take on our scholarly work.

Sincerely,

*H Pastides*

Harris Pastides
President, University of South Carolina

AS a statement of the University of South Carolina's values and its expectations of community members, the Carolinian Creed is at the heart of life at the university. But how did it come to be? And what does it really mean? This chapter reviews the development of the creed; examines its tenets, or principles, as well as related topics; and describes ways to practice and promote it.

# University Rules

For more than 100 years, the University of South Carolina had just one rule governing the conduct of its students. The Honor Principle, as it was called, stated, "Every Carolina student is expected to conduct himself as becoming to a gentleman or a lady, not only in the class room but in his or her dealings with others at all times" (University of South Carolina, 1930). As the institution evolved, however, the Honor Principle was not enough, and in response, USC developed a number of policies. The additional regulations were necessary to ensure that the university provided a learning environment that would help advance its mission while meeting the expectations of students and their parents and the requirements of government and accrediting agencies. By the 1960s, Carolina had amassed around 100 pages of policies prohibiting students, faculty, and staff from a variety of behaviors and actions.

In the late 1980s, a series of disturbing incidents rocked college and university campuses across the United States that alarmed USC administrators. Studies at the time showed an alarming increase of racial, anti-Semitic and sexual assault incidents, and researchers described the 1980s as "a time of increasing intergroup conflict on college campuses" (Berg-Cross, Starr, & Sloan, 1993). Distressed by the trend, USC administrators sought to learn why this behavior was increasing and what could be done to prevent it from happening at Carolina.

Administrators performed a "cultural audit" of the university and gathered a group of students, faculty and staff, charging them with examining students' relationships with each other, defining Carolina's values and its expectations of

**STUDENT BODY TRADITIONS**

Every college has certain traditions which are an essential part of college life. You may not like them now. Later you will see the point and will be glad that you followed them.

1—All Carolina men speak to all other Carolina men wherever they meet. Learn to say "Hello" and then say it.

3—All members of the student body stand and remove their hats while singing or while the band plays the Alma Mater.

4—All freshmen must wear the regulation cap throughout their freshman year.

5—No man shall wear a block "C" unless he has been awarded one by the Athletic Board. High school letters shall not be worn on the Carolina campus.

7—All Carolina men sit in the "Carolina Cheering Sertion" of the bleachers at football games.

8—Students give preference to those merchants who back Carolina by advertising in the college publications.

9—Colors are worn by all students thruout Fair Week.

10—"We Hail Thee Carolina" is sung only on fitting occasions and with due reverence to the institution.

## THE CAROLINA COED CODE

The "Carolina Coed Code" from 1966-1967 includes a list of rules, including no slacks outside the residence halls, making your bed before going to class, and not leaving the residence halls alone after dark. Students were also forbidden to visit Taverns, Hotels, or places of Public Amusement, without special permission first obtained from the President.

community members and devising a way to communicate these to the community.

While other colleges and universities at the time resorted to passing restrictive codes of speech and conduct, the members of USC's task force wanted to do something different. Rather than writing an exhaustive list of forbidden actions and their resulting punishments, the USC group highlighted the university's community standards and the values the university expects its community members to espouse in their relationships with each other. The process took two years and resulted in the Carolinian Creed, which was approved by the university's governing bodies and presented to the Carolina community in October 1990.

## An expression of university values and expectations

Vice President for Student Affairs Dennis Pruitt, who led the development of the creed, wrote:

> ...the creed focuses not on minimum standards for student behavior or a list of things students should not do but on understanding, appreciating, and living the values of civility, compassion, empathy, and openness. The creed reflects a concern for *all* members of the university community as individuals, providing each with membership in our community and a genuine sense of inclusion. Lastly, the creed calls for each member of the campus community to be the best he or she can be by reflecting individual faith in the enduring values and shared ideals it expresses. Adhering to the creed is not something we *need* to do, it is something we *want* to do. (Pruitt, 1996)

Since its adoption, the creed has been infused in all facets of university life. Its words are cast in bronze on a marker at the top of the historic Horseshoe. It is presented to each incoming class at fall convocation and incorporated in classes, activities, and events across campus. It is celebrated each year during USC's Carolinian Creed and Diversity Week. And it distills into a few statements exactly what it means to be a Carolinian.

ADHERING TO THE CREED IS NOT SOMETHING WE NEED TO DO; IT IS SOMETHING WE WANT TO DO.

- Dennis Pruitt
Vice President for Student Affiars,
Vice Provost and Dean of Students

# The Carolinian Creed

The community of scholars at the University of South Carolina is dedicated to personal and academic excellence. Choosing to join the community obligates each member to a code of civilized behavior.

As a Carolinian...

I will practice personal and academic integrity;

I will respect the dignity of all persons;

I will respect the rights and property of others;

I will discourage bigotry, while striving to learn from differences in people, ideas, and opinions;

I will demonstrate concern for others, their feelings, and their need for conditions which support their work and development.

Allegiance to these ideals requires each Carolinian to refrain from and discourage behaviors which threaten the freedom and respect every individual deserves (Carolinian Creed, 2015).

## *The tenets*

### I will practice personal and academic integrity

A person who acts honestly and in accordance with his or her beliefs and values demonstrates personal integrity, a characteristic that is vital to positive relationships with others and to successful membership in a community. Academic integrity is necessary for USC and all higher education institutions to fulfill their missions of teaching and scholarship. It refers to the practice of truthfully presenting one's own academic work for evaluation and avoiding dishonest behaviors that give an unfair advantage (Honor Code Student FAQ, 2015).

# Academics with honor

USC's Honor Code is the university's academic policy. It states, "It is the responsibility of every student at the University of South Carolina Columbia to adhere steadfastly

to truthfulness and to avoid dishonesty, fraud, or deceit of any type in connection with any academic program" (Honor Code, 2015). Examples of behaviors that would violate the Honor Code include:

- Giving or receiving unauthorized assistance on an assignment
- Using another person's words or ideas without proper acknowledgment
- Using materials or information without authorization
- Accessing the contents of past exams without authorization.

Integrity, honesty, and cheating are not concerns exclusive to higher education. Colleges and universities exist within the larger society and student and faculty conduct are reflections of larger societal beliefs and attitudes. Recently, there has been considerable attention paid to the perceived decline of personal integrity in today's world. It is difficult to open the paper each morning without reading tales of CEOs that have acted unethically, athletes that have gained an unfair advantage by using performance-enhancing drugs, or other acts of dishonesty or cheating. And while acts of academic dishonesty are as old as colleges themselves, there has been increased attention in recent years to rising incidents of cheating on college campuses. McCabe (2005) found that more than half of all students surveyed acknowledge at least one incident of serious cheating in the past academic year and more than two thirds admit to one or more questionable behaviors, such as collaborating on assignments when specifically asked for individual work.

## To Cheat or Not to Cheat

When students are asked to discuss why they should act with integrity when it comes to academics, many respond that they would be cheating themselves. This is certainly a valid point. If you are not learning the material, you will not be gaining the knowledge of what you need to learn to be successful. In addition, having a mark on your transcript that indicates you violated the academic integrity code will cast a shadow on your character and make it much harder for you to find a job or get into graduate school. You may also receive a failing grade for the course.

Cheating also impacts more than just the cheater. The entire academic community at the University of South Carolina will suffer if cheating is rampant. Cheating impacts students who are honestly working to make good grades and it provides an unfair advantage in competition for jobs, scholarships, or admission to graduate school. Also, if an institution gets pegged with a reputation for cheating, the prestige of that institution and value of the degrees of current students and the thousands of alumni who came before will be damaged, thus diminishing the value of everyone's degree. Cheating is unjust, because it undermines the good faith efforts of those acting with integrity, and it violates student rights that arise from the implicit (if not explicit) social contract created when they voluntarily become a member of the university community. According to Daniel Wueste (2008), "Cheating thwarts the aspirations for genuine excellence of individual students and the university" (p. 21).

Common sense indicates that cheating is not ethical, though many rationalize it as appropriate behavior. In his book *The Cheating Culture*, David Callahan (2004) suggests four reasons why people are likely to cheat:

- Increased pressures to set oneself apart (e.g., more competition for spots in elite colleges, entry into graduate school, promotions at work)
- Bigger rewards for winning (CEOs inflating earnings' reports, athletes looking for a bigger contract or even just trying to stay in the pros)
- Greater temptation as it becomes easier to cheat and not get caught
- A mistaken belief that everyone is doing it

But why should you act with integrity? Why should you not cheat? Do people follow the rules because it is the right thing to do, or do they follow the rules because they are afraid to get caught? The renowned theorist of moral development, Lawrence Kohlberg, posited three developmental levels that explain why people follow the rules or do the right thing. The first level, characterized by most young children, is the avoidance of punishment. These individuals are motivated to follow the rules to avoid getting in trouble, but often believe that the action is not wrong if you do not get caught.

The second level explains individuals who try to do the right things in order to live up to the expectations of others, to gain approval, and to maintain an image of being a good person. The highest level is where individuals do what is right based on the extent to which they promote fundamental values. Acting with integrity is, thus, a social contract (Evans et al., 2010). It is this higher-order thinking that Carolina students should use when making the decision to do their academic work honestly.

Cheating for any reason, including the ones above, carries huge risk. Violating the Honor Code can lead to serious consequences—a failing grade, a mark on your transcript, suspension or expulsion and a stain on your reputation that could make it hard for you to be admitted to another school or hired by an employer. And by cheating on an assignment, you're cheating yourself out of the education you and your family have made a significant investment in and the knowledge and skills you'll need to be successful in life after college.

Aside from the risks and negative consequences, there's a more fundamental reason not to cheat: it's wrong. Cheating violates the social contract—the implicit agreement for the good of the community—you enter into when you enroll at Carolina. Acting to uphold this value of integrity is something that Carolina students should aspire to in their lives at the university.

## I will respect the dignity of all persons

Respecting the dignity of all persons requires believing that all people have inherent worth and treating them as the valuable individuals they are. This fair and compassionate treatment of individuals is necessary no matter their similarities or differences, a topic discussed further in chapter 8, Clarifying Your Values and Identity. A commitment to this tenet requires avoiding any behavior that denies or threatens the dignity of others. Those behaviors include intimidation, harassment, discrimination, hazing and violence, among others (USC, 1990).

IN A SURVEY OF FIRST-YEAR USC STUDENTS, 35% OF RESPONDENTS REPORTED THAT THEY CHEATED ON AN EXAM OR ASSIGNMENT DURING THEIR LAST YEAR OF HIGH SCHOOL.

*Source*: CIRP Freshman Survey, Higher Education Research Institute.

## Hazing

The University of South Carolina defines hazing as "any activity, undertaken by a group or a member of a group, which subjects members to harassment, intimidation, physical exhaustion, pain, undue mental fatigue or distress, or mutilation or alteration of parts of the body" (Hazing, 2015). We most commonly associate hazing with Greek letter organizations, but the truth is that hazing can happen in any group. According to the hazing prevention organization StopHazing, more than half of students who participate in teams, groups or student organizations experience some type of hazing while in college (Allan & Madden, 2008a). Examples of common types of hazing include:

- Heavy alcohol consumption
- Wearing odd items of clothing (e.g., bright hats, fanny packs)
- Silence periods with implied threats for violation
- Having to memorize trivial bits of information
- Carrying unnecessary objects at all times
- Sleep deprivation
- Public humiliation
- Acts of personal servitude

Allan and Madden (2008b) discovered that, despite the serious nature of some of these acts, 95% of students who labeled their experiences as hazing did not report them to officials. These students reported being afraid of negative consequences for themselves or their groups or being ostracized by group members for reporting hazing (Allan & Madden, 2008b). But the real consequences of hazing can be far more severe.

HazingPrevention.org (2015) stated that 71 percent of students who report being hazed have suffered negative consequences, including declining grades, diminished physical and mental health, erosion of trust and personal relationships, post-traumatic stress disorder and, most tragically, even death.

Hazing is illegal, it violates university policy and it's dangerous. That is why students at USC are prohibited from

### HAZING HOTLINE

To report hazing, call 803-777-5800 and give a detailed description of the occurrence. Reports can be made anonymously, but the more information shared, the more successful the university will be in addressing the problem.

 803-777-5800

engaging in hazing and required to report any occurrence. To make a report – even an anonymous one – call the hazing hotline at 803-777-5800 and leave a detailed description.

## Sexual assault

A recent report commissioned by the U.S. Department of Justice found that nationwide, one in five women and one in 16 men are the victims of sexual assault while in college (Krebs, Lindquist, Warner, Fisher & Martin, 2007). Sexual assault can happen to anyone regardless of age, gender, sexual orientation, ethnicity, religion and appearance. But it is never the survivor's fault, and it's never tolerated at the University of South Carolina, which has a number of resources available 24/7 to help you learn how to prevent sexual assault and to support survivors in the tragic event that an assault occurs.

According to the University of South Carolina, "sexual assault is any form of sexual contact that occurs without consent and/or through the use of force, threat of force, intimidation, incapacitation or coercion" ("Definitions," 2015). Consent is defined as "clear, conscious, willing and affirmative agreement to engage in sexual activity." Examples of sexual assault can include:

- Touching an unwilling person's intimate parts or touching them with yours
- Having sex with someone who is intoxicated, unconscious, or otherwise incapacitated
- Forcing, threatening or intimidating someone into engaging in sexual activity
- Exploiting a person's physical or mental condition to have sex with them

If you or someone you know has experienced sexual assault, there are three important things to know:

1. We believe you.
2. It's not your fault.
3. You are not alone. USC has resources to help.

STOP SEXUAL ASSAULT

Learn how you can prevent sexual assault, support survivors and report an assault in the tragic event that one occurs by visiting:

sc.edu/stopsexualassault

YES!
Consent is only a clear and uncoerced "Yes."

## Resources for Survivors

### University support

Survivors of sexual assault are guaranteed certain rights, including assistance from university offices. USC Police can help survivors get restraining orders and orders of protection. It is important to keep in mind that reporting an assault is different from prosecuting it. To report an assault, call 803-777-4215 or, in an emergency, 911.

USC Sexual Assault and Violence Intervention & Prevention is a *confidential resource*. Trained advocates are on call 24/7 to provide support, information, and referrals to survivors. Advocates also can assist with class schedule and room changes if needed. You can call 803-777-8248 during the workday or USC police after hours and ask for the SAVIP advocate.

### Additional support

Another confidential resource is Sexual Trauma Services of the Midlands. They have advocates on call 24 hours a day, and you can reach them by calling 803-771-7273.

### Medical attention

Palmetto Richland Hospital (confidential resource) — Medical attention is critical. Visit the ER at 5 Medical Park or call 803-434-6628.

### Counseling

USC Counseling and Psychiatry (confidential resource) — Seek help from one of USC's professional counselors, psychologists or psychiatrists. Call 803-777-5223.

### Campus judicial support and investigation

USC Office of Student Conduct — Conduct staff members can provide no-contact orders, conduct investigations, evaluate conduct charges and determine appropriate resolutions. Call 803-777-4333.

### Title IX rights and process assistance

USC Title IX coordinator — Title IX protects students' rights to an educational environment free from discrimination, including sexual assault. Call 803-777-3854.

**DRINKING ISN'T CONSENT.**
Consent is only a clear and uncoerced "Yes."

**DATING ISN'T CONSENT.**
Consent is only a clear and uncoerced "Yes."

**CLOTHING ISN'T CONSENT.**
Consent is only a clear and uncoerced "Yes."

### *Preventing sexual assault*

As members of the Carolina community, we all have a responsibility to create a safe campus environment. Ways to step in and speak up to prevent harm are discussed at the end of this chapter. To learn more about what you can do to prevent sexual assault and how to support a survivor with compassion, visit sc.edu/stopsexualassault.

# I will respect the rights and property of others

Respecting a person's dignity and respecting his or her rights and property are related. The second follows naturally from the first. In a community, however, members share responsibility for respecting not only the property of individuals, but also the property that is meant to be shared by the community. Community members must always consider how their actions (or inactions) affect the individuals and the larger group those individuals comprise.

To uphold this tenet, Carolinians must not misappropriate, steal, vandalize or otherwise damage property that does not belong to them. They must also avoid violating another person's rights, including those of expression and privacy (University of South Carolina, 1990).

# Campus safety

The University of South Carolina's campus is patrolled by a team of highly trained, sworn law enforcement officers and composed of a community of caring individuals. But, like every college campus, it does attract some crime. Property crimes – particularly car break-ins and the theft of books, electronics and other personal belongings – comprise the majority of crime on USC's campus. Fortunately, there are steps you can take to protect yourself, your property and your community. The university's Division of Law Enforcement and Safety, which includes the USC Police Department, suggests the following safety tips (Safety Tips, n.d.):

- Trust your instincts. If a place or situation doesn't feel right, it probably isn't. Leave.
- Avoid shortcuts and isolated areas when walking after dark.
- Don't walk alone after dark. Early evening to late evening, travel only in groups of three or more in well-lit and heavily traveled areas. Use the APO Escort Service (803-777-DUCK) or call for a police escort (803-777-4215).
- When traveling in your vehicle, keep windows up and doors locked.
- When you park your car, don't leave your belongings in sight.
- Never venture into or through dark or undesirable neighborhoods.
- Familiarize yourself with emergency call box locations.
- Don't carry large sums of cash.
- If you see something or someone suspicious, contact USC police at 803-777-4215 or use the nearest emergency call box.

**RAVE GUARDIAN**

Download the free safety app RAVE Guardian, which turns your mobile phone into a portable emergency call box.

 **sc.edu/safety**

# Protecting Your Property
## *Protecting Your Books*

Book theft continues to be a serious problem on college and university campuses. Individuals who steal textbooks generally do so for the primary purpose of converting them into ready cash at the local campus bookstore. Take a few easy steps to minimize opportunity. Never leave your books unattended. Once you purchase your books and are certain that they are the correct books for your courses, write your name in each book along with an additional identifying characteristic only you know. Do this in a couple of places within the book. Should your books be lost or stolen and turn up at the local bookstore, you then can identify them as yours. Remember all new books for a particular course look the same. By placing your name and an additional identifying characteristic somewhere in the book, you personalize the item in a manner that will assist, if necessary, with future identification.

## Protecting Your Bicycle

Many University students choose to avoid the parking crunch and use alternate forms of transportation. One popular alternative is the bicycle. It is important to take steps to secure your bike with an adequate locking device manufactured specifically for the security of bicycles. A U-lock type bicycle lock is recommended to properly secure your bicycle. Registration is required for all bicycles on campus and is provided free to all students. Parking Services will assist you with this process. You will be provided with a decal as well as the opportunity to engrave a personal mark somewhere on your bicycle. This office will also help you locate your bicycle serial number and provide you with a card so you can maintain a record of this information. Moped registration is also required.

## Protecting Your Residence Hall Room and Personal Items

Many students live on campus, particularly during their first year. If you are one of these students, take time to become familiar with security policies and procedures that pertain to your particular residence hall. Remember to get in the habit of locking your room (a practice that you probably did not follow while living at home) even if you are going down the hall for a few minutes. It takes less than a minute to remove items from an unlocked room. If you see suspicious activity in or around your residence hall, report it to your resident mentor or the campus police. Reduce your risk of theft of laptops and other personal items by purchasing STOP security tags from the information desk at Russell House. These tags contain a unique bar code, making your item personally identifiable and are attached with adhesive that makes the tag virtually impossible to remove if stolen. Underneath the tag is a stolen property tattoo that cannot be removed without defacing the item.

In the event you are the victim of a crime, call USC police immediately. Dial 911 and tell the operator you are on the USC campus or call 803-777-4215 to speak to USC police dispatch. Try to give a good description of the perpetrator and remain in a safe area until help arrives.

USC POLICE

sc.edu/safety

facebook.com/USCPD

@USCPD

@CarolinaAlert

@USCPD

# I will discourage bigotry, while striving to learn from differences in people, ideas, and opinions.

Bigotry is defined as intolerance toward those who hold different ideas, beliefs or opinions from one's own. But, inviting differing viewpoints and perspectives is required for learning and development. In fact, the ability to wrestle with and analyze these multiple perspectives is a marker of a true scholar and what we hope every Carolinian will strive toward. Pledging to uphold this tenet requires an attitude of inclusion and "affirmative support for equal rights and opportunities for all" (University of South Carolina, 1990), regardless of their age; sex; gender identity; race; religion; sexual orientation; disability; ethnic or cultural heritage; socioeconomic status; or political, social or other affiliation or non-affiliation.

## Diversity and Inclusion

At the University of South Carolina, we believe that diversity and inclusion are necessary to achieve academic and institutional excellence. Every student, faculty and staff member not only matters—it is their unique perspective that is the core of our strength and our success.

At the University of South Carolina, diversity and inclusion help create the vibrant, welcoming campus we are known for, and they are necessary for academic and institutional excellence. But what do we mean by diversity and inclusion? Lydia Dishman (2015) reports that Millennials view diversity as the "blending of different backgrounds, experiences and perspectives." Inclusion, then, is the creation of an environment that prizes and encourages active participation from people with these different traits. These definitions are certainly appropriate for our campus.

Everything that makes you you -- including your ethnicity, religion, sex, gender identity, sexuality, family history, cultural heritage, socioeconomic standing and unique experiences

AS PRESIDENT OF THE UNIVERSITY, I ENVISION THE UNIVERSITY OF SOUTH CAROLINA AS A PLACE WHERE OUR DIVERSITY IS NOT ONLY MEASURED IN NUMBERS, BUT ALSO IN THE INCLUSIVE AND WELCOMING CLIMATE THAT WE PUT ON DISPLAY EACH AND EVERY DAY IN OUR COMMUNITY.

- Harris Pastides, President, University of South Carolina

-- contributes to the diversity of USC's campus. Be aware of how these traits inform your beliefs and perspectives, and be willing to share how they have influenced you. Also, take time to consider how others' opinions are shaped by their backgrounds, and be eager to listen to and learn from them. Strive to keep an open mind and consider alternate viewpoints. Your college experience will be enriched by the variety of people you meet and the things they teach you.

# I will demonstrate concern for others, their feelings, and their need for conditions which support their work and development.

As an individual with innate dignity, inherent rights and valuable ideas and opinions, each person also has complex feelings and a need for particular conditions that support their success. Recognizing those -- and reacting with compassion and support -- takes empathy, the ability to identify what others are feeling and to feel it with them from their perspective (Shankman & Allen, 2008). To uphold this tenet, Carolinians must be compassionate and considerate of others, show care for their safety and well-being and avoid behaviors that are insensitive or that make others feel unsafe or unwelcome (University of South Carolina, 1990).

## *Civility*

In his book *Choosing Civility: The Twenty-five Rules of Considerate Conduct*, Forni (2002) defines civility in the following way:

> Civility is a form of goodness; it is gracious goodness. But it is not just an attitude of benevolent and thoughtful relating to other individuals; it also entails an active interest in the well-being of our communities and a concern for the health of the planet on which we live.

It is this "active interest in the well-being" of the Carolina community described in this tenet of the Carolinian Creed.

And it's easy to act with civility when everyone agrees with you. But on a campus as diverse as USC's with people whose backgrounds, viewpoints and beliefs are so different, there's bound to be disagreement. What then?

The answer is dialogue, which David Bohm (2004) identifies as a free exchange of ideas. Dialogue, says Bohm, is very different from debate, which pits opposing sides against each other in an attempt to come out on top. In dialogue, the aim is to understand, to consider all perspectives and to come to a shared agreement. When you're in a disagreement with someone, respect each other's dignity and rights and do not resort to hostility or judgment. Instead, work toward dialogue rather than debate and follow these tips for civil disagreements:

- Don't confuse being right with being happy
- Compromise
- Check in frequently
- Don't fight to hurt
- Keep focus
- Have a sense of humor

By using these strategies, acting in accordance with the second tenet of the Carolinian Creed, "I will respect the dignity of all persons," seeking to understand rather than to win and striving to find common ground, you can discuss any issue with civility.

## Confronting harmful behavior

A community affords its members certain privileges, but it also obligates them to a number of responsibilities. In the last line of the creed, Carolinians' greatest responsibility is described when they are implored not only to "refrain from" but also, critically, to "discourage behaviors which threaten the freedom and respect every individual deserves" ("Carolinian Creed," n.d.). The university requires members of the Carolina community to "confront and challenge, and respond to, or report [those] behaviors whenever or wherever they're encountered" (University of South Carolina, 1990).

50 PERCENT OF PEOPLE HAVE ENDED A FRIENDSHIP BECAUSE ANOTHER PERSON WAS UNCIVIL. AMONG THOSE WHO BELIEVE THAT CIVILITY IS GETTING WORSE, 59% OF PEOPLE BELIEVE THE INTERNET AND SOCIAL MEDIA ARE PARTIALLY TO BLAME ("CIVILITY IN AMERICA," 2013).

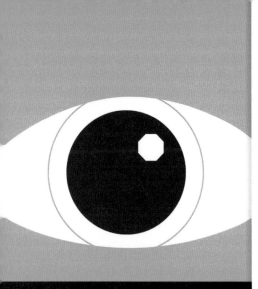

AN ACTIVE BYSTANDER IS A PERSON WHO SEES A NEGATIVE SITUATION OR EVENT AND INTERVENES IN SOME WAY TO PREVENT HARM.

STAND UP CAROLINA

Learn more about being an active bystander by taking part in USC's training, Stand Up Carolina. For presentation dates or to schedule one for your group, call:

 803-777-8248

Today, this notion of confronting, challenging, responding to or reporting harmful behavior is described by the concept of bystander accountability. An accountable, or active, bystander "is a person who sees a negative situation or event and intervenes in some way to prevent harm" ("Definitions," n.d.). Most commonly discussed in the field of prevention -- particularly as it relates to bullying and sexual assault -- the idea of bystander accountability can be applied to any harmful or potentially harmful situation.

### How to intervene

Often, we think of intervening as physically stepping in to a situation to stop it – jumping in to break up a fight, for example. While that is one example of bystander intervention, there are many others, and you should do what's safe and comfortable for you. When you see something that looks wrong, consider:

- Calling 911 if it's especially dangerous.
- Asking the potential victim, "Are you okay?"
- Telling the perpetrator, "Cut it out," or "That's not cool."
- Using humor to defuse the situation.
- Creating a distraction.
- Asking someone else for help.

It doesn't really matter what you do, only that you do *something*. Doing what you can to stop a negative situation – whether you're doing so directly or discreetly – can make an enormous difference in someone's life, and it's a hallmark of a community that cares for one another.

## Character matters

What business is it of a university to expect its community members to aspire to the Carolinian Creed's ideals? It is the most important business. The university was founded in 1801 as a means to "create harmony in the state by providing a learning environment typified by the finest human qualities, such as mutual respect, integrity, and selflessness" (Pruitt, 1996). The university motto translated from Latin reads, "Learning humanizes character and does not permit it to be cruel." In selecting this phrase, written by the poet Ovid, to be inscribed on the university seal in 1803, university founders proclaimed their expectation that a Carolina education would foster not just intellect, but also character.

USC cultivates its community members' character development within and beyond the classroom. Carolinians are involved in work to advance causes such as social justice, cultural appreciation, environmental sustainability, civic engagement and shared responsibility for our world. Through academic pursuits, leadership and service, Carolinians strive to understand, appreciate and improve their community.

## Practicing and promoting the creed

There are numerous examples of USC students, faculty and staff practicing the tenets of the Carolinian Creed through acts of service, compassion and citizenship.

In recent years, students have led the founding of two important efforts to assist their fellow Carolinians. The campus food bank, Gamecock Pantry, provides food to students in need. Carolina Closet loans clothing to students who couldn't otherwise afford to buy professional attire for job and internship interviews.

Student leaders wrote an open letter to the Carolina community in 2014, denouncing online incivility. In their letter, the students said that anonymous commenting through apps like Yik Yak enables people "to lose integrity, promote bigotry, and disrespect the rights and property of others" ("Student Leaders," 2014). The students urged their peers to use social media in ways consistent with the creed.

But practicing and promoting the Carolinian Creed doesn't have to be a large public effort. Other ways include:

- Volunteering as a note taker for Student Disability Services to help students with visual, hearing or learning disabilities
- Showing support for LGBTQ students by becoming a Safe Zone Ally

The university seal highlights Carolina's motto "Emollit Mores Nec Sinit Esse Feros," which means "Learning humanizes character and does not permit it to be cruel."

The student members of the Carolina Judicial Council pass out Random Acts of Creed cards to encourage other students to engage in simple, everyday acts of kindness, compassion, integrity and respect.

## CREEDx

CREEDx, a presentation of brief talks modeled after TED Talks and TEDx, is one of the highlights of Carolinian Creed Day, held each March. In an uplifting and inspirational program, select students, faculty and staff share personal messages about what the tenets of the creed mean to them. CREEDx won the 2015 national Innovation Award from the Association for Student Conduct Administration.

- Taking a class to learn more about an unfamiliar religious or spiritual tradition
- Signing up to be a conversation partner for international students learning English
- Serving the community on a Service Saturday or through an Impact Weekly Service Project
- Attending the Oxfam Hunger Banquet to learn more about hunger and income inequality
- Visiting sc.edu/stopsexualassault to learn how to prevent sexual assault and help survivors
- Joining Carolina Judicial Council to hear student conduct cases
- Practicing the safety tips at sc.edu/safety and downloading the Rave Guardian app
- Encouraging friends and colleagues to seek help from the many available USC resources

## Conclusion

The Carolinian Creed expresses the University of South Carolina's values, expectations and the ideals to which all members of the Carolina community should aspire. It is a guide for making decisions and taking actions, and as USC Professor Joel Stevenson said in his 2015 CREEDx talk, "It's a way to live your life."

## REFLECTION QUESTIONS

1. Imagine the University of South Carolina without the Carolinian Creed. How would community values be known? How would community members' behaviors be different?

2. Describe a time you saw someone else act in a way that upheld one or more tenets of the Carolinian Creed. How did you react? How could you show appreciation and encouragement when others act in accordance with the creed?

3. Describe a time you acted in a way that was inconsistent with one or more tenets of the Carolinian Creed. Why did you behave that way? What could you have done differently?

4. The Carolinian Creed was developed amidst a wave of negative attitudes, damaging behavior and illegal incidents on college campuses across the U.S. Do you see similarities in today's college culture? How could you apply the tenets of the Carolinian Creed to preserve a healthy campus environment or create positive change?

## RESOURCES

**Office of Academic Integrity** . . . . . . . . . (803) 777-4333
Byrnes Building, Suite 201
http://www.sc.edu/academicintegrity/

**Office of Student Judicial Programs** . (803) 777-4333
Byrnes Building, Suite 201
http://www.sc.edu/osjp

**Sexual Assault and Violence Intervention and Prevention** . . . . . . . . . . . . . . . . . . . . . . (803) 777-8248
Thomson Student Health Center
https://www.sa.sc.edu/shs/savip/

**The Carolinian Creed**
http://www.sa.sc.edu/creed/

**University Ombudsman**
http://www.sc.edu/ombuds/

**Safety & Transport**

**USC Police Department** . . . . . . . . . . . . . (803) 777-4215
Emergency . . . . . . . . . . . . . . . . . . . . . . . . . . . . . . .911
1415 Henderson Street
http://les.sc.edu/

**Victim/Witness Coordinator** . . . . . . . . . (803) 777-7786

**Blue Ribbon Taxi Cab Corporation** . . . (803) 754-8163
http://originalblueribbontaxi.com/

**Carolina Alert**
http://carolinaalert.sc.edu/

**Carolina Cab**
https://www.sa.sc.edu/sg/carolina-cab/

**Checker Yellow Cab Company** . . . . . . . . (803) 799-3311
http://checkeryellowcab.com/

**RAVE Guardian**
http://les.sc.edu/crime-prevention-and-safety-resources/mobile-safety-app/

**Shuttlecock (Campus Shuttles)** . . . . . . (803) 777-1080
http://www.sc.edu/vmps/shuttle.html

**Walk Home Cocky**
https://www.sa.sc.edu/sg/walkhomecocky/

# REFERENCES

Allan, E. A., & Madden, M. (2008a). Hazing in view: College students at risk [infographic]. Retrieved from http://www.stophazing.org/infographics/

Allan, E. A., & Madden, M. (2008b). Hazing in view: Student reporting, perceptions, and prevention [infographic]. Retrieved from http://www.stophazing.org/infographics/

Berg-Cross, L., Starr, B. J., & Sloan, L. (1993). Race relations and polycultural sensitivity training on college campuses. In L. Whitaker & J. Pollard (Eds.) *Campus violence: Kinds, causes, and cures* (pp. 151-175). Binghamton, NY: Haworth Press.

Bohm, D. (2004). *On dialogue.* New York: Rutledge Classics.

Callahan, D. (2004). *The cheating culture: Why more Americans are doing wrong to get ahead.* New York: Harcourt, Inc.

Civility in America (2013). Weber Shandwick. Retrieved from http://www.webershandwick.com/uploads/news/files/Civility_in_America_2013_Exec_Summary.pdf

Definitions (n.d.). University of South Carolina: Retrieved from http://www.sc.edu/about/initiatives/safety/stop_sexual_assault/training/definitions/index.php

Dishman, L. (2015, May 18). Milennials have a different definition of diversity and inclusion. Retrieved from http://www.fastcompany.com/3046358/the-new-rules-of-work/millennials-have-a-different-definition-of-diversity-and-inclusion

Evans, J. E., Forney, D. S., Guido, F. M., Patton, L. D., & Renn, K. A. (2010). *Student development in college: Theory, research and practice.* San Francisco, CA: Jossey-Bass.

Forni, P. M. (2002). *Choosing civility: The twenty-five rules of considerate conduct.* New York: St. Martin's Press.

Hazing (n.d.). University of South Carolina Office of Fraternity and Sorority Life: Retrieved from https://www.sa.sc.edu/fsl/hazing-2/

Hazing and its Consequences (n.d.). HazingPrevention.org: Retrieved from http://hazingprevention.org/home/hazing/hazing-and-its-consequences/

Higher Education Research Institute. (2010). *Findings from the 2009 administration of the Your First College Year (YFCY): National aggregates.* Retrieved from http://www.heri.ucla.edu/PDFs/pubs/Reports/YFCY2009Final_January.pdf

Honor Code Student FAQ (n.d.). University of South Carolina Office of Academic Integrity: Retrieved from http://www.housing.sc.edu/academicintegrity/stufaq.html

Krebs, C., Lindquist, C., Warner, T., Fisher, B., & Martin, S. (2007) The campus sexual assault study: Final report. Retrieved from https://www.ncjrs.gov/pdffiles1/nij/grants/221153.pdf

McCabe, D. (2005). *Levels of cheating and plagiarism remain high, honor codes and modified codes are shown to be effective in reducing academic misconduct.* Retrieved from http://www.academicintegrity.org/

Pruitt, D. (1996, May-June). The Carolinian's Creed. *About Campus,* 27-29.

Safety Tips (n.d.). University of South Carolina Division of Law Enforcement and Safety. Retrieved from http://les.sc.edu/crime-prevention-and-safety-resources/safety-tips/

Shankman, M. L., & Allen, S. J. (2008). *Emotionally intelligent leadership: A guide for college students.* San Francisco, CA: Jossey-Bass.

Student Leaders Denounce Online Incivility (2014, Nov. 21). University of South Carolina: Retrieved from http://www.sc.edu/uofsc/announcements/2014/11_students_denounce_yikyak.php#.VYmIBPlVhHw

The Carolinian Creed (n.d.). University of South Carolina. Retrieved from http://www.sa.sc.edu/creed

University of South Carolina Office of Student Conduct and Academic Integrity (n.d.). The Creed at Carolina: Your guide to the values of the Carolina community [brochure].

University of South Carolina (1930). *The Carolina student's handbook.* Retrieved from http://digital.tcl.sc.edu/cdm/ref/collection/ssh/id/217

University of South Carolina (1990). *The Carolinian's Creed* [Poster].

University of South Carolina Honor Code (n.d.). University of South Carolina Division of Student Affairs. Retrieved from http://www.sc.edu/policies/ppm/staf625.pdf

Wueste, D. (2008). Unintended consequences and responsibility. *Teaching Ethics,* 13-24.

# CHAPTER 10

# Wellbeing

## Dear First-Year Student,

Welcome to the University of South Carolina! I am glad you have chosen Carolina to be your home for the next few years. It is my alma mater, and, while here, I developed many healthy habits that continue to this day.

One of the great things about being in college is independence. Without parents to tell you when to get up, what to eat, or how to manage your time, the first few months on your own can be a challenge. However, this time is also an opportunity to cultivate healthy behaviors and routines that will last a lifetime. Fortunately, the University of South Carolina has a variety of resources available for you to attain and maintain wellness in body, mind, and spirit during your collegiate career.

At the full-service Thomson Student Health Center, you can see a physician if you are not feeling well, but the Center provides so much more. Students may fill prescriptions, meet with a registered dietitian, and get flu or allergy shots. In addition, the Campus Wellness office provides blood pressure, body composition, and fitness assessments; exercise consultations; and a variety of programs related to nutrition, physical activity, sexual health, stress management, and disease prevention. Finally, the Counseling and Psychiatry office is here whenever you feel the need to talk with a professional about personal challenges.

This campus provides many opportunities for physical activity. From walking the beautiful Horseshoe to playing intramural sports, there is something for everyone. The Strom Thurmond Wellness and Fitness Center is a state-of-the-art fitness facility where students can take group exercise classes, climb a rock wall, swim, learn to kayak, and work out in the weight room.

Carolina Dining provides ample places to eat on campus and offers many healthy choices. Campus Wellness registered dietitians can help you learn how to eat nutritious meals and snacks while navigating your busy days.

Another aspect of college life may involve engaging in risky behaviors, including using alcohol or other drugs, developing sexual relationships, and walking alone at night from popular hangouts like Five Points. There are a range of University services, including sexual health educators with Campus Wellness who can answer your questions about developing and maintain healthy relationships.

Another aspect of the wellness wheel depicted in this chapter is spirituality. The University is rich with faith-based groups and places to worship. You are sure to find your spiritual home.

I wish you all the best as you embark upon your Carolina journey!
To your health,

*Marguerite O'Brien*

Marguerite O'Brien
Director, Wellness, Prevention & Advocacy

**OFTEN,** when students are asked to describe their personal wellness, they automatically talk about their physical activity and nutritional habits. While these are two very important health components, wellness is far more comprehensive than what you eat and how much you exercise. The University of South Carolina defines wellness as a holistic, well-balanced approach to living that involves the mind, body, and spirit. Carolina cares about you and your personal wellness because it has a direct impact on your academic success as well as your quality of life.

With an understanding that wellness means more than being free of illness or disease, healthy Carolinians are those who make a commitment to seven dimensions of wellness:

## PHYSICAL WELLNESS

Respecting and caring for your body. Applying knowledge, motivation and skills toward enhancing personal fitness and health.

## SOCIAL WELLNESS

Contributing to your human and physical environment for the common welfare of and social justice within your community.

## EMOTIONAL WELLNESS

Striving to meet your emotional needs constructively, responding resiliently to emotional states and the flow of life events. Taking responsibility for your own behavior and having the ability to form interdependent relationships based on mutual commitment, honesty, and respect.

## INTELLECTUAL WELLNESS

Having a curiosity and strong desire to learn. A lifelong process of creating and reflecting upon experience, staying stimulated with new ideas and sharing.

## SPIRITUAL WELLNESS

Searching for meaning, value, and purpose resulting in hope, joy, courage, and gratitude. Encourages one to develop a personal faith and to seek the divine in all things.

## OCCUPATIONAL WELLNESS

Combining who you are called to be and what you are called to do. Finding the place where your deep desires and gifts meet the needs of the community.

## ENVIRONMENTAL WELLNESS

Being aware of the state of the earth and the effects of daily habits on the physical environment. Respecting all of creation and the beauty and balance of nature.

If one component within the Dimensions of Wellness is not developed, you may feel like your life is unbalanced. The Wellness Wheel Inventory at the end of this chapter will help you evaluate your wellbeing within the seven dimensions. You may find that you are not devoting adequate time to each of these areas, and we hope you will use this as an opportunity to reflect on ways you can foster your overall wellbeing.

# Personal Wellness

You have likely heard that students go through several important transitions when they enter college. One significant area of change involves developing new habits and behaviors related to your personal health and wellness. Now is the time to decide how you will engage in essential wellness activities for this next chapter of your life. The benefits of engaging in healthy behaviors go beyond the expected physical health outcomes. In reality, the connections between positive wellness and personal and academic success are numerous, including as means to manage stress (Ruthig, Marrone, Hladkyz, and Robinson-Epp, 2011) and to develop positive sleep patterns (Trockel, Barnes, and Egget, 2000). The choices you make now will impact your long-term habits and overall attitude.

This chapter provides a collection of strategies and resources to help you achieve overall personal wellness. As you read, you will have a number of opportunities to reflect on how the decisions you make now will impact the rest of your college experience. The chapter begins by addressing some of the following key questions that many first-year students pose related to wellbeing in the first year college:

- Will I really gain the "Freshman 15"?
- Do I really need eight hours of sleep?
- How should I handle stress?

The chapter also addresses key topics such as alcohol consumption, sexual health, and financial wellness.

Because many USC students are from places outside of South Carolina, it's important to think about acclimating to our unique blend of humid and warm weather. Temperatures have been as high as 113 degrees in Columbia. One way to be sure you are taking care of yourself, whether it's exercising outside or walking between classes, is to be properly hydrated. There are many water hydration systems located around the campus, including the Russell House University Union and the campus residence halls. Make sure you carry a water bottle with you and fill up regularly at one of the water stations.

# Will I Really Gain the "Freshman 15"?

The "Freshman 15," an assumption that you will gain 15 pounds during your first year of college, is actually a myth. Many researchers have tested this hypothesis and found that the expected amount of weight gain for first-year students is actually closer to 2-3 pounds (Hoffman, Policastro, Quick, & Lee, 2006; Mihalopoulos, Auinger, & Klien, 2008). While the weight increase is not as dramatic as originally believed, it can still be challenging for many new students to maintain a healthy weight. As you get older, you metabolism naturally begins to slow down, and staying up late to study or spending time with friends often means eating late at night when it is harder to burn off calories. Also, you may have been very active in high school, but find you are participating less in physical activities in college. When determining if you are on the right track in terms of your physical health, it helps to reflect on how your current activity levels compare to your prior experience. Consider the characteristics of your current exercise patterns, including the frequency, intensity, and variety of activities pursued. In case you are not pursuing physical activity in the ways you would prefer, ask yourself how you can make a personal commitment to change or improve your behavior.

The first step towards meeting your exercise goals is to make a plan of action. Research shows those who create strategies to support their exercise goals, such as scheduling personal activity time into your weekly responsibilities or purchasing exercise equipment or clothing, achieve greater success than those who do not (Spencer, Adams, Malone, Roy, & Yost, 2006). To help you make a plan, be sure to check out the many resources USC offers to help you achieve optimal personal wellness through physical activity.

## Top Ways to Get Active at USC

- Join an intramural or club sport sponsored through USC's Campus Recreation department. By participating in these peer-to-peer structured activities, students are charged with creating the experience, and also practice skill development and interpersonal communication through interactions with teammates and officiating staff. You also have the opportunity to initiate your own intramural or club sport. In fact, that's how the Quidditch and Ultimate Frisbee clubs were created. Opportunities for participation can be found on their website: https://campusrec.sc.edu/sport-clubs/

- Engage in physical activity on your own, or through less structured methods. For instance full-time students have access to the Strom Thurmond Wellness and Fitness Center as well as the Blatt PE Center. Both facilities are equipped with state-of-the-art strength and conditioning equipment as well as pools, basketball courts, and group exercise classes. The Strom Thurmond Wellness and Fitness Center also provides a climbing wall, indoor track, outdoor pool, and sand volleyball courts. Campus Wellness offers fitness assessments and one-on-one exercise consultations for individuals that are new to the workout scene or are looking to change their current practices.

- Take advantage of the many established walking paths on our campus of 480 acres. Be sure to check out the walking and running maps for suggested paths around our campus: http://www.sa.sc.edu/healthycarolina/

- Take a physical activity class for credit. Benefits of participating in these courses include opportunities to improve skill development through lessons taught by technical experts, meeting new people with an interest in similar activity, and having a variety of course offerings to choose from. Some examples of course offerings are judo, swing dance, and triathlon training. Be sure to check out the course schedule each semester to see what opportunities exist. Many of the courses are listed under PEDU (Department of Physical Education and Athletic Training).

Students enjoy the outdoor pool at the Strom Thurmond Wellness and Fitness Center.

# Do I really need eight hours of sleep?

Now that you have the freedom to choose when you go to sleep and when you get up, how many hours of sleep do you really need? The National Sleep Foundation (2015) recommends 7-9 hours of sleep for younger adults, ages 18-25. The effects of lost sleep are numerous, but also less likely to be visible until an extended period of time has passed. A recent study found that changes in sleep influenced a student's Grade Point Average (GPA) as students who stayed up late had lower GPAs than those who went to bed earlier in the evening (Taylor, Vatthauer, Bramoweth, Ruggero, & Roane, 2013). Experts have also found that students who receive less sleep tend to have a more negative disposition that can leave you feeling angry or even sick (Lund, Reider, Whiting, & Prichard, 2010).

Think about your current activities and how they distract you from going to sleep earlier. To get better sleep consider:

- Reducing the amount of caffeine ingested at night, and be wary of energy drinks and over-caffeinating during daytime hours.
- Avoiding long naps during the day as they can inhibit your ability to fall asleep consistently during nighttime hours.
- Reducing the use of technology before going to sleep as increases in exposure to light through technology devices can make sleeping more difficult.
- Increasing your physical activity. The energy absorbed through exercise during the day can help regulate sleep patterns at night. For this reason, it is also important to realize that engaging in physical activity too close to bedtime can increase difficulty in falling asleep as your heart rate may still be elevated. A general rule of thumb is to quit activity 2-3 hours before falling asleep.

# How should I handle stress?

Significant changes in life can naturally result in increased stress. It is important to note that not all stress is bad, and in fact, two different types of stress exist. Eustress is defined as "good" stress in that it serves as a motivator to be positive and productive. Conversely, distress can be detrimental since negative emotions can overwhelm actions or behaviors, and thus lead to increased tension or worry (McGowan, Garner, & Fletcher, 2006). Transitioning to college while adjusting to all of its "new"ness can be daunting. In addition, you are likely making important decisions that influence your daily living for the first time in your life. Whether you are making short-term decisions, or dealing with large-scale life events, it is important to understand how stress can impact your overall wellness. On the next two pages, you will find some of the top strategies for managing and responding to stress. The challenge lies in recognizing when you need to use them and having the ability to actually do so in spite of your stress.

## *Anxiety*

Students report that anxiety is one of the top factors negatively impacting their academic performance. Anxiety disorders are one of the most common ailments on college campuses, with 13% of Gamecocks reporting that they were diagnosed or treated for an anxiety disorder in 2013. It is important to be able to recognize what may be "common" worries versus an anxiety disorder.

Symptoms of anxiety include:

- Excessive anxiety and worry that occurs more days than not
- Difficulty controlling the worry
- Trouble making decisions or putting off decisions
- Feeling restless or "on edge"
- Difficulty concentrating or mind going blank
- Feeling tired or fatigued
- Frequent irritability
- Muscle tension
- Difficulty falling or staying asleep, or unsatisfying, restless sleep

# TOP 10 STRATEGIES SUCCESSFUL PEOPLE EMPLOY WHEN EXPERIENCING STRESS

## 1 THEY APPRECIATE WHAT THEY HAVE

Taking time to contemplate what you're grateful for actually improves your mood. Reflection on what you are thankful for reduces the stress hormone cortisol by 23%. Research conducted at the University of California, Davis found that people who worked daily to cultivate an attitude of gratitude experienced improved mood, energy, and physical well-being.

## 2 THEY AVOID ASKING "WHAT IF?"

"What if?" statements only add to a pile of stress and worry. Things can go in a million different directions, and the more time you spend worrying about the possibilities, the less time you'll spend focusing on taking action that will calm you down and keep your stress under control. Calm people know that asking "what if?" will only take them to a place they don't want—or need—to go.

## 3 THEY STAY POSITIVE

Positive thoughts help make stress intermittent by focusing your brain's attention onto something that is completely stress-free. Think about your day and identify one positive thing that happened, no matter how small. If you can't think of something from the current day, reflect on the previous day or even the previous week. Or perhaps you're looking forward to an exciting event that you can focus your attention on. The point here is that you must have something positive that you're ready to shift your attention to when your thoughts turn negative.

## 4 THEY DISCONNECT

Technology enables constant communication and the expectation that you should be available 24/7. Given the importance of keeping stress intermittent, it's easy to see how taking regular time off the grid can help keep your stress under control. Forcing yourself offline and even—gulp!—turning off your phone gives your body a break from a constant source of stress.

## 6 THEY SLEEP

Not enough can be said about the importance of sleep to increasing your emotional intelligence and managing your stress levels. When you sleep, your brain literally recharges, shuffling through the day's memories and storing or discarding them (which causes dreams), so that you wake up alert and clear-headed. Your self-control, attention, and memory are all reduced when you don't get enough—or the right kind—of sleep. Sleep deprivation raises stress hormone levels on its own, even without a stressor present. Stressful projects often make you feel as if you have no time to sleep, but taking the time to get a decent night's sleep is key to helping to get things under control.

## 5 THEY LIMIT THEIR CAFFEINE INTAKE

Drinking caffeine triggers the release of adrenaline. Adrenaline is the source of the "fight-or-flight" response. The fight-or-flight mechanism sidesteps rational thinking in favor of a faster response. When caffeine puts your brain and body into this hyper aroused state of stress, your emotions overrun your behavior. The stress that caffeine creates is far from intermittent, as its long half-life ensures that it takes its sweet time working its way out of your body.

## 7 THEY SQUASH NEGATIVE SELF-TALK

A big step in managing stress involves stopping negative self-talk in its tracks. The more you focus on negative thoughts, the more power you give them. Most of our negative thoughts are just thoughts, not facts. You can bet that your statements are not true any time you use words like "never," "worst," "ever," etc. When you find yourself believing the negative and pessimistic things, your inner voice says, stop what you're doing and write down what you're thinking. Once you've taken a moment to slow down the negative momentum of your thoughts, you will be more rational and clear-headed in evaluating their authenticity. Identifying and labeling your thoughts as thoughts by separating them from the facts will help you escape the cycle of negativity and move toward a positive new outlook.

## 9 THEY BREATHE

The easiest way to make stress intermittent lies in something that you have to do every day anyway: breathing. When you're feeling stressed, take a couple of minutes to focus on your breathing. Close the door, put away all other distractions, and just sit in a chair and breathe. The goal is to spend the entire time focused only on your breathing, which will prevent your mind from wandering. Think about how it feels to breathe in and out. If staying focused on your breathing proves to be a real struggle, try counting each breath in and out until you get to 20, and then start again from 1. You will be surprised by how calm you feel afterward and how much easier it is to let go of distracting thoughts that otherwise seem to have lodged permanently inside your brain.

## 8 THEY REFRAME THEIR PERSPECTIVE

Stress and worry are fueled by our own skewed perception of events. You cannot control your circumstances, but you can control how you respond to them. So before you spend too much time dwelling on something, take a minute to put the situation in perspective. A great way to correct this unproductive thought pattern is to list the specific things that actually are going wrong or not working out. Most likely you will come up with just some things—not everything—and the scope of these stressors will look much more limited than it initially appeared.

## 10 THEY USE THEIR SUPPORT SYSTEM

It's tempting to attempt tackling everything by yourself. To be calm and productive, you need to recognize your weaknesses and ask for help when you need it. This means tapping into your support system when a situation is challenging enough for you to feel overwhelmed. Everyone has someone who is on their team, rooting for them, and ready to help make the most of a difficult situation. Identify these individuals in your life and make an effort to seek their insight and assistance when you need it. Asking for help will alleviate your stress and strengthen your relationships with those you rely upon.

- Experiencing moments of sudden terror or fright which can feel paralyzing
- Having frequent thoughts of bad things happening that are unwarranted or baseless
- Removing oneself from situations or engaging minimally due to worries/fears

Anxiety disorders are often treated with therapy (both individual and group), medication, mindfulness strategies, or a combination of these. Even though anxiety disorders are highly treatable, only about one-third of people suffering from an anxiety disorder receive treatment. If you think it is interfering with your daily living or you are not feeling like yourself, you probably would benefit from talking to a counselor.

## Depression

Many people experience the first symptoms of depression during their college years. Unfortunately, college students who have depression are not often getting the help they need. They may not know where to go for help, or they may believe that treatment won't help. Others don't get help because they think their symptoms are just part of the typical stress of college, or they worry about being judged if they seek mental health care. Depression is a medical illness and treatments can be very effective. Early diagnosis and treatment of depression can relieve depression symptoms, prevent depression from returning, and help students succeed in college and after graduation. The following section details symptoms of depression.

The symptoms of depression vary. If you are depressed, you may feel:

- Sad
- Empty
- Hopeless
- Worthless
- Restless
- Anxious
- Helpless
- Guilty
- Irritable
- Tired

You may also experience one or more of the following:

COUNSELING AND
PSYCHIATRY SERVICES
AT CAROLINA

**Counseling Services**

 803-777-5223

 Close-Hipp Building, 5th Floor

**Psychiatry Services**

 803-777-1833

 Thomson Student Health Center, 3rd Floor

- Loss of interest in activities you used to enjoy
- Aches, pains, headaches, cramps, or digestive problems that do not go away
- Lack of energy
- Loss of appetite or eating too much
- Problems concentrating, remembering information, or making decisions
- Problems falling sleep, staying asleep, or sleeping too much

The University of South Carolina's Student Health Services, specifically the Counseling & Psychiatry Services, offers mental health services to students. In 2013, the American College Health Association–National College Health Assessment (NCHA) of University of South Carolina students found 25% of students reported feeling "so depressed that it was difficult to function" at some time in the past year. As you can see, these symptoms can significantly impact your academics, social life, dating relationships, physical health, or daily functioning.

## Suicidal Ideation

Suicide is the third leading cause of death for young adults ages 15 to 24 (CDC, 2014). Each year, caring students recognize and respond to signs of mental health issues and suicide risk by connecting students in crisis with the appropriate resources. Being there for your friends and peers could help save a life. Therefore, it is important to know the signs of a suicidal person, the resources, and how to respond.

The warning signs of suicide include:

- Ideation: Threatening to hurt or talking of wanting to hurt or kill him/herself
- Increased alcohol or drug use
- Expressing no reason for living or no sense of purpose in life
- Anxiety, agitation, inability to sleep or sleeping all the time
- Feeling trapped like there is no way out
- Hopelessness, feelings of despair
- Withdrawal from family, friends, and society

- Uncontrolled rage and anger
- Acting reckless or engaging in risky activities
- Dramatic mood swings

If you observe any of these warning signs, you can help by:

- Being actively involved in getting the person connected with treatment, assisting him or her in making an appointment or walking with them to the appointment if needed
- Talking to your friend about your concerns. Be direct, but gentle and non-judgmental
- Asking if they are thinking about suicide
- Listening and being available
- Offering support and hope
- Taking action, such as informing housing staff, parents, police or a university official

If a student is talking about suicide or is at immediate risk for harming him or herself, call 911, University Law Enforcement & Safety at 803-777-4215, or CHDC at 803-777-5223. You can also inform your resident mentor, housing staff, and file a Behavioral Intervention Team report at www.sc.edu/bit. Stay with the person until help arrives. Never ignore comments about suicide or be sworn to secrecy.

# Financial Wellness

Finances can be overwhelming for students, particularly when you transition to college and managing your money becomes more of your responsibility. Increased pressure to find a job and cover college expenses can contribute to feeling overwhelmed and stressed regarding your finances. A 2012 study examined the top stressors college students face and found that four of the top five were all related to finances. In fact, some students were so stressed about finances it actually impacted their academic performance (Trombitas, 2012).

This feeling of stress might come from not understanding personal finance or believing there is little you can do to control your situation. However, there are many aspects of your personal finances that you can control, and much of it begins with gaining a basic understanding of your financial picture.

Knowing where to start is sometimes the hardest part. Below are the top five best practices first-year students should do to increase their financial wellness:

- Create and utilize a budget
- Consider ways to safely begin establishing consumer credit
- Understand how you are financing your education
- Consider the financial implications of academic decisions
- Find a trusted resource

**Create and utilize a budget.** Budgeting is one of the most important, yet basic, financial skills you can learn. Utilizing a budget allows you to plan for tuition, every day expenses, and even emergencies. The easiest place to start is by tracking and comparing your income and expenses. Income is everything you have coming in, including stipends, part-time work, financial aid overage checks, etc. Your expenses include everything you purchase or spend money on, regardless of how big or small. Keep in mind, there are different types of expenses based on their frequency and purpose. These include:

- **Monthly fixed** - expenses that do not change month to month, such as a car payment or rent for off-campus housing. These expenses are easy to plan for because they will be the same amount each month.
- **Monthly variable** - expenses you pay each month, but fluctuate in price. Examples of these types of expenses include groceries, utility bills (depending on the apartment complex), and gasoline. While still occurring each month, these expenses can be harder to plan for because they fluctuate in amount.
- **Period** - expenses that do not occur monthly, such as textbooks, tuition, or doctor visits. These are the hardest to plan for and often the most forgotten. Period expenses can be budget breakers because we tend to not plan for them, even though we know they are going to occur.

- **Discretionary** - expenses that are not necessary, such as eating out with friends and entertainment. Discretionary expenses are often defined as our "wants" rather than our "needs."

Tracking your income and expenses is the fastest way to learn where your money is going. Once you have identified your income and expenses, the next step is to evaluate your financial picture. Are you spending too much money on items without realizing it? Or do you have money leftover that you can start saving now for an emergency fund or loan repayment?

If you find you are concerned with your ability to make ends meet, you have two options: increase your income or decrease your expenses. Evaluate where you can cut back, and brainstorm creative ways to decrease expenses. For example, if you have a car, consider alternative ways to travel to work or around campus, which can save you money on gas and parking. You can also utilize a textbook rental service instead of purchasing, when possible. Student deals and discounts at restaurants, events in Columbia, and even local businesses can help you save money if you find you are spending too much on discretionary items.

Your other option is to increase your income. Could you take on a part-time job? Are there work-study opportunities available? Visit the Career Center to learn more about additional part-time work opportunities.

Tracking your income and expenses allows you to create a baseline from which you can build your budget. Budgeting is the process of planning or estimating your expenses based on your financial goals. When it comes to budgeting, there are a variety of tools and strategies you can use, and it is important to find one that works best for you. You can utilize a paper budget, such as the one found on page 233, or you can also take advantage of online budgeting tools such as Excel workbooks or any of the mobile apps available. There are also a variety of strategies you can use to guide how much of your income you should be spending on various types of expenses.

## STUDENT WORK OPPORTUNITIES.

Visit the Career Center website to find information on student work opportunities.

 sc.edu/career

## SCHOLARSHIPS

Visit the Student Financial Aid and Scholarships website to learn about scholarships and how you qualify.

 sc.edu/financialaid

One place to start is with the commonly used 50-20-30 rule. This strategy provides a guide for what percentage of your take-home pay should be allotted for your financial obligations, needs, and wants. Keeping track of multiple categories in a budget can be overwhelming, and this method helps to simplify the process.

The 50-20-30 rule is simple, and applies only to your take-home pay:

- 50% goes towards needs, such as housing, food, and utilities
- 20% goes towards your financial obligations, such as saving and debt repayment
- 30% goes towards lifestyle choices, such as hobbies, interests, and travel

Another benefit of this strategy is that it helps ensure you are identifying and meeting your financial priorities, such as housing and savings, while still retaining some funds for your hobbies and interests. While this is a great strategy for identifying your priorities and streamlining your budget, keep in mind the 50-20-30 rule is just a starting point, and might not necessarily be a realistic solution for your individual situation.

**Consider ways to safely begin establishing credit.** Using credit is the act of making purchases using money borrowed from a lender. Credit is considered to be a debt incurred anytime you use money now and repay that money later, with a common example being a credit card. To build credit means that you are demonstrating, over time, that you can responsibly borrow and repay money from lenders.

Demonstrating good consumer credit is important because it is necessary to make major purchases down the road, such as a car or home. Additionally, prospective employers and landlords may also look at your credit history to determine whether you are a responsible consumer. The level of responsibility indicated by your credit information can often be a determining factor for qualifying for future borrowing, as well as how much you are charged in interest when borrowing. Building and maintaining strong credit

## CREDIT SCORE VS. CREDIT REPORT

Two terms you may have heard before are credit score and credit report, and it is important to understand the difference between the two, as they are the two ways your credit is illustrated.

- A **credit report** is a detailed listing of your credit history. Among other things, it includes a summary of all the places from which you have borrowed money, such as credit cards and loans, as well as any outstanding payments you might have.
- A **credit score** is a numerical representation of your credit report, and ranges from 300-850.

can be a tricky process for those who do not realize how this type of debt works.

The safest and easiest way to build consumer credit is to consistently and responsibly use a small amount of it over a long period of time. This establishes a strong credit history that proves you are capable of borrowing and repaying money. One strategy for building consumer credit is using a credit card. However, opening a credit card can be risky if you are not prepared for the responsibility it requires. It is important you speak with someone and do your research prior to opening a line of credit, as credit card offers and policies can be confusing, causing you to make mistakes without realizing it. If you are considering a credit card, be sure to:

- Find a card that does not have fees associated with it (e.g., no annual fee).
- Look for a card that has a low APR (annual percentage rate). The APR is roughly how much interest you will be charged in the event you do not pay your bill in full, each month. Be sure to read the fine print, because many companies will advertise using *teaser rates*, low rates that typically only apply to the first six months or a year, and then drastically jump up to a much higher rate (e.g., a 0% introductory interest rate that jumps to 20% after a certain period of time).
- Make a few small purchases on your card that you know you can pay in full. Never charge more than what you can repay in full each month so that you can avoid interest and penalties. One strategy is to identify a monthly expense that is lower in amount and only charge that expense on your card. This strategy is effective because it is a recurring charge that you can plan for and one you know you can pay in full each month.

When it comes to credit, the most important thing is that it is used safely. Future lenders look at this financial history to determine whether or not you are eligible for credit, strong interest rates, or other types of financial plans. Unfortunately, damaging your credit can be done fairly quickly and sometimes unknowingly. However, the process of building (and rebuilding) credit is a much harder and time consuming

## HOW DOES INTEREST WORK?

Credit card interest is considered a type of compound interest, meaning the amount accrued in interest is added back to the original amount you owed. For example, let's say you own a credit card that has a 10% interest rate. If you spend $100 on that card but you only make the minimum payment, the next month you will owe $110, and the month after that you will owe $121. The interest is charged to the new total amount, which will increase each month because the initial payment was not made in full. This is why it is so important to only charge small amounts that you know you can pay in full each month.

## FINANCIAL LITERACY CONSULTATIONS

The Student Success Center staff will meet with you one-on-one to discuss a variety of important financial topics, including money management, building and managing credit, moving off-campus, and financial planning for study abroad. You can make an appointment by visiting the Student Success Center's website.

sc.edu/success/
appointments.html

process. Educating yourself now on what steps you can take to safely build and manage credit is important so that you are not limited down the road.

Strategies for building your credit are important, but understanding what can damage it is just as important. There are a variety of ways your credit can be damaged, so consider the following:

- Take precautions when signing up for credit offers used in advertisements. These offers are designed to be appealing but often carry penalties and high fees, included only in the fine print of the application. Additionally, do not sign up for credit cards simply to earn free goods.
- Do not sign up for multiple credit cards in an effort to quickly build consumer credit. Each time you sign up for a line of credit, it is called a "hard inquiry" and can slightly damage your credit. Additionally, the more lines of credit you have, the harder it is to successfully manage each one, which could cause you to accrue too much debt.
- Store credit cards (such as Gap or J. Crew) are the same as traditional credit cards, but often carry much higher interest rates. If you already possess these types of cards, it is best to speak with someone about the safest way to close the accounts without further damaging your credit. Avoid signing up for these cards, if you have not already, because the process and impact are the same as applying for any other type of credit card.
- Do not leave any bills unpaid. Unpaid bills, such as a phone or medical bill, get reported to collection agencies, who in turn report the delinquencies to credit agencies.

**Understand how you are financing your education.** Paying for college can be one of the biggest financial stressors for a student. Only 35% of South Carolina freshmen indicated they were confident in their ability to finance their college education, and 82% of first-year students indicated there was a good chance they would get a job to help pay for college expenses (CIRP, 2014). While there is a lot to consider when

## DIRECT SUBSIDIZED LOANS VERSUS DIRECT UNSUBSIDIZED LOANS

**Direct Subsidized Loans** are federal loans available for students who demonstrate a financial need. The amount you are eligible to borrow cannot exceed your individual need. Interest does accrue with these loans, but while you are in college it is subsidized (paid for) by the federal government, as long as you are enrolled at least part-time. The interest is also subsidized for the first six months after graduation and during a period of deferment. Once the grace or deferment period is over, you begin making payments on the loan.

Students are also eligible for **Direct Unsubsidized Loans**. However, the ability to qualify is not dependent on a student's financial need. Interest rates for these loans are not subsidized, so the borrower is responsible for the interest payments once the loan is disbursed. You do have the option of deferring the interest payment, but doing so causes the interest to then be added to the original amount of the loan, increasing your debt significantly.

# FINANCIAL AID AND SCHOLARSHIPS

The mission of the Office of Student Financial Aid and Scholarships (OSFAS) is to educate and assist students and their families in the application procedures necessary to secure the funding that they need and to provide leadership to the university in obtaining and administering federal, state, institutional and privately funded financial aid and scholarship resources for which they are eligible.

Estimate and understand your college-related costs each year. If it appears you will need additional finances, contact the OSFAS and investigate options for resolving any concern. The University's only application for financial aid is the Free Application for Federal Student Aid (FAFSA). It must be submitted each year and the priority application deadline is April 1st. Recognize that any loan that you accept will require repayment; never borrow more than you absolutely need.

It is essential that you watch for communications from OSFAS and understand any notifications you receive. Plan carefully; meet all deadlines, and be sure you understand the requirements for any loans or scholarships you are receiving or wish to receive.

If you are a scholarship recipient, there is generally a grade point average needed to renew your award; usually, the required GPA is a 3.0.

If you are receiving financial aid, you must achieve a level of Satisfactory Academic Progress (SAP) in order to maintain eligibility.

 (803) 777-8134

 sc.edu/financialaid

 **1714 College Street**
8:30am-5:00pm
Office closed to the public 12:30-5:00 Wednesday afternoons; phone and email contact remain available

financing your education, there are steps you can take now to help ensure you are:

- Do your research and determine which college expenses are required, and which ones are not.
- Only borrow what you need. Every dollar you borrow is a dollar you will have to repay, plus interest. Keep your borrowing consistent with your needs so that you do not end up owing more than necessary upon graduation.
- Save extra earnings for loan repayment. Saving now can be hard, especially if you are trying to make ends meet with your other expenses. However, saving should be a priority, and every little bit helps. Get into the habit of saving early and contribute more when you are able.
- Look for university/departmental scholarships that focus on programs of study, interests, and hobbies. Determine if there are other ways to keep costs down throughout college.
- Do what it takes to maintain your scholarships during college so that tuition payments do not become unexpected expenses. If you lose a scholarship because of poor academic performance, that is a large additional expense that you might not be prepared to cover.

It is important to devote time to understanding your loans and scholarships, as well as what it will take to maintain them throughout your time in college.

**Consider the financial implications of your academic decisions.** Decisions you make can impact you in a variety of ways, including financially. Have you ever considered that dropping a class could have a financial impact? Dropping too many credits can impact your Satisfactory Academic Progress (SAP), and therefore your eligibility for loans and scholarships. If you become ineligible for loans and scholarships that cover your tuition, you will find yourself in a situation where you have to determine alternative ways to finance your education.

**Find a trusted resource.** Keep in mind, many of these suggestions are simply general rules of thumb. It is important

# College Budget

| Income | Current | |
|---|---|---|
| Job Earnings #1 | | |
| Job Earnings #2 | | |
| Financial Aid | | |
| Allowance | | |
| Gifts | | |
| Tax Refunds | | |
| Interest | | |
| Total Income | | |

| Variable Expenses | Current | Projected |
|---|---|---|
| Food | | |
| Electricity | | |
| Gas | | |
| Phone Bill | | |
| Other | | |
| Total Variable Expenses | | |

| Fixed Expenses | Current | Projected |
|---|---|---|
| Rent | | |
| Car Payment | | |
| Internet/Cable Bill | | |
| Tuition | | |
| Misc. (Parking Pass, Organization Dues) | | |
| Other | | |
| Total Fixed Expenses | | |

| Periodic Expenses | Current | Projected |
|---|---|---|
| Doctor visits | | |
| Car Repairs | | |
| Textbooks | | |
| Personal Care | | |
| Other | | |
| Total Periodic Expenses | | |

| Discretionary Expenses | Current | Projected |
|---|---|---|
| Social (meals out, movies) | | |
| Shopping (clothes, electronics) | | |
| Gifts | | |
| Charity | | |
| Travel | | |
| Misc. | | |
| Total Discretionary Expenses | | |

| | | |
|---|---|---|
| Total Income | | |
| Total Expenses | | |

*Source*: Catherine Greene, 2016

to seek individual advice from a trusted mentor or resource. Everyone's financial situation is different, and taking the time to understand your specific situation is crucial. Start by locating resources that focus on money management and strategies for budgeting and managing your credit. Find a trusted mentor, whether it is a family member, friend, or someone on campus, who you can talk to when you have questions or concerns related to personal finances. The Student Success Center also offers Financial Literacy Consultations for students enrolled at the University.

Always remember, there is a difference between financial education and advice. Anytime you are ready to make a decision that could impact your finances, it is important to talk with someone who is trained and able to give you the appropriate information you will need to make a smart decision.

Educating yourself now might help prevent you from making mistakes that will prevent you from achieving goals you set for yourself. Decisions you make can also have a lasting impact on you and your ability to achieve your financial goals, so it is important to be sure you begin educating yourself sooner rather than later.

## Alcohol Use and Other Drugs

USC cares deeply for its students and wants to provide a safe environment to support students on their journey towards personal and academic success. In the past, our campus has experienced drug and alcohol related tragedies that have negatively impacted our close-knit community. While such unfortunate events can never be completely eliminated, it is important to practice responsible behaviors and intervene on behalf of others when necessary. You are beginning to make friends and establish new relationships on a college campus. We want you to be equipped with information to help you make the best decisions for a safe and responsible social environment. Beyond the apparent personal safety reasons, there are many positive reasons to engage in responsible behaviors, including those that relate to your academic success.

The Carolina campus takes these misbehaviors very seriously. The Office of Student Conduct and Academic Integrity manages the reported misbehaviors and it's important to know there are significant policies and procedures in place that our campus supports and follows. Students can be charged for alcohol and drug offenses if found responsible, and the outcome can be costly (see image on p. 238).

## Blood Alcohol Content

Different types of alcoholic beverages have varying amounts of alcohol, and many exotic or mixed drinks (e.g., Long Island Iced Tea, punch, fishbowls) can contain more than the standard drink alcohol levels. Being aware of the amount and type of alcohol you are drinking will dramatically increase your ability to make healthy and safe decisions about alcohol.

The following factors directly impact an individual's blood alcohol content (BAC) and the rate of intoxication:

*Number of drinks consumed*—Your body can only metabolize one standard drink per hour so the speed at which you drink directly impacts your level of intoxication. Instead of participating in drinking games, alternate each alcoholic drink with a nonalcoholic, non-caffeinated drink, such as water or a sports drink.

*The speed at which you drink and the time spent drinking*—Your body metabolizes alcohol more effectively when consumption is spaced over longer periods of time.

*Your body weight*—The more an individual weighs the more water they have within their system to dilute the alcohol.

*Your body composition*—Men and women have different body compositions and, therefore, metabolize alcohol differently. Women are more likely to have higher BAC levels than men after drinking the same quantity of alcohol.

*Eating before drinking*—Consuming a full or heavy meal (bread, protein) before drinking will slow down the rate of alcohol absorption in your system.

## STAND-UP CAROLINA SUGGESTS THE FOLLOWING GUIDELINES

- Take a buddy with you every-where when you go out, especially after-hours.
- If you get separated from your friends, make a pact beforehand that everyone will communicate with friends once back home safely. Expect follow-up if not heard from (and vice-versa).
- If you see something out of the ordi-nary, alert someone of authority. Also, don't forget to use the campus call boxes that are strategically located around our campus. It's hard to travel very far without seeing one. Remember the slogan, "if you see something, do something."

Retrieved from: https://www.sa.sc.edu/shs/savip/stand-up/

*Types of drinks consumed*—Alcoholic drinks that contain carbonation cause an individual to become intoxicated more rapidly.

As a student at the University of South Carolina you are a member of a larger family often referred to as the Carolina or Gamecock Community. As a member of this community you are expected to follow the guidelines set forth by the *Carolinian Creed*. If you suspect that someone is suffering from the consumption of too much alcohol, it is important to get this student help as quickly as possible. An intoxicated person should never be left alone! For anyone exhibiting signs of alcohol poisoning, seek medical attention immediately by dialing 911. The acronym "CUSP" is a memorable way to identify symptoms of those experiencing alcohol poisoning:

**C**old, clammy, pale, or bluish skin
**U**nconscious or unable to be roused
**S**low or irregular breathing
**P**uking repeatedly or uncontrollably

If someone has passed out from too much drinking, try to keep the individual sitting up (back against a wall). If the person must lie down, keep the individual on his or her side with the head turned to the side (fetal position, if possible). Prevent the person from rolling onto his or her back, and watch for choking. The number one reason an intoxicated person dies is because they aspirate or choke on their own vomit.

If you live on campus in a residence hall, you will want to inform your resident mentor (RM) or any other on-duty University Housing staff if someone has been drinking too much. When unhealthy decisions are made about alcohol, it is important that help is received as quickly as possible. As a member of the Carolina community, taking care of each other is a top priority.

If you do choose to drink alcohol, we want you to be equipped with commonsense tips to help you be as safe as possible.

- Eat a meal before going out. The meal will help absorb the alcohol so you are less likely to feel the effects.
- Take your cell phone with you wherever you go and be sure to program the USC police department into your phone: 803-777-4215.
- Know what you are drinking: make or order your own drinks, and be sure to always monitor your drinks so no one else is ever in control of its contents.
- Be sure to drink plenty of fluids that do not have alcohol. A good rule of thumb is to always take time to consume water between alcoholic beverages.
- Do not mix alcohol and other drugs. Otherwise, the effects are compounded and likely unexpected, thus placing you in an unsafe situation.
- Always have a plan for the evening. Know where you are going and who will be driving you to these locations. A designated driver is an absolute must; know that alternate transportation options are available in case your original plan has to change.
- Remember, USC sponsors late night transportation through the Five Points shuttle service and Carolina Cab.
- Lastly, know your limits. When you are not in control of yourself or the situation, then you are placing yourself in a dangerous setting.

Beyond caring for yourself, there are additional steps that should be taken to prevent negative consequences from occurring to you or your community. It's important we look to each other to help build a safe environment. During orientation or another early campus experience, you likely heard about the "Stand-Up Carolina" initiative. As a reminder, the campus community encourages its members to be active bystanders. Please see chapter X about the Carolinian Creed that addresses bystander accountability.

## STANDARD DRINK SIZES

BEER     12 OZ.

WINE     5 OZ.

LIQUOR     1 OZ.

## KNOW
--WHAT'S IN--
YOUR CUP

## A STANDARD DRINK IS:

ONE 12-OUNCE BEER

ONE 5-OUNCE GLASS OF WINE

1 ½ OUNCE OF 80 PROOF LIQUOR (CONSIDERED 40% ALCOHOL BY VOLUME)

1 OUNCE OF 100-PROOF LIQUOR (CONSIDERED 50% ALCOHOL BY VOLUME)

# HOPE THAT BEER WAS TASTY...

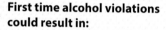

## GETTING A TICKET FROM LAW ENFORCEMENT

**Purchase, consumption, or possession of alcohol under 21 could result in:**

- Fines exceeding **$400**
- Driver's license suspension
- Possible loss of scholarship

**Total cost of a diversion program:**

- Alcohol Education Program (AEP): **$400**
- Pre-Trial Intervention (PTI): **$400**
- Upon completion the courts will expunge the record, which is worth it to save your future career.

**Driving under the influence could result in:**

- 3 months jail time
- Fines exceeding **$2,000**
- Permanent criminal record
- Suspension of driver's license
- Alcohol education program

## CONSEQUENCES FROM USC STUDENT CONDUCT

**First time alcohol violations could result in:**

- **$400** fine
- Alcohol education class

**Additional violations could result in:**

- **$350** fine
- Substance education counseling
- Suspension (for 3rd offenses)

**When will my parents find out?**

- Student Conduct will call your parents during your meeting with a conduct administrator if you are under 21.

# IT'S A COSTLY DECISION.

## Adderall and Non-Prescription Drugs

For some students, the need for prescription drugs, such as Adderall, is necessary to address diagnosed health conditions. However, the prevalence of nonmedical use of drugs on college campuses is growing (NCHA, 2015). A common perception of prescription stimulants is the support they provide to help individuals focus on required tasks, such as studying or writing. However, there are additional characteristics or behaviors that have emerged in association with the use of non-prescription drugs, including excessive drinking and use of other drugs, skipping classes, and lower GPAs (Arria, O'Grady, Caldeira, Vincent, and Wish, 2008). Despite assumptions that use of non-prescription drugs can be relatively safe, the health risks are great. Students who are prescribed these drugs yet provide these substances to others, as well as students receiving and using these drugs without a prescription, are subject to disciplinary actions.

## Tobacco-Free

USC Columbia is a completely tobacco free campus. All forms of tobacco use are prohibited on all USC leased, owned and controlled property and in vehicles parked on USC property. Since the start of the Tobacco-free initiative, the number of documented smoking incidents has decreased significantly. Beyond the aesthetics of our campus environment, the stoppage of smoking has promoted important positive effects on individual and collective health. For example, smoking can be linked to other behaviors, including drinking alcohol and using other drugs. It can be difficult to stop smoking, so USC offers many options to support students, faculty, and staff in their efforts to quit smoking. Be sure to check out Carolina's Tobacco Treatment Program and Tobacco Cessation Coaching Programs offered through Student Health Services.

# TOBACCO FREE USC

A Healthy Campus to Live, Learn, Work and Play

To learn more about Tobacco Free USC, visit the following website:

 **sa.sc.edu/healthycarolina/ initiatives/tobacco**

# Sexual Health

There is a misperception among college students that your peers are having frequent sex with numerous sexual partners. In fact, the most recent results show 74% of students had one or zero sexual partners in the last academic year (ACHA, 2015). Abstinence is the best way to protect yourself from unexpected pregnancies or sexually transmitted infections (STI's). In addition, we want you to be aware of additional options that are available to you if you choose to engage in sexual activity. The Types of Contraception chart on page 241 describes the types of contraception methods available, including important details about effectiveness and methods to access.

## Sexually Transmitted Infections (STI)

STIs are infections transmitted through sexual contact. A person with an STI can potentially infect others without showing signs of disease or infection. Many signs and symptoms of STIs are mild and can be easily overlooked, so testing is crucial. Even though many students take all the necessary precautions to practice safer sex, things can still go wrong. Having a basic understanding of the most common sexually transmitted infections and diseases and their corresponding symptoms can alert you to problems at an early stage. This may help you avoid complications that could arise from treatment delays.

## Communicating With Your Partner

If you are currently sexually active or plan to become sexually active in the future, the most important part of a sexual relationship is open communication with your partner. Healthy sexual relationships include trust as well as an ability to express your needs and wants to others. Prior to becoming sexually involved with a new partner, it is important to have an open and honest conversation regarding past sexual partners and sexually transmitted infections. Definitions of common sexual terms (abstinence, intercourse, foreplay, STIs) may differ from person to person; therefore, open communication is essential. On the next page, you will find helpful tips for communicating with your partner about sex.

# TYPES OF CONTRACEPTION

| METHOD | DOES IT PROVIDE PROTECTION AGAINST STI/HIV? | DO I NEED A PRESCRIPTION | EFFECTIVENESS (BASED ON CORRECT AND CONSISTENT USAGE) |
|---|---|---|---|
| Abstinence | Yes | No | 100% |
| Cervical Cap | No | Yes | 86% effective for women who have never been pregnant |
| | | | 71% effective for women who have given birth vaginally |
| Contraceptive Injection (Shot) | No | Yes | 99% |
| Diaphragm | No | Yes | 94% |
| Female Condom | Yes | No | 95% |
| Implant | No | Yes | 99% |
| IUD (intrauterine device) | No | Yes | 99% |
| Male Condom | Yes | No | 98% |
| Vaginal Ring | No | Yes | 99% |
| Patch | No | Yes | 99% |
| Oral Contraceptive (the pill) | No | Yes | 99% |
| Spermicide | No | No | 85% |

*Source*: Planned Parenthood.

# TIPS FOR COMMUNICATING WITH YOUR PARTNER ABOUT SEX

- To reach mutual understanding and agreement on sexual health issues, choose a convenient time when you will both be free of distractions.

- Do not use alcohol/drugs to reduce your inhibitions.

- Use "I" statements when talking. For example, "I feel that abstinence is right for me at this time." Or, "I would feel more comfortable if we used a condom."

- Be assertive! Do not let fear of how your partner might react stop you from talking with him/her.

- Be a good listener. Let your partner know that you hear, understand, and care about what she/he is saying and feeling.

- Understand that success in talking does not mean one person getting the other person to do something. It means that you both have said what you think and feel, respectfully and honestly, and that you have both listened respectfully to each other.

- Be patient with your partner, and remain firm in your decision that talking is important.

- Avoid making assumptions. Ask open-ended questions to discuss relationship expectations, past and present sexual relationships, contraceptive use, and testing for STIs, including HIV, among other issues.

- Avoid judging, labeling, blaming, threatening, or bribing your partner. Don't let your partner judge, label, blame, threaten, or bribe you.

- Do not wait until you become sexually intimate to discuss safer sex with your partner. In the heat of the moment, you and your partner may be unable to talk effectively.

- Stick by your decision. Don't be swayed by lines like, "If you loved me, you would have sex with me." Or, "If you loved me, you would trust me and not use a condom."

The two most common concerns students have when engaging in a sexual relationship are pregnancy and sexually transmitted infections. Abstinence and condoms are the only two methods of contraception that protect against both pregnancy and STIs. Also, using both a hormonal and barrier method is recommended. The chart on the preceding page provides an illustration of the numerous types of contraception available.

# Health Care

As an enrolled student, you are provided affordable, convenient access to primary healthcare through Student Health Services. This campus service supports student success by offering primary care, wellness education, mental health counseling, and sexual assault violence prevention services to the Gamecock community. Most services are covered by the student health fee included in tuition.

The student health fee pays for:

- Healthcare provider visits at the Thomson Student Health Center's General Medicine Center and Women's Care
- Access to wellness care and education, including nutrition consults, stress management services, and exercise consultations
- Ten one-on-one annual individual visits with trained psychologists, family/marriage therapists, and social workers at the Counseling & Psychiatry Center
- Urgent care response to campus medical emergencies through our EMT First Responders program
- Access to 24/7 sexual assault advocates

You have access to board-certified physicians with a wide range of specialties (e.g., internal medicine, emergency medicine, family medicine, pediatrics, obstetrics and gynecology, psychiatry), nurse practitioners, registered nurses, and other health professionals. Additional fees apply if you need lab work, x-rays, psychiatric services, physical therapy, sports medicine or pharmaceutical products at the health center.

# Conclusion

This chapter focused on the importance of establishing personal wellness habits and suggested methods for engaging in associated healthy behaviors. By concentrating on overcoming the identified challenging aspects of wellness experienced during the early stages of college, you will be well situated to develop a stronger disposition supporting holistic health across your lifespan.

Each dimension of wellbeing contributes to your own sense of wellness or quality of life, and each affects and overlaps the others. At times one may be more prominent than others, but neglect of any one dimension for any length of time has adverse effects on overall health. Utilize the many resources at Carolina to start your pursuit of a balanced life. As a Gamecock, we are all in this together.

# WELLNESS WHEEL INVENTORY

| Read each statement below and check the box that most accurately describes you at this point in your life. | Seldom or never 1 | Sometimes 2 | Usually or often 3 | Always 4 | Totals |
|---|---|---|---|---|---|
| I engage in physical activity at least three times per week. | | | | | |
| I eat a healthy, well balanced diet. | | | | | |
| I avoid tobacco, drugs, and excessive alcohol consumption. | | | | | |
| I seek appropriate medical care when necessary. | | | | | |
| I eat five servings of fresh fruits and vegetables each day. | | | | | |
| I avoid eating foods high in simple sugars, salts, and fat. | | | | | |
| **Physical Wellness Total** | + | + | + | = | |
| I have healthy, supportive friendships and family relationships. | | | | | |
| I communicate effectively with friends, family, and coworkers. | | | | | |
| When I have a conflict with another person, I try to resolve it in an honest, assertive manner. | | | | | |
| I respect lifestyles and cultures different than my own. | | | | | |
| It is important to me to contribute to the well-being of others in my family and social network. | | | | | |
| I can say No to someone without feeling guilty. | | | | | |
| **Social Wellness Total** | + | + | + | = | |
| I am aware of a wide range of feelings in myself. | | | | | |
| I recognize my personal limitations and accept help when necessary. | | | | | |
| I have the skills to cope with daily challenges and stressors. | | | | | |
| I feel positive about myself and my life. | | | | | |
| I am autonomous but able to create meaningful and satisfying relationships with others. | | | | | |
| I avoid people who are "down" all the time and who bring those around them down. | | | | | |
| **Emotional Wellness Total** | + | + | + | = | |
| I challenge myself mentally with stimulating ideas and activities on a regular basis. | | | | | |
| I am able to solve problems and think independently. | | | | | |
| I have the opportunity to learn new concepts in my personal or professional life. | | | | | |
| I pursue interests that are important to me. | | | | | |
| I enjoy spending time learning new things. | | | | | |
| I take time to read for enjoyment and relaxation. | | | | | |
| **Intellectual Wellness Total** | + | + | + | = | |
| My actions align with my personal values and beliefs. | | | | | |
| I feel a sense of inner peace and strength. | | | | | |
| I feel my life has purpose and meaning. | | | | | |
| I have faith in something greater than myself. | | | | | |
| I look for and work towards balance. | | | | | |
| Morals, ethics, and principles guide my actions. | | | | | |
| **Spiritual Wellness Total** | + | + | + | = | |
| I am satisfied with my work (e.g., volunteer, part-time). | | | | | |
| I am satisfied with my current major. | | | | | |
| I am comfortable with my current professional goals. | | | | | |
| I am able to contribute unique talents and skills to my work. | | | | | |
| My major and studies align with my needs and strengths. | | | | | |
| I feel comfortable making short- and long-term goals. | | | | | |
| **Occupational Wellness Total** | + | + | + | = | |
| I try and reduce the amount of pollution I generate. | | | | | |
| I regularly reuse containers, bags and batteries when possible. | | | | | |
| I recycle paper, glass, aluminum and plastic. | | | | | |
| If I see a safety hazard, I take the steps to fix the problem. | | | | | |
| I am aware of my surroundings at all times. | | | | | |
| I am involved in socially responsible activities to protect the environment. | | | | | |
| **Environmental Wellness Total** | + | + | + | = | |

# PERSONAL WELLNESS WHEEL

After you have completed your inventory, take a moment to color in your wheel. Use your score from each Wellness Total to shade in the corresponding portion of your Personal Wellness Wheel.

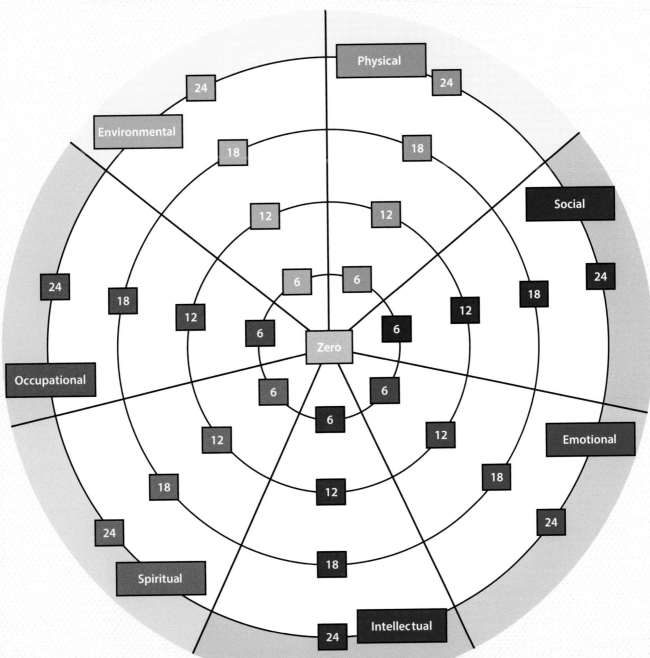

# STUDENT HEALTH SERVICES

Student Health Services provides a patient-centered, holistic approach to health care. Students can access general medical care, women's care, sports medicine, physical therapy, counseling and psychiatric services, radiology and laboratory services, a pharmacy, wellness services, and sexual assault and violence intervention and prevention programs. Students can make appointments (www.sc.edu/myhealthspace), fill prescriptions (www.sc.edu/myrxspace or download the PocketRx app) and contact a victim's advocate 24 hours a day, 7 days a week. Visit our website www.sa.sc.edu/shs for more information about our events, programs and services.

## MEDICAL SERVICES

General medicine provides primary and urgent health care and is staffed by board-certified physicians and licensed nurse practitioners. Women's care is staffed by board-certified gynecologists and licensed women's health nurse practitioners. Our Sports Medicine physician is board-certified in sports medicine and family medicine. You must have a referral to meet with our licensed physical therapist.

When you visit general medicine, students will be assigned to a primary care physician, who will be part of a care team as part of the Patient Centered Medical Home Model. The care teams work as a single unit to implement and develop treatment plans and seek to combine the medical providers' skills with counselors, case managers, social workers, nutritionists, pharmacists, wellness professionals, advocates and other Student Health Services support staff. The goal of the care teams is to promote health, prevent disease and enhance student success.

## ANCILLARY SERVICES

Coinciding with our medical services, we also provide ancillary services, including a laboratory, radiology department, allergy, immunization and travel services and a pharmacy. We also offer our First Responders program, which is an urgent care response unit of nationally-registered EMTs available 24/7 during the fall and spring semesters and 7 a.m. – midnight during summer and breaks.

## MENTAL HEALTH SERVICES

Counseling & Psychiatry's counseling services provide you a safe place to speak privately and confidentially with a trained counselor about a variety of concerns. Psychiatric services include board-certified psychiatrists who provide emotional support through psychotherapy, medication management and referrals.

## PREVENTION, WELLNESS AND ADVOCACY SERVICES

Campus Wellness offers convenient and accessible programs and services that support and encourage striving for optimal health by incorporating healthy behaviors into daily living; programs include nutritional consultations, exercise consultations and sexual health consultations. The Sexual Assault and Violence Intervention & Prevention office presents on and encourages discussion about interpersonal violence and being accountable bystanders. The SAVIP office also accompanies students for support (if desired by the individual) for those who have experienced sexual assault, domestic and dating violence, stalking, harassment or a hate crime.

 803-777-3175

 sa.sc.edu/shs

 **The Thomson Student Health Center is located between the Russell House University Union and the Bull Street Garage**

## REFLECTION QUESTIONS

1. This chapter begins by identifying the seven dimensions of wellness. Which of these are the lowest priority for you? Alternately, which dimensions are the highest priority? Why?

2. Have you found yourself staying up later or feeling more tired since you arrived at USC? If so, which of the suggestions offered in this chapter would be most helpful in addressing this?

3. The chapter introduces and explains concepts such as anxiety, depression, and suicidal ideation. At what point would you seek help for yourself or a friend if you observed the warning signs that were listed for each of these?

4. A portion of this chapter focuses on how to build a strong credit score. What are some reasons that credit is so important to establish while you are in college?

5. What is the biggest money drain that you have experienced since coming to college? What could you do to prevent this?

6. What are the top two stressors in your life right now? How can you take steps to reduce your stress?

7. What is one thing from this chapter you can do moving forward to make your well-being more of a priority in college? In what ways would this contribute to your overall success in college?

## REFERENCES

American College Health Association-National College Health Assessment (ACHA-NCHA). (2007). *Data highlights*. Retrieved from http://www.acha-ncha.org/data_highlights.html.

American College Health Association-National College Health Assessment (ACHA-NCHA). (2015). Undergraduate students reference group data report. Retrieved from http://www.acha-ncha.org/docs/NCHA-II_WEB_SPRING_2015_REFERENCE_GROUP_EXECUTIVE_SUMMARY.pdf

Arria, A. M., O'Grady, K. E., Caldeira, K. M., Vincent, K. B., & Wish, E. D. (2008). Nonmedical use of prescription stimulants and analgesics: Associations with social and academic behaviors among college students. *Journal of Drug Issues, 38*(4), 1045-1080.

Hoffman, D. J., Policastro, P., Quick, V., Lee, S. (2006). Changes in body weight and fat mass of men and women in the first year of college: A study of the "Freshman 15". *Journal of American College Health, 55*(1), 41-45.

Lund, H. G., Reider, B. D., Whiting, A. B., & Prichard, J. R. (2010) Sleep patterns and predictors of disturbed sleep in a large population of college students. *Journal of Adolescent Health, 46*(1), 124-132.

McGowan, J., Gardner, G., & Fletcher, R. (2006). Positive and negative affective outcomes of occupational stress. *New Zealand Journal of Psychology, 35*, 92-98.

Mihalopoulos, N. L., Auinger, P., Klien, J.D. (2008). The freshman 15: Is it real? *Journal of American College Health. 56*(5). 531-534.

Ming, X., Koransky, R., Kang, V., Buchman, S., Sarris, C., & Wagner, G. C. (2011). Sleep insufficiency, sleep health problems and performance in high school students. *Clinical Medicine Insights: Circulatory, Respiratory and Pulmonary Medicine, 5*, 71-79.

National Sleep Foundation. (2015). National Sleep Foundation's updated sleep duration recommendations: Final report. *Journal of the National Sleep Foundation, 1*(4), 233-243.

Ruthig, J.C., Marrone, S., Hladkyj, S., & Robinson-Epp, N. (2011). Changes in college student health: Implications for academic performance. *Journal of College Student Development, 52*(3), 307-318.

Taylor, D. J., Vatthauer, K. E., Bramoweth, A. D., Ruggero, C., & Roane, B. (2013). The role of sleep in predicting college academic performance: is it a unique predictor? *Behavioral Sleep Medicine, 11*(3), 159-172. Doi: 10.1080/15402002.2011.602776

Trockel, M.T., Barnes, M.C., & Egget, D.L. (2000). Health-related variables and academic performance among first-year college students: Implications for sleep and other behaviors. *Journal of American College Health, 49*, 125-131.

# RESOURCES

## General Wellness Resources on Campus
**Student Health Services**

Thomson Student Health Center
http://www.sa.sc.edu/shs
Emergencies ...............................911
General Medicine Center/Laboratory/
Radiology ........................ (803) 777-3175
Women's Care ................... (803) 777-6816
Pharmacy ....................... (803) 777-4890
Immunizations/Travel Clinic/Allergy
Clinic............................ (803) 777-9511

## Alcohol & Drugs
**Substance Abuse Prevention &**
**Education** ...................... (803) 777-3933
Strom Thurmond Wellness &
Fitness Center, 3rd Floor
http://www.sa.sc.edu/sape
**Tobacco Cessation** ................... (803) 777-6518
https://www.sa.sc.edu/shs/cw/tobacco/
**Tobacco Free USC**
https://www.sa.sc.edu/healthycarolina/
initiatives/tobacco/

## Campus Wellness
.................................. (803) 576-9393
Strom Thurmond Wellness &
Fitness Center,1st floor
https://www.sa.sc.edu/shs/cw/

## Counseling and Psychiatry
**Counseling Services** ................ (803) 777-5223
Close-Hipp Building, 5th Floor
https://www.sa.sc.edu/shs/cp/
**Psychiatry Services** .................. (803) 777-1833
Thomson Student Health Center, 3rd Floor
https://www.sa.sc.edu/shs/cp/

## Financial Literacy
**Student Success Center** ............. (803) 777-0684
Thomas Cooper Library-- Mezzanine Level
http://www.sa.sc.edu/ssc/

## Healthy Carolina
**Healthy Carolina** .................... (803) 777-4752
http://www.sc.edu/healthycarolina

## Hospitals
**Palmetto Baptist Medical Center** .... (803) 296-5010
**Palmetto Health Richland Hospital** .. (803) 434-6350

## Physical Fitness & Nutrition
**Carolina Dining** ...................... (803) 777-6339
https://uofsc.sodexomyway.com/
**Outdoor Recreation**.................. (803) 576-9397
http://campusrec.sc.edu/orec
**Registered Dietitian** ................. (803) 777-3175
Thomson Student Health Center
**Solomon Blatt Physical Education**
**Center** ........................... (803) 576-9375
https://campusrec.sc.edu/
solomon-blatt-physical-education-center/
**Strom Thurmond Wellness & Fitness**
**Center** ........................... (803) 576-9376
https://campusrec.sc.edu/
strom-thurmond-wellness-and-fitness-center/
**USDA Choose My Plate**
http://ChooseMyPlate.gov

## Sexual Assault & Violence Intervention Prevention
**Sexual Assault & Violence Intervention**
**Prevention** ...................... (803) 777-8248
Thomson Student Health Center
http://www.sa.sc.edu/shs/shvp/
**USC Police Department** .............. (803) 777-4215
1415 Henderson Street
http://les.sc.edu/
**American Social Health Association** . (919) 361-8400
**STI Resource Center Hotline** ......... (800) 227-8922
www.ashastd.org
**Planned Parenthood**................. (800) 230-7526
2712 Middleburg Drive, Suite 107 . (803) 256-4908
Columbia, SC 29204
http://www.plannedparenthood.org
**Sexual Trauma Services of the Midlands**
**Hotline** .......................... (803) 771-7273
http://www.stsm.org/

## Stress Reduction
**Massage Therapy Appointments** .... (803) 576-9393
**Biofeedback Appointments** ......... (803) 777-5223

# CHAPTER 11

# Employability

# UNIVERSITY OF
# SOUTH CAROLINA

*Dear First-Year Student,*

During your time here at USC you will be challenged academically, socially, intellectually and you will have the opportunity to chart your career path. Know that the resources are all here for you to thrive. This chapter provides information to help you begin the process of developing your career plan and to increase your employability.

The key to career planning is recognizing that it is never too early to start. The process can seem daunting but when taken on early and with assistance, it is attainable. Conducting exploration activities, confirming choices, and gaining experience have made securing employment and acceptance to graduate and professional school the norm for our graduates.

In this chapter you will learn about the importance of not only career planning but also of developing relationships, gaining experience, putting your academic subject to work, acquiring transferable skills, and developing emotional intelligence. The Career Center employability model will help you better understand what employability is and how you will achieve your career goals.

Know that as a student at Carolina, you have a career coach at the Career Center ready to provide assistance. Career Center career coaches are trained to guide you through the process of making a career decision, help you stay focused and motivated, and help you overcome obstacles you will naturally face. Additionally, your career coach can help you develop a Four Year Student Plan, explore career options using a career assessment, assist you in finding a job shadowing or externship opportunity to learn about the world of work, and answer all your questions about career exploration. Remember that the Career Center helps all students in all majors, regardless of career goals and regardless of the level of career focus. We are here for students who don't know what they want to do, as well as for those who already know their goals. To ensure you are successful, take advantage of the resources of the Career Center early and often!

Take advantage of the outstanding faculty and staff who want to help you. Learn about our excellent alumni because they are always willing to help. Don't forget that friends and family members can also be excellent resources in achieving your career goals! I look forward to hearing your success story.

Best wishes,

*Thomas J. Halasz*

Tom Halasz
Director, Career Center

# Engaging in Career Planning... It's Never Too Early to Start

As you approach this chapter, you may say to yourself, *"Career planning? Why is there a chapter about career planning in here? I'm just a first- year student. I don't need to start thinking about that yet."* On the contrary, early career planning has never been more important and complex than it is in today's job market and is crucial in maximizing your college experience.

# Understanding the Current Landscape

The Great Recession of 2008 had a significant impact on the job market. In 2008 and 2009 the U.S. labor market lost 8.4 million jobs, increasing the overall unemployment rate from roughly 5% to 10%. This was the most dramatic employment contraction (by far) of any recession since the Great Depression of the 1930s (Economic Policy Institute, 2014).

When looking at age groups during and following the recession, the unemployment rate was highest among workers aged 25-34, not only because there were fewer jobs available, but also because many of those expected to retire in the early 2010s held on to their jobs and did not free up opportunities for others to enter the market.

Even five years after the recession officially ended, a study in September of 2014 showed that only about a dozen states had unemployment rates better than before the recession started (National Public Radio, 2014).

According to data from the U.S. Census Bureau and U.S. Bureau of Labor Statistics, 44% of recent college graduates aged 22-27 were unemployed or under-employed (Abel, Deitz, & Su, 2014). Underemployment could mean being employed in less than a full-time position or having a position in which the employee has education, experience, or skills beyond the requirements of the job. Needless to say,

the recession has made for an extremely difficult job market over the past half decade.

**The good news is that the market IS rebounding!** Unemployment rates continue to improve, new jobs are being created, and opportunities for younger generations will grow as those in the baby boomer generation begin to retire and others move up to replace them.

Those entering the labor market in the next decade will be greeted with both great challenges and tremendous opportunity. While the number of opportunities is increasing, the *nature* of those opportunities is also changing. Rapid technological advancements and access to an ever-expanding wealth of information has drastically altered both the way work is performed today and the skills that workers need to possess.

In many cases the "entry level" position of today is equivalent to a position that was once held by someone who already had 3-5 years of professional work experience. Candidates will need to be further prepared to enter the workforce – even more than the college graduates of the past.

Understanding the labor market and what it takes to be employable (work-place ready) is important to student success. This will be covered in greater detail throughout this chapter.

## Getting a Better Job

More than 86% of incoming freshmen in a 2014 nation-wide survey ranked "to be able to get a better job" as a very important reason they decided to go to college (Eagan et al., 2014). In fact, they ranked this higher than all other reasons, including "to gain a general education and appreciation of ideas" and "to be able to make more money."

But herein lies the challenge. Simply *attending* college itself does not guarantee a better job. Granted, college graduates fare much better than those who did not attend college in terms of employment and earnings, but students who believe that "just showing up" to college is enough, will all-too-soon learn that the degree alone is not sufficient and that intense competition still exists among the college educated.

Positioning yourself for success in the workforce is a complex process involving a number of components and it requires forethought and intentionality. In other words, if you want to be able to get a better job, you will need to know the steps to take to accomplish this and get started early enough to realistically accomplish all that is involved before you graduate.

The purpose of this chapter is to help you better understand employability and career planning, as well as to suggest strategies and resources you can use to navigate your own career path.

# Employability? What's That?

*Employability, career-readiness* and *work-place ready* are all terms that have been elevated in the media in recent years. As students and their families concern themselves with whether or not there will be a job available at the end of the college journey, employers are equally concerned about whether or not there will be graduates available who are equipped to meet their needs.

The University of South Carolina serves as a bridge to bring students and employers together, preparing students along the way. To address the issue of career-readiness, the university has identified an employability model for its students, which includes a definition of employability: **Employability** is having a set of skills, knowledge, understanding and personal attributes that make a person more likely to choose, secure and retain occupations in which they can be satisfied and successful (Dacre Pool & Sewell 2007, 2012).

The model itself is designed to help students identify the key foundational components in which they need to engage so that they can **CREATE** the conditions that will lead to employability.

## *Prioritizing and Self Management*

It's important to note here that *you* are the one who will create the conditions that will lead to your employability. While academic advisors, career coaches, academic major department offices, dean's offices and other campus offices

> STUDENTS WHO BELIEVE THAT "JUST SHOWING UP" TO COLLEGE IS ENOUGH, WILL ALL-TOO-SOON LEARN THAT THE DEGREE ALONE IS NOT SUFFICIENT AND THAT INTENSE COMPETITION STILL EXISTS AMONG THE COLLEGE EDUCATED.

are all resources which can provide information, help prevent and resolve difficulties, give insight into possible alternatives, and suggest new opportunities, you must understand the employability model and take the initiative to manage the process. Career planning and preparing for the workplace should be a self-driven endeavor in which students take advantage of the services and resources available to them. College is filled with a wealth of opportunities and choices and it is critical that students make appropriate and informed decisions and manage their priorities, which starts first with establishing priorities. Chapter 3 on time management and goal setting can be quite useful in this process.

## USC Employability Model
### *It starts with a firm foundation*

USC's employability model presents six foundational components that, when engaged in with reflection, will lead to self efficacy, self confidence, and self esteem, and ultimately enhance your employability. In other words, if you wish to secure and retain an occupation in which you can be satisfied and successful, you should be proactive and intentional about each of the following:

## FOUNDATION #1:
## Career Planning

*Student understands career development process and establishes and implements a structured plan for active, self-driven participation in career development activities to include self assessment, workplace exploration and job search preparation.*

### *A goal without a plan is just a wish*

There is a popular adage often attributed to Benjamin Franklin: *If you fail to plan, you are planning to fail*. It is not without intent that the above statement about career planning indicates that students will first *establish* a plan and then *implement* their plan. In fact, the core of the career planning concept is the word *plan*.

> EMPLOYABILITY IS HAVING A SET OF SKILLS, KNOWLEDGE, UNDERSTANDING AND PERSONAL ATTRIBUTES THAT MAKE A PERSON MORE LIKELY TO CHOOSE, SECURE AND RETAIN OCCUPATIONS IN WHICH THEY CAN BE SATISFIED AND SUCCESSFUL.
>
> Dacre Pool & Sewell 2007, 2012

# University of South Carolina Employability Model

*Adapted with permission from the CareerEDGE Model of Graduate Employability (Dacre Pool & Sewell, 2007)*

"Employability is having a set of skills, knowledge, understanding and personal attributes that make a person more likely to choose, secure and retain occupations in which they can be satisfied and successful."

Dacre Pool & Sewell
2007; 2012

Whether or not a student finds employment can be impacted by factors both inside and outside the model (i.e. a downturn in the market, selection of major/degree or the range and quality of experiences gained by the student.)

## Employability

**Self-efficacy:**
One's **belief in one's own ability** to successfully perform the tasks required to **achieve specific goals**.

**Self-esteem:**
One's sense of self worth.

**Self-confidence:**
One's strength of belief in their overall aptitude for success - **a general sense of self-assurance.**
*(self-efficacy plays an important part in determining self-confidence.)*

## Reflection, Integration & Evaluation

| **Career Planning** | **Relationships** | **Experience (Life & Work)** | **Academic Subject Knowledge, Skills & Understanding** | **Transferable Skills** | **Emotional Intelligence** |
|---|---|---|---|---|---|
| Student understands career development process and **establishes and implements a structured plan** for active, self-driven participation in career development activities to include **self assessment, workplace exploration** and **job search preparation.** | Student strategically establishes network by **developing relationships** with university faculty and staff, academic advisors, career coaches, alumni, mentors and practitioners. Student **establishes appropriate online presence and connections** (i.e. LinkedIn). | Student actively participates in **high impact, experiential practices** such as parttime employment, internships, co-operative education, study abroad, service learning, and research in order to develop technical knowledge related to various career paths. | Student demonstrates mastery of both their academic program (major/degree) requirements and the Carolina Core (general education) requirements through **successful academic performance** and **degree attainment.** | *(list below taken from NACE Job Outlook Spring 2015)* <br><br>**Student is able to:** <br>1) Work in team structure; <br>2) Make decisions & solve problems; <br>3) Communicate verbally; <br>4) Plan, organize & prioritize work; <br>5) Obtain & process information; <br>6) Analyze quantitative data; <br>7) Demonstrate technical knowledge related to job; <br>8) Demonstrate proficiency w/ computer software programs; <br>9) Create/edit written reports; <br>10) Influence others (leadership). | Student develops emotional literacy (the ability to monitor and appropriately label both their own and other's emotions and apply emotional information to guide thinking and behavior), through **exposure to emotional intelligence theory and exercises.** |

# handshake

The Career Center has an online integrated job search resource center that allows students and alumni to search part-time job, full-time job, internship and co-op postings, view and apply for opportunities to interview with employers on campus, and access employer and Career Center events. All students and alumni have free access and should take advantage of this great tool!

Visit the Career Center website for more information.

 sc.edu/career/handshake

## JOB FAIRS

The Career Center hosts approximately ten job fairs a year, including specialty events for students interested in science, engineering, technology, health professions, education and more!

For a complete listing of events see:

sc.edu/career

---

The key to this component is to first recognize that there is an actual process you can use to determine what you might want to do occupationally, and then take the appropriate steps to get there. The Career Center provides numerous staff and resources to aid you in this effort.

## Decide it. Experience it. Live it.

The mission of the Career Center at USC is *to educate and empower students in their development of lifelong career management skills*. They do so through a three-step approach where they work to help students:

### Decide it. (Self Assessment)

- Identify career-related skills, interests and values
- Learn about career options
- Explore majors

### Experience it. (Workplace Exploration)

- Gain exposure to the world of work through shadowing and informational interviews
- Find work experiences (part-time jobs, internships or co-ops) related to career and/or academic interests

### Live it. (Job Search Preparation)

- Prepare for and execute a job search or plan for graduate school
- Learn about opportunities to interact and network with employers

Of course career planning is much more involved than this. More will be covered on the career planning process later in this chapter.

# FOUNDATION #2: Relationships

*Student strategically establishes network by developing relationships with university faculty and staff, academic advisors, career coaches, alumni, mentors and practitioners. Student establishes appropriate online presence and connections (e.g., LinkedIn).*

In a nutshell, "who you know" is still a very important component to your success. While having great contacts may not help students who haven't engaged appropriately in all of the other foundational components of the employability model, it can certainly go a long way in expanding your opportunities.

## The power of weak ties

In her book, *The Defining Decade: Why Your Twenties Matter and How to Make the Most of Them Now*, Dr. Meg Jay cites a famous social networking study conducted by Stanford professor Mark Granovetter. Granovetter found that "weak ties" (people we see occasionally or rarely) were often more important than "strong ties" (family and close friends) because weak ties can give us access to social networks where we don't otherwise belong (Jay, 2012). Students who spend most of their time with the same five friends are likely missing out on the new ideas and opportunities that stem from these less known connections. Strategically developing new connections—even with those defined only as casual acquaintances—may ultimately be the catalyst to helping you achieve your career goals.

## It's not just who, but how

As important as *who you know* is *how you manage the relationship*. Relationships, in and of themselves, will not help you meet your goals, so it is important that you not only think strategically about who to get to know, but also consider carefully the content of your interactions. Students who intentionally share information with contacts about what they are studying, career paths of interest, where they hope to intern, attend graduate school, or live one day, increase the likelihood of opening the door for potential leads and connections that can help down the road.

## Establishing an appropriate online presence

Online networking plays an integral part of many individual's web of connections. Just as important as it is to proactively use online networks to establish connections, you should also remember that others may be looking for you (and at you) online. Taking steps to establish an appropriate, *professional* online presence is critical. You can start by creating profiles in online networks specifically designed for professional use, such as LinkedIn. At the same time, you should not underestimate the impact that other social networking tools could have on your job prospects if these present an image of you that is less than professional. For example, data show that one in ten young people have been rejected for a job because of their social media profile (On Device Research, 2013). The Career Center at the University of South Carolina is a helpful resource for students who wish to learn more about establishing an appropriate online presence.

# FOUNDATION #3:
# Experience (Life & Work)

*Student actively participates in high impact, experiential practices such as part-time employment, internships, co-operative education, study abroad, service-learning, and research in order to develop technical knowledge related to various career paths.*

The importance of hands-on learning has intensified in recent years as employers need workers with practical knowledge who are ready to hit the ground running when they start a job. There is a consensus among practitioners in higher education that beyond-the-classroom learning in many ways serves as a laboratory where you can put theory you have learned in the classroom to practice, allowing you to develop many of the valuable skills (more on these skills later) that employers seek. See chapter 5 to learn more about USC Connect and beyond-the-classroom learning at Carolina.

## SPUR CONNECTIONS

Spur Connections is a mentor program designed to assist USC students and alumni in learning more about various job positions and industries. USC students and alumni can search the Spur Connections database and contact individuals nationwide and even around the world who are working in various fields or pursuing graduate/professional study. Once a connection is made students can set up opportunities for e-networking, information interviewing, and/or job shadowing.

For more information, see:

 sc.edu/career/
spurconnections

## Considering What's Most Heavily Weighted

When it comes to experiences, generally speaking, employers have indicated that internships and employment during college are the most heavily weighted attributes they consider when evaluating graduates for hire (Chronicle of Higher Education, 2012).

Many employers have expressed that students who have had one (or more) internship experiences upon graduation are the most competitive applicants for their organization. It is important to employers that you will have had exposure to, experience working in, and have been previously evaluated in, a professional work-place setting.

In some cases, employers have indicated that they no longer visit college campuses to recruit entry-level talent; instead they visit college campuses to recruit interns or co-operative education students, then seek to covert those students to full-time hires. In fact, the 2015 Internship & Co-op Survey from the National Association of Colleges & Employers (NACE) showed that 51.7% of interns and 37.8% of co-op students were converted to full-time hires (NACE, 2015a).

INTERNSHIPS AND EMPLOYMENT DURING COLLEGE ROSE TO THE TOP OF THE LIST AS THE MOST HEAVILY WEIGHTED ATTRIBUTES CONSIDERED BY EMPLOYERS.

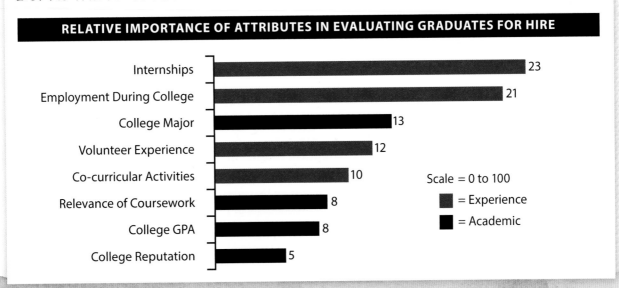

**RELATIVE IMPORTANCE OF ATTRIBUTES IN EVALUATING GRADUATES FOR HIRE**

| Attribute | Value |
|---|---|
| Internships | 23 |
| Employment During College | 21 |
| College Major | 13 |
| Volunteer Experience | 12 |
| Co-curricular Activities | 10 |
| Relevance of Coursework | 8 |
| College GPA | 8 |
| College Reputation | 5 |

Scale = 0 to 100
= Experience
= Academic

> EMPLOYERS HAVE INDICATED THAT INTERNSHIPS AND EMPLOYMENT DURING COLLEGE ARE THE MOST HEAVILY WEIGHTED ATTRIBUTES THEY CONSIDER WHEN EVALUATING GRADUATES FOR HIRE (CHRONICLE OF HIGHER EDUCATION, 2012).

Needless to say, pursuing an internship or co-op experience during college is a very good way for students to potentially find a future full-time employer as well as to determine if a career path is right for you!

## The Decision is Highly Personal

In spite of the clear importance of internships in the job preparation process, determining the specific types of experiences you should pursue during your college years does vary widely depending on both your particular personal and career goals.

For example, a study abroad experience may be highly valued by employers with global operations, while undergraduate research experience may be of significant value to admissions committees for graduate schools. Engaging in volunteer activities or service learning may be of personal importance to you. Selecting the best options for gaining life and work experience is a highly relative and personal decision, and you may wish to discuss your options with a career coach in the Career Center or a professor in your field.

# FOUNDATION #4:
# Academic Subject Knowledge, Skills & Understanding

*Student demonstrates mastery of both their academic program (major/degree) requirements and the Carolina Core (general education) requirements through successful academic performance and degree attainment.*

At the heart of the college experience, as well as at the center of the employability model, is the pursuit of an academic credential. Employers and students alike rely on the education a student receives in college to prepare the student for work in specific fields. While not every position requires a specific degree path for entry, certainly very many do. For example, students who wish to be chemical engineers would be wise to major in chemical engineering, students who wish to be accountants would be best prepared by a major in accounting, but for those interested in many other positions, any

## EXPLORING YOUR OPTIONS

When it comes to gaining hands-on work experiences as a USC student, both internships and cooperative education (co-ops) are forms of experiential education that integrate knowledge and theory learned in the classroom with practical application and skill development in a professional work setting. Review the table below to compare and contrast your options and learn the steps for pursing each.

| Option | Internships | | | Co-ops | |
|---|---|---|---|---|---|
| | **Independent Internship** | **Academic Internship** | **Career Center Internship** | **Parallel Co-op** | **Alternating Co-op** |
| **In a Nutshell** | • Usually the length or equivalent of a single fall semester, spring semester or summer (can repeat semesters)<br>• May be part-time or full-time<br>• May be paid or unpaid<br>• May or may not be eligible for academic credit<br>• May or may not be reflected on your academic transcript | | | • Provides *multiple* (2-3) work terms (semesters/summer) for the same employer spanning one or more calendar years<br>• May be part-time or full-time<br>• Guaranteed to be a paid experience<br>• Coordinated by the USC Career Center<br>• Will be reflected on your academic transcript (zero credits earned)<br>• Most popular in the following industries: science, technology, math, engineering and business | |
| **Bottom Line** | Find an internship and pursue it on your own. | Earn (and pay for) academic credit for your internship experience. | Enroll in the Career Center's Community Internship Program (CIP) to ensure full-time student status and gain official University recognition for your internship. | Enroll in the Career Center's Cooperative Education (Co-op) Program to ensure full-time student status and gain official University recognition for your co-op. | |
| **University Affiliation** | No. You will not have an advocate from the University should any issues arise. | Yes. You will have a faculty/staff advocate should any issues arise. | Yes. You will have a Career Center advocate should any issues arise. | Yes. You will have a Career Center advocate should any issues arise. | |

continued on next page

continued from previous page

# Experience it. Internships and Co-ops at USC

| Option | Internships | | | Co-ops | |
|---|---|---|---|---|---|
| | Independent Internship | Academic Internship | Career Center Internship | Parallel Co-op | Alternating Co-op |
| Full-time Student Status | No. If interning during a fall or spring semester and not taking a full load of classes, you will lose your full-time student status. | Depends. Student may or may not have full-time student status depending on the total number of academic credit hours being earned during the term in which he/she interns. Students who need full-time student status have the option to simultaneously enroll in a Career Center internship. | Yes. If interning during a fall or spring semester and not taking a full load of coursework, the Career Center will assist you in maintaining full-time student status. | Yes. As long as you are still enrolled in a full load of classes while co-oping part-time you will maintain your full-time student status. | Yes. When co-oping full-time during a fall or spring semester, the Career Center will assist you in maintaining full-time student status. |
| Academic Credit | None. | Will be determined by the department which offers your major. Most academic departments will want to see the position description and verify that the work you will be doing is related to your course of study. The number of credit hours you may earn (and will pay for) varies by academic department. | While appearing on your academic transcript, internships through the Community Internship Program are zero-credit, meaning that you neither earn, nor pay for, academic credit. | While appearing on your academic transcript, co-op positions are zero-credit, meaning that you neither earn, nor pay for, academic credit. | |

# Experience it. Internships and Co-ops at USC

| Option | Internships | | | Co-ops | |
|---|---|---|---|---|---|
| | Independent Internship | Academic Internship | Career Center Internship | Parallel Co-op | Alternating Co-op |
| University Recognition | No recognition of the experience on your academic transcript. | By enrolling in a course for credit, the experience will indirectly appear on your academic transcript reflected through the title of the internship course in which you enroll. | By enrolling in the Community Internship Program (even during the summer), the experience will appear on your academic transcript as *Career Center Internship*. | By enrolling in the Career Center's Cooperative Education (Co-op) Program the experience will appear on your academic transcript as *Career Center Cooperative Education*. | |
| Part-time / Full-time | Either. | Either. The number of hours you must work may vary by academic department. | The student may work **part-time** (20 hours a week or 240 hours a term) or **full-time** (40 hours a week or 480 hours a term). | The student **works part-time** (20 hours a week or 240 hours a term) while attending school full-time for two or three consecutive semesters. | The student **works full-time** (40 hours a week or 480 hours a term) for two or three terms (semesters), alternating terms of work and school. |

continued on next page

# Experience it. Internships and Co-ops at USC

| Option | Internships | | | Co-ops | |
|---|---|---|---|---|---|
| | Independent Internship | Academic Internship | Career Center Internship | Parallel Co-op | Alternating Co-op |
| **Paid / Unpaid** | Either. | Either. | Required to be paid, unless with non-for-profit organizations. | Always paid. The average co-op salary is:<br>• Overall: $17.16/hr<br>• Engineering & Computing: $27.59 | |
| **Personal & Professional Development** | Unknown. | Varies by academic department. | All CIP interns will complete an internship preparation workshop, establish desired learning outcomes, receive an on-site mid-semester site visit from a Career Center staff member, be formally evaluated by the internship workplace supervisor, and participate in a post internship reflection workshop. | All co-op students will complete a co-op preparation workshop, establish desired learning outcomes, receive an on-site mid-semester site visit from a Career Center staff member, be formally evaluated by the co-op workplace supervisor, and participate in a post co-op reflection workshop. | |
| **Action Steps** | We recommend pursuing one of the remaining four options which provide University Affiliation. | To explore obtaining academic credit for your internship, review the list of internship contacts by academic department at www.sc.edu/career. | To explore enrolling in the Career Center's Community Internship Program, visit the Career Center's website: www.sc.edu/career. (Note: certain pre-requisites must be met to qualify.) | To explore enrolling in the Career Center's Co-op Program, visit the Career Center's website: www.sc.edu/career. (Note: certain pre-requisites must be met to qualify.) | |

# Experience it. Internships and Co-ops at USC

## WHY IS UNIVERSITY AFFILIATION AND FULL-TIME STUDENT STATUS IMPORTANT?

Obtaining University affiliation for your internship or co-op provides several important advantages for you. Not only does having a University advocate stand to improve the overall quality of your experience, but having your internship or co-op appear on your academic transcript will legitimize the experience in the eyes of future employers.

Maintaining your full-time student status at the University during an internship or co-op term has critical implications for your financial aid, health insurance, access to student services (such as housing and/or football tickets) and more. Without maintaining full-time student status during an internship, you would have to reapply for admission to USC upon completion of the experience.

## HOW DO I FIND AN INTERNSHIP OR CO-OP?

Searching for an internship or co-op is great practice for finding a full-time job. You should be proactive in the search process but will have numerous resources at your disposal. Some of the more common ways students find opportunities include:

- Handshake (Career Center online job posting system)
- Job Fairs (Career Center or Academic Department sponsored)
- Career Center Web Resources (the internship category provides links to numerous online internship databases)
- Academic Departments
- Networking

Visit the Career Center during drop-in hours, Monday-Friday, 1-4pm for assistance with getting started!

## NEXT STEPS

As you ease into your first year at USC, your primary focus should be to identify and narrow career paths of interest. In some cases it is helpful to do this prior to pursuing an internship or co-op. In other cases the internship or co-op itself will assist you in clarifying your career interests. Recommended steps for first-year students include:

- Be proactive in your exploration of industries and career options by following the 4-step Career Decision Making Model outlined in this chapter.
- Complete a job shadow or informational interview through Spur Connections and/or participate in Pathways to Professions where the Career Center coordinates a visit to an employer site for a group job shadow. These are often precursors to an internship or a co-op.
- Begin drafting a resume and cover letter for use with internship/co-op applications and have these reviewed by Career Center staff.
- Participate in mock interviews through the Career Center to prepare for internship and co-op interviews.

number of different degree options might get them there. Following are some important career considerations as you develop an academic plan:

## It's about Depth & Breadth: The T-shaped model

Gone are the days when major alone was a student's only concern. Even the chemical engineering major, who has a fairly linear career path, has much more to consider. Employers today are looking for candidates in the context of the T-shaped model. (See image on p. 267.) They need workers who have both *in-depth* knowledge, skills and understanding in one discipline, allowing them to be analytic thinkers and problem solvers within that realm, as well as having a *wide breadth* of general understanding of, and ability to communicate with specialists in, other disciplines and functional areas. This is precisely why all students at USC will take coursework in the Carolina Core (see Chapter 4 for more information of the Carolina Core), as well as in their designated major.

Not to be overlooked is the option to pursue a minor, or cognate, that can complement your major. It will be helpful to consider how unique combinations—especially those crossing more than one college or school at USC—might enhance your competitiveness for various positions. Even the choice of specific electives can be a selling point when speaking with employers (or graduate schools) about your candidacy.

For example, a student with a long-term goal of working in healthcare administration might major in public health (Arnold School of Public Health) with a minor in business (Darla Moore School of Business) and take elective courses in nutrition, food production and purchasing (College of Hospitality, Retail and Sport Management). A student interested in environmental policy might major in environmental studies with a minor in political science (both in the College of Arts & Sciences) while taking elective courses in public relations (School of Journalism and Mass Communications). Finally, a student interested in marketing (Darla Moore School of Business) might round out his or

# THE T-SHAPED MODEL

**BOUNDARY CROSSING COMPETENCIES**
Teamwork, communication, perspective, networks, critical thinking, global understanding, project management, etc.

**ME**

**MANY DISCIPLINES**
Understanding & communications

**MANY SYSTEMS**
Understanding & communications

**DEEP IN AT LEAST ONE DISCIPLINE**
Analytic thinking & problem solving

**DEEP IN AT LEAST ONE SYSTEM**
Analytic thinking & problem solving

Source: Collegiate Employment Research Institute. (n.d.)

her degree with a minor in applied computing (College of Engineering & Computing) by choosing the web development, database technology or project management track.

It is worth noting the significance of technology in today's workplace. Most jobs today involve the use of technology to enhance and support their processes. Students with both a solid understanding of a specific discipline and the ability to apply technology to achieve workplace goals will have an advantage over those with less developed technological skills.

## Balancing Passions with Practicality

Most students cannot imagine working full-time for the 50 years following graduation. It may sound unbelievable, but this is exactly what is happening in the world of work today; people are working longer for a variety of reasons, chief among them is the fact that people are living longer. Therefore, it is crucial that you choose a major you enjoy that will provide you with essential and multiple marketable skills within a larger field of work because returning to school to pursue a degree you wish you had earned in the first place can be costly and difficult to manage later in life.

Those who work in the Career Center make it a priority to help students identify a course of study that will lead them to career paths related to that student's interests, skills, values and passion. However, career coaches also understand the importance of balance and the benefit of choosing options that are a good fit for the student in the context of the realities of supply and demand in the current and the future marketplace. The ideal scenario involves a student pursing a course of study that he or she loves, while also having a keen understanding of the potential competitiveness of their selected pathway(s).

# FOUNDATION #5:
# Transferable Skills

Each year, the National Association of Colleges & Employers (NACE) surveys employers of college graduates nationwide about trends in college recruiting. In the spring of 2015

NACE identified the top 10 essential skills employers were seeking in new college graduates (NACE, 2015b).

Accordingly to their survey, a student **should be able to:**

1. Work in team structure;
2. Make decisions and solve problems;
3. Communicate verbally;
4. Plan, organize and prioritize work;
5. Obtain and process information;
6. Analyze quantitative data;
7. Demonstrate technical knowledge related to the job;
8. Demonstrate proficiency with computer software programs;
9. Create and edit written reports;
10. Influence others (leadership).

## The Only Thing Constant is Change

The majority of today's graduates can expect to hold 12-15 distinct positions in the course of their work-life, potentially in three to four different fields. Transferable skills are those which can be easily transferred from position to position and are valued by employers in many settings. Even as the nature of work itself changes rapidly, the majority of the skills identified in the NACE survey above are highly transferable across many settings. Most employers value a candidate who can demonstrate they are well-versed in the skills listed above.

## Seeking Opportunities for Growth

It is important to keep in mind that most skills are developed over time and must be intentionally cultivated and honed. Fortunately, the university setting provides an ideal location for you to practice these skills. Opportunities abound for skill development through coursework, class projects, internships or employment during college, volunteerism, campus involvement and leadership positions.

# FOUNDATION #6: Emotional Intelligence

*Student develops emotional literacy (the ability to monitor and appropriately label both their own and other's emotions and apply emotional information to guide thinking and behavior), through exposure to emotional intelligence theory and exercises.*

Of course it makes sense that employers want to hire candidates who are emotionally aware and able to use their awareness of emotions to shape both how they view and respond to various workplace situations. Many refer to this as managing emotions or even attempt to sum it up by calling it *maturity*, but it is much more complex than that. You should not underestimate the fact that emotional intelligence was singled out and given its own category as a foundational component of the employability model.

Like the transferable skills referenced in this chapter, emotional intelligence must be developed and practiced. It is worth exploring further, and resources such as Stephen Covey's (2013), *The 8th Habit: From Effectiveness to Greatness*, address approaches to developing your emotional intelligence.

## Reflection, Integration & Evaluation

Assuming that you fully understand the importance of engaging in each of the six foundational components of the **CREATE** Employability Model, the next steps are for you to *reflect* on your experience with each of these components, consider how you might *integrate* these seemingly individual components into a larger whole, and *evaluate* how each will help to position you for where you want to go.

While developing in each of the six components is in and of itself important, it's critical that you are able to articulate what you learned to others, for example, on your resume or in a job interview. You have a number of resources on campus for engaging in reflection, integration, and evaluation, but you should particularly seek out the guidance of Career Center staff who are well versed in working with students to synthesize and articulate experiences in the context of preparation for entry into the workforce.

## Self-Efficacy, Self Esteem & Self-Confidence

The final layer of USC's employability model is the development of self-efficacy, self-esteem and self-confidence.

It is important that you believe that you have the ability to perform the tasks required to achieve specific goals (self-efficacy). Further, you must also have a general belief that you are likely to succeed (self-confidence), and finally, you must believe that you deserve to succeed (self-esteem). Each of these goes a long way in getting you where you want to go.

Fortunately, the college experience provides ample opportunity for students to develop in these attributes. Specifically, as students engage in the various components of the employability model they will prepare themselves to become more employable and with increased preparation comes increased confidence.

# Every Piece Matters

The key to fully appreciating USC's employability model is understanding that every piece of the model is important. If any one of the pieces is missing or deficient, you are at risk of not being employable.

## How will I get there?

At this point of the chapter, you may be thinking *"Okay, so I understand **why** I need to be actively engaged in career planning early, and I'm clear on **what** is involved in the process of making myself employable, but I'm still not sure **how** I will actually figure out what I want to do or ultimately how I will get there."*

The remainder of this chapter will focus on answering these questions.

As was noted in the employability model earlier, a key foundational component of becoming more employable is to (1) understand the career planning process and (2) establish and implement a structured plan for active, self-driven participation in career development activities.

### RESUME & INTERVIEW PREPARATION

By the end of your first year, you may wish to draft a resume and start developing your interviewing skills to assist in the search for internship/co-ops, the application process for campus leadership opportunities, or even for use with scholarship applications.

The Career Center provides **OptimalResume**, a customized online resume development tool to help students get started. They also provide sample resumes and cover letters for students to view online at sc.edu/career/resume.html

Likewise, the Career Center provides numerous resources on interview preparation, including **InterviewStream**, a mock-interview program through which students can practice and digitally record practice interviews using web cam technology. See sc.edu/career/interviewing.html

The process of deciding on a career is complex and comprehensive. It is not something you can do in one sitting or in a short period of time. In order to make an informed career decision, it is helpful to follow the four-step process below. Even a student who feels fairly-well decided in their major and/or career selection can benefit from a review of the following in an effort to seek confirmation of their choice.

# Career Decision Making: Four-Step Model

## Step 1: Develop Self-Awareness and Understanding: Who Am I?

Answering this question involves a thorough investigation of your background, interests, values, feelings, abilities, needs, ambitions, achievements, and lifestyle. The better you can articulate who you are and what you want, the more likely it is that the decisions you make will be informed choices that lead to success and happiness in a future career. Chapter 8 discusses how you can clarify and better understand your personal values and others.

Each new experience provides a unique opportunity to deepen your self-awareness, which develops over time as you engage in reflection and think about your interactions with others and the world. Sustained effort and attention to making meaning out of experiences will lead to enhanced self-awareness.

Staff members at the Career Center use assessments, interviews, and career coaching sessions to help students gather information about themselves and integrate what they have learned into a meaningful whole. Assessments such as the Strong Interest Inventory (assesses interests), Myers-Briggs Type Indicator (personality type inventory that assesses psychological preferences), Work Values Inventory (assesses work-related values) and FOCUS (comprehensive tool assessing multiple components), are available to guide you through many aspects of this process. These assessment tools are not designed to tell you what to be or what major to choose; instead, they indicate how your interests, personality, or values relate to various occupations.

FOUR STEP MODEL

1) WHO AM I?

2) WHAT IS OUT THERE?

3) HOW DO I FIT?

4) WHAT IS MY PLAN OF ACTION?

## Step 2: Acquire Knowledge of Fields of Study and Careers: What Is Out There?

The answer to this question requires extensive investigation and research. Becoming aware of the career options available may both help to inform selection of a major and determine an initial career path. The University of South Carolina offers more than 70 undergraduate majors and minors from which you can choose. Reviewing the Undergraduate Bulletin, exploring college and school websites, and talking with professors, upper-level students majoring in fields of similar interest, and academic advisors can all be good sources of information about majors and minors.

The world of work is so vast and ever-changing, the job or field you will be entering after graduation may not yet exist. Further, many of the jobs of today will soon be obsolete! Investigating the possibilities in the work world can be very helpful in charting a path and can be gathered through activities such as researching career literature, informational interviews, job-shadowing experiences, visiting the workplace, and viewing media presentations regarding careers. The Career Center's resource room and online resources, as well as their connections to mentors and employers through specialized programs, will be rich sources of information for you.

## Step 3: Synthesize Information and Make Choices: How Do I Fit?

Arriving at an answer of where you fit in will require you to synthesize all accumulated information to determine a good fit in a potential career. Once you have engaged in significant and intentional self-awareness and have investigated career options available in the current and future job market, you are ready to begin processing and choosing a major and career direction. Making choices can be a difficult process, so it is helpful to test out thoughts with others. Staff members at the Career Center, as well as academic advisors, can assist you in this process. Others who are close to you or who have known you for many years can be helpful as well. Finally, friends and family members can serve as sounding boards as you synthesize information and tentatively test out possibilities.

### COMPARE & CONTRAST CAREERS

The U.S. Department of Labor has developed *The Occupational Outlook Handbook*, which includes the following information on hundreds of different types of jobs:

- Training and education needed
- Earnings
- Expected job prospects
- Job duties
- Working conditions

In addition, the Handbook offers job search tips, links to information about the job market in each state, and more. For more information, visit http://www.bls.gov/oco.

> THE WORLD OF WORK IS SO VAST AND EVER-CHANGING, THE JOB OR FIELD YOU WILL BE ENTERING AFTER GRADUATION MAY NOT YET EXIST. FURTHER, MANY OF THE JOBS OF TODAY WILL SOON BE OBSOLETE! INVESTIGATING THE POSSIBILITIES IN THE WORK WORLD CAN BE VERY HELPFUL IN CHARTING YOUR PATH.

## FOUR YEAR STUDENT PLAN

For a more in-depth four year student timeline see sc.edu/career/tipsheets.html and click on Four Year Student Plan.

## Step 4: Develop an Effective Plan for Achieving Goals: What Is My Plan of Action?

Once you have made a decision on a major and one or more potential career paths, developing a plan can be energizing and exciting. In addition to making careful academic course choices and considering strategies for achieving academic success, an action plan should include all of the components of the employability model as well as elements of the first three steps of the career decision making model. (Who am I? What's out there? How do I fit?)

Effective job search skills will also be necessary to assist you in achieving your goals. Programs offered by the Career Center and personalized sessions with staff members can help you develop a resume, refine your interviewing style and technique, identify key people to serve as references, learn how to search for a job, and generally learn how to put your best foot forward.

As you move through the four step career decision making model, you should draft goals to guide you in making progress on your journey. Studies show that those who write down their goals, develop written action commitments for each goal, and share their commitments with others, are much more likely to achieve their goals (Anderson, 2013). When developing goals, the use of SMART goals is highly recommended. SMART stands for Specific, Measurable, Attainable, Realistic and Timely. A *specific* goal has a much greater chance of being accomplished than a general goal. Also, providing criteria for yourself that you will be able to *measure* and one that is *attainable* is important. You will want your goal to be *realistic*, so that you are actually able to reach it. Finally, setting a *timeframe* is a necessary step if you plan on accomplishing your goal.

## Conclusion

Whatever a student's needs regarding career exploration, the Career Center is available to help. They are prepared to address the career-related needs of students from the time they are admitted to the University until after they graduate.

## SMART GOAL (SPECIFIC, MEASURABLE, ATTAINABLE, REALISTIC, AND TIMELY)

## AVAILABLE CAMPUS RESOURCES

| ACTION STEPS | DEADLINE | CHECK WHEN COMPLETED |
|---|---|---|
| 1. | | |
| 2. | | |
| 3. | | |
| 4. | | |
| 5. | | |

## POSSIBLE OBSTACLES I MAY FACE IN TRYING TO REACH MY GOALS

## A Real-Life Example of Using the Career Decision Making Model

*While the Four-Step Career Decision Making Model presented in this chapter provides a useful framework for making decisions, the process may still feel quite ambiguous to you. Let's follow along with a fellow Gamecock, Emily, and see how she managed the career planning process during her first year at USC.*

When Emily arrived on campus as a first-year student she was undeclared, and considering a major in education, psychology, or journalism. She knew she enjoyed communicating and interacting with people, and the idea of writing, teaching, or helping others was appealing to her. Beyond that she wasn't at all sure how to narrow it down, so she decided to visit the Career Center to get help with choosing a major. After speaking with a Career Development Coach, Emily agreed that it made sense to remain undeclared until the following semester while taking some time to tackle the first two steps of the Career Decision Making Model.

### Step 1: Develop Self-Awareness and Understanding: Who Am I?

The first goal Emily set was to take a variety of career assessments offered through the Career Center. In doing so, she learned the following about herself:

**Strong Interest Inventory:** This instrument largely confirmed Emily's interest in working with people and helping others, but also indicated a strong bend toward creativity and persuasion. In addition to advertising managers, fundraising directors, non-profit organizers, and college admissions officers, Emily was surprised to see that she had similarities to professionals who were medical social workers, hospital admissions managers, and public health educators.

**Myers Briggs Type Indicator:** After taking this personality assessment, Emily received further clarification that people with the same personality type as she often pursued careers in communication, education, human/social services, health care, and business.

**Work Values Inventory:** This inventory was particularly eye-opening for Emily. She learned that it was important to her to pursue work which would allow her to help society on a large scale (versus helping small groups of people), create new ideas and programs, make decisions about courses of action or policies, and most importantly, be assured of a reasonable level of job security in the future.

### Step 2: Acquire Knowledge of Fields of Study and Careers: What Is Out There?

Over the remainder of her fall semester and for the first several months of her spring semester, Emily committed herself to learning more about career options. Using the link to the U.S Department of Labor's *Occupational Outlook Handbook* provided in this chapter, Emily began to research various career options and was surprised to learn how many of the fastest growing jobs of the future were in healthcare. The *Handbook* also provided all of the basics of each job she reviewed: job description, work environment, median pay, education required, job outlook, and more.

Emily used her Career Center Handshake account to search for alumni who worked in professions she was interested in exploring. She reached out and conducted information interviews with several professionals and signed up to attend a group site visit to the South Carolina Department of Health and Human Services through the Career Center's *Pathways to Professions* program.

## Step 3: Synthesize Information and Make Choices: How Do I Fit?

In the spring semester, Emily scheduled a follow-up appointment with her Career Development Coach. Through careful processing with her Career Development Coach, Emily gradually began to put the pieces together. She began to understand that both her interests and personality type drew her toward careers that involved communication and helping others by way of sharing information or exerting influence. While the health professions was a recurring theme in her research and was clearly a strong fit for her value of job security, she just didn't feel she had the academic skills needed to pursue a hands-on career in medicine.

With her Career Development Coach encouraging her to review course descriptions through the Undergraduate Bulletin, Emily began to rule out majors one by one until she had narrowed her options to public relations, public health, and political science. Further conversations with family members and first-year advisor led her to a tentative decision of majoring in Public Relations with a minor in Health Promotion, Education and Behavior. While Emily still wasn't sure *exactly* where this would lead, she had visions of serving as a public relations manager for a hospital, a lobbyist for a government agency, or even working for a pharmaceutical company.

## Step 4: Develop an Effective Plan for Achieving Goals: What Is My Plan of Action?

With a tentative plan in place, Emily took to the task of setting goals for the years ahead. In keeping with the foundational components of the USC Employability Model, her list included the important elements of Relationships, Experience, and Transferable Skills.

Emily searched the online listing of student organizations for ways she could get more involved on campus and found the Changing Carolina Peer Leader position. She made a list of faculty she wanted to meet and scheduled an appointment with the Office of Pre-Professional Advising to learn more about preparing for law school. Lastly, Emily promised her Career Development Coach that she would return to meet with him at least once a semester to make sure she was staying on track. She also set a deadline to start working on her resume and to begin exploring internship opportunities for her sophomore year.

Emily was comfortable knowing her plan could still change slightly, but she felt confident that she was making an *intentional* and *informed* decision and was well on her way to creating the conditions that would lead to her employability!

# Career Center

## FIRST-YEAR STUDENT CAREER PLANNING CHECKLIST

*Planning adequately for your professional future requires an early start, commitment and intentionality. Take a few moments to consider the following statements. Determine where you're currently at in the career planning process and steps you might need to take during your freshman year.*

### Explore major and career options.

| | | |
|---|---|---|
| Yes | No | I have researched the majors/minors available to me and discussed this with my Career Development Coach. |
| Yes | No | I have taken an interest inventory to determine the types of activities I would enjoy at work. |
| Yes | No | I have taken a work values inventory to determine the factors that will be most important to me in my work. |
| Yes | No | I have taken a personality inventory to determine how my personality type may impact my work. |
| Yes | No | I have met with my Career Development Coach to discuss how my interests, values and personality type might influence my career choice. |
| Yes | No | I have thoroughly explored career fields I'd like to know more about. |

### Gain exposure to and experience in the workplace.

| | | |
|---|---|---|
| Yes | No | I have communicated directly with people who are in career fields I'd like to know more about. |
| Yes | No | I have visited employer sites of interest for a "behind-the-scenes" view of what it's all about. |
| Yes | No | I am aware of resources at USC that can assist me in finding part-time jobs, internships and co-ops. |

### Start preparing now to live out your career goals.

| | | |
|---|---|---|
| Yes | No | By the end of my freshman year I plan to write a resume based on Career Center guidelines. |
| Yes | No | By the end of my freshman year I will attend a job fair to start learning more about employers and their opportunities. |
| Yes | No | I've connected to the Career Center through social media. |

### Recommended Action Plan

- Review the Undergraduate Bulletin at http://bulletin.sc.edu/
- Take the Strong Interest Inventory
- Take the Work Values Inventory
- Take the Myers Briggs Type Indicator
- Schedule an appointment with your Career Development Coach to discuss your career options
- Visit the Career Center Resource Room and online web resources at http://tinyurl.com/ccexplorecareers
- Search http://www.sc.edu/career/spurconnections/ for mentors
- Sign up for an externship (day-long group site visit) to an employer site
- Schedule an appointment with your Career Development Coach to discuss how to gain experience
- See http://www.sc.edu/career/resume.html
- See http://www.sc.edu/career/Jobfairs3.html
- Follow us on Twitter/ Like us on Facebook: UofSCCareers

USC CAREER CENTER | THOMAS COOPER LIBRARY, LEVEL 5 | (P) 803.777.7280 | (F) 803.777.7556
CEC SATELLITE | 1A01 SWEARINGEN BLDG. | (P) 803.777.1949 | (F) 803.777.1946
WWW.SC.EDU/CAREER | CAREER@SC.EDU

UNIVERSITY OF
SOUTH CAROLINA

## REFLECTION QUESTIONS

1. Review the Employability Model on page 255. Which of the foundational components have you engaged in and how? How might you get started on those in which you have not yet engaged?
2. What is an example of an appropriate online professional presence? Have you ever considered how your social media accounts affect your employability? If so, how?
3. Identify at least two people (names or roles) you would like to establish an intentional connection with in the coming year who can assist you with career planning.
4. What types of work activities do you prefer (e.g., working with people, organizing or analyzing data, creating ideas, doing hands-on or practical activities)? Are there any specific examples from your previous work or co-curricular experiences that you particularly enjoyed doing?
5. Pick six of the ten transferable skills outlined on page 269. Which three do you feel you have already developed? Which three do you hope to develop or enhance during your time at USC? What are some ways you might do this?
6. What job or career characteristics (e.g., salary, location, advancement) will be most important to you after college? List three to five. What occupations or career fields are a good fit for these values?
7. What knowledge do you currently have about the market trends of your intended career path(s) in terms of supply and demand? (i.e., What career fields will offer the most work opportunities in the next 5-10 years?) Where can you find good information about the occupations or career fields that interest you?
8. What majors or minors are offered at the University of South Carolina that could help you reach your occupational goals?
9. What impact does the T-shaped Model have on your career decision process?
10. What types of career-related work experiences (i.e., internships, part-time or summer jobs, cooperative education experiences) as well as co-curricular activities (e.g., student organizations) will best assist you in reaching your career goals?

## RESOURCES

**Career Center** . . . . . . . . . . . . . . . . . . . . . . . (803) 777-7280
Thomas Cooper Library, Level 5
http://www.sc.edu/career/
Email: career@sc.edu

**Office of Pre-Professional Advising** . . (803) 777-5581
Sumwalt College, Room 208
http://www.sa.sc.edu/oppa/

**Student Success Center** . . . . . . . . . . . . . . (803) 777-0684
Thomas Cooper Library-- Mezzanine Level
http://www.sa.sc.edu/ssc/

**University Advising Center** . . . . . . . . . . (803) 777-1222
Close-Hipp Building, Suite 102
http://www.sc.edu/advising/

## REFERENCES

Abel, J. R. Deitz, R., & Su, Y. (2014). Are recent college graduates finding good jobs? *Current Issues in Economics and Finance, 20*(1), 1-8.

Anderson, N. (2013). Five ways to make your new year's resolutions stick. *Forbes.* Retrieved from: http://www.forbes.com/sites/financialfinesse/2013/01/03/5-ways-to-make-your-new-years-resolutions-stick/

Chronicle of Higher Education. (2012, December). The role of higher education in career development: Employer perceptions. Retrieved from https://chronicle.com/items/biz/pdf/EmployersSurvey.pdf

Collegiate Employment Research Institute. (n.d.) *T-Shaped Professionals.* Retrieved from http://www.ceri.msu.edu/t-shaped-professionals/

Covey, S. (2013). *The 8th habit: From effectiveness to greatness.* New York, NY: Free Press.

Dacre Pool, L., & Sewell, P. (2007). The key to employability: Developing a practical model of graduate employability. *Education & Training, 49*(4), 277-289.

Eagan, K., Stolzenberg, E. B., Ramirez, J. J., Aragon, M. C., Suchard, M. R., & Hurtado, S. (2014). *The American freshman: National norms fall 2014.* Los Angeles: Higher Education Research Institute, UCLA.

Economic Policy Institute. (n.d.) *The Great Recession.* Retrieved from http://stateofworkingamerica.org/great-recession/

Jay, M. (2012). *The defining decade: Why your twenties matter—and how to make the most of them now.* New York: Twelve.

National Association of Colleges and Employers (NACE). (2015a). *2015 Internship & Co-op Survey: Executive summary.* Bethlehem, PA: National Association of Colleges and Employers.

National Association of Colleges and Employers (NACE). (2015b). *Job outlook spring 2015 update.* Retrieved from https://www.naceweb.org (available to NACE members only)

National Public Radio. (2014, September 4). The unemployment rate in every state, before and after The Great Recession. Retrieved from http://www.npr.org/sections/money/2014/09/04/345796900/the-unemployment-rate-in-every-state-before-and-after-the-great-recession

On Device Research. (2013). Facebook costing 16-34s jobs in tough economic climate. Retrieved from https://ondeviceresearch.com/

# INDEX

# S